HEXHAM

THROUGH TIME

Stan Beckensall

AMBERLEY PUBLISHING

Acknowledgements

Many people have photographs of old Hexham, and I would thank some of those who have helped over the years with the material in the book, especially Colin Dallison, Ray Dallison, Peter Robson, Terry Robson, Matthew Hutchinson, the late Morton Charlton, Hilton Edgar, and George Johnson.

Also I thank the *Hexham Courant*, Hexham Museum Service, the Rectors and PCCs of Hexham Abbey, Sarah Parker and Joe Pettican. To my son Julian for technical help.

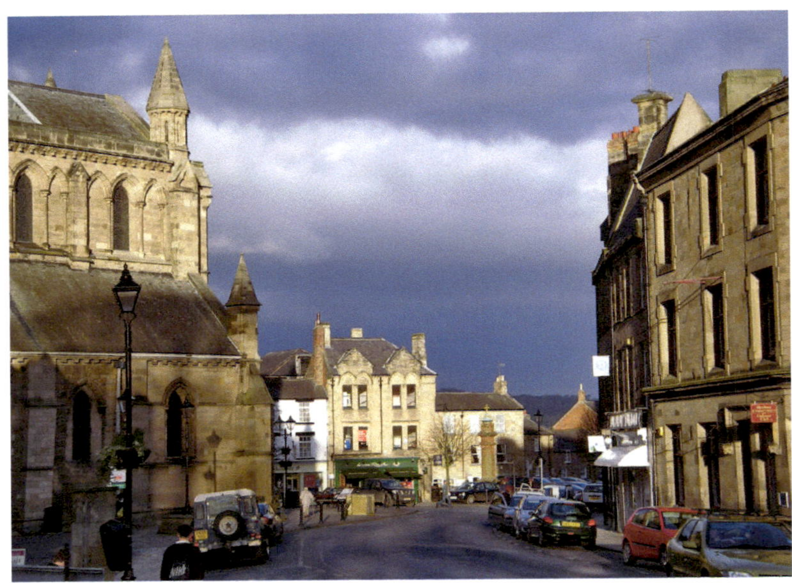

First published 2012

Amberley Publishing
The Hill, Stroud
Gloucestershire, GL5 4EP

www.amberley-books.com

Copyright © Stan Beckensall, 2012

The right of Stan Beckensall to be identified as the Author of this work has been asserted in accordance with the Copyrights, Designs and Patents Act 1988.

ISBN 978 1 4456 0843 3

All rights reserved. No part of this book may be reprinted or reproduced or utilised in any form or by any electronic, mechanical or other means, now known or hereafter invented, including photocopying and recording, or in any information storage or retrieval system, without the permission in writing from the Publishers.

British Library Cataloguing in Publication Data.
A catalogue record for this book is available from the British Library.

Typeset in 9.5pt on 12pt Celeste.
Typesetting by Amberley Publishing.
Printed in the UK.

Appointed GPSR EU Representative: Easy Access System Europe Oü, 16879218
Address: Mustamäe tee 50, 10621, Tallinn, Estonia
Contact Details: gpsr.requests@easproject.com, +358 40 500 3575

Introduction

Hexham's existence is mainly the result of the building of an important Anglo-Saxon monastery by St Wilfrid on land given to him by Queen Etheldreda in the seventh century. Before that the glacial terrace on which it is built overlooking the Tyne Valley to the north was known as the Hagustald's land, that of the youngest son of a noble who could not inherit from his father and had to seek a place for himself. We do not know what the land looked like then, but the underlying geology was made up of pebbles, gravel, sand and glacial clay, cut by streams flowing to the river.

The river valley has been important throughout prehistoric and Roman times, within the Roman Wall 'corridor', giving access to the hinterland, to the fertile soils of the valley and to the extensive woodland spreading from it. It was suitable for animal husbandry and for patches of cultivated land that could feed a market that demanded these products, so the town of Hexham, grafted onto the priory ground, provided such a market as well as houses and tracks leading to it.

As the town grew, buildings developed with different functions around the Market Place in defined areas: the Moothall and Old Gaol had their enclosed land which was for civil functions, connected to the Market from the east. The houses, shops and workshops clustered together in concentrated spaces around the Market Place on strips of land that can still be traced, running at an angle to the roads. The Priory had its own borders in the form of a wall, but outside it there was a separate church facing the market, built for the townspeople; it gradually fell into decay.

Although Hexham had small industries that included iron working, it was largely famous from the thirteenth century onwards for tanning, especially later with the manufacture of gloves, for which the local cattle and sheep provided skins. On the outskirts were lead and galena industries that attracted itinerant labour, so it no surprise to find from early census returns that people were attracted from other parts of the country to settle there.

The Abbey is the most dominantly-beautiful and oldest of Hexham's buildings, surrounded by parkland, but there are also medieval and some seventeenth-century buildings surviving that help us to see some of the developments of the town over a long period.

Some of its visible history and what does not survive can be attributed to Hexham's position as a town in the Border zone between England and Scotland, for even when other parts of the country were at peace, the Border was not. Henry VIII's dissolution of the monasteries allowed the Priory church to continue to exist, but the monastic buildings were acquired by the Lord of the Manor. Today a huge project has been launched to re-unite these confiscated buildings with the Abbey.

The coming of the railways and the developments of roads have helped to change the nature of the townscape. Traditional industries have been replaced by large factories such as Egger for turning trees into woodchip, large allotment gardens have been built on for the use of a variety of small industries, a supermarket and leisure centre, but Hexham has still managed to keep vital parts of its past safeguarded whilst new housing has spread away from the historic centre and allowed it to be one of the most attractive towns in Northumberland. When we read in documents about the lack of hygiene in the mid-nineteenth century and realise what a filthy place the town was, we become aware of how far we have travelled.

The pictures and comments in this book will give an idea of what used to be and what is.

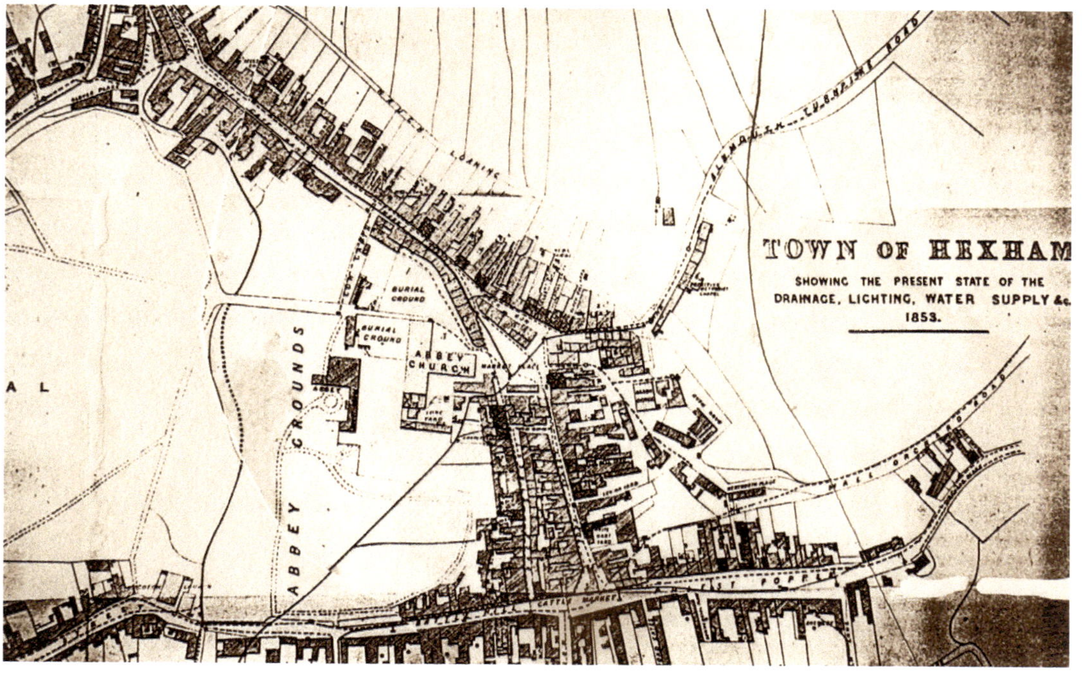

Hexham from the Air I

Rawlinson's map of 1853 that accompanied his survey of Hexham to apply the Public Health Act shows the extent of the town then. The roads focus on the Market Place. To the north there are fields before the Tyne is reached. Buildings are concentrated.

The air photograph shows that basically the pattern of building at the centre remains the same, with the Abbey (left) and civic buildings (right) around the market, but the riverside is now extensively developed.

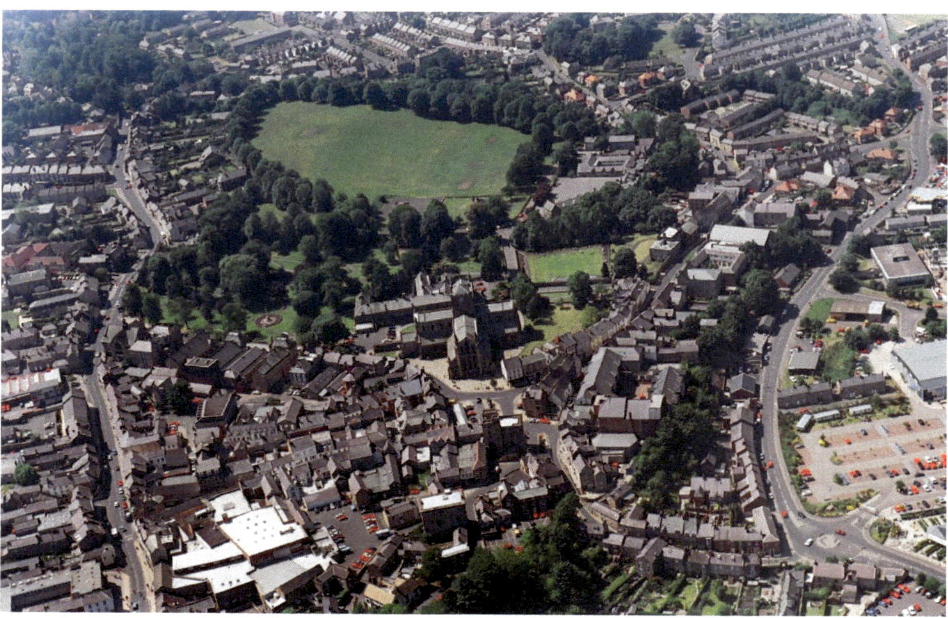

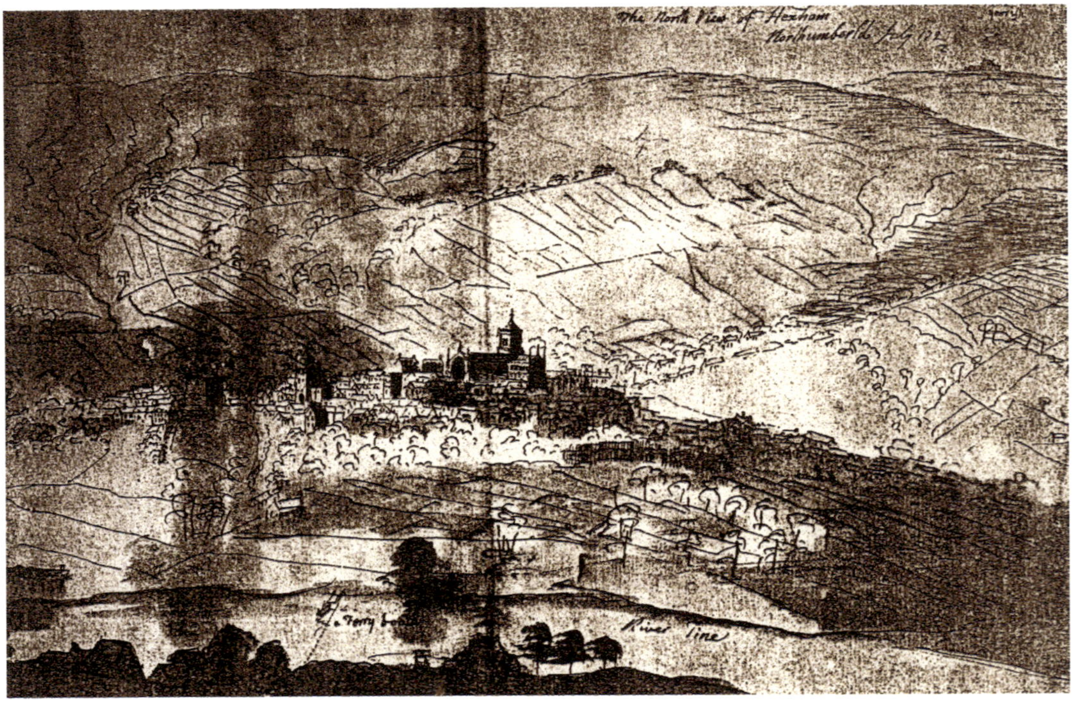

Abbey I

The view across the river from the north is of the Sele (still an open space today) and the Abbey in 1772.

Today the Abbey still dominates the skyline, the riverside includes a green space and a pleasant public walk, golf course and railway, with the rest of the haugh (flat, alluvial land) taken over by industries, retail stores, car parks and a leisure centre.

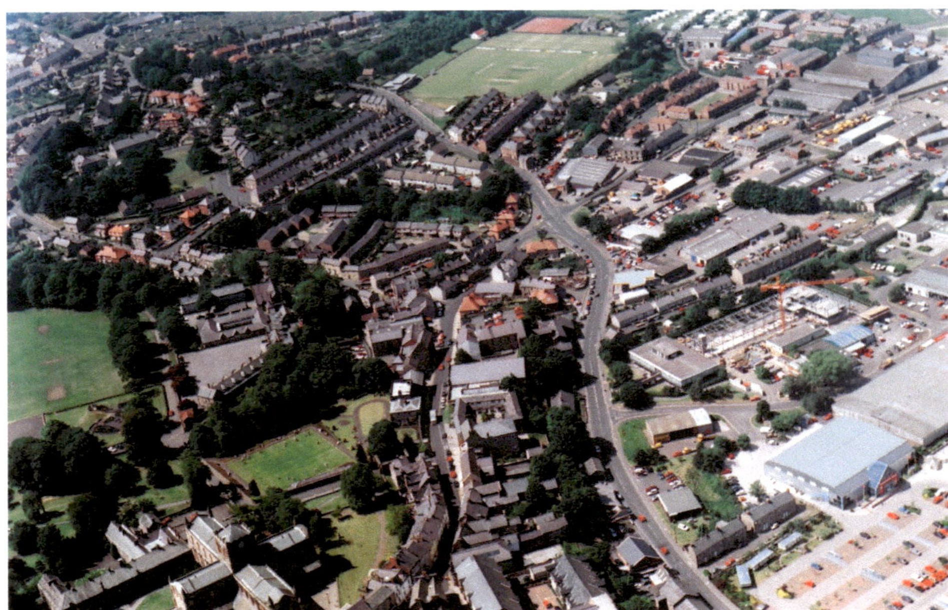

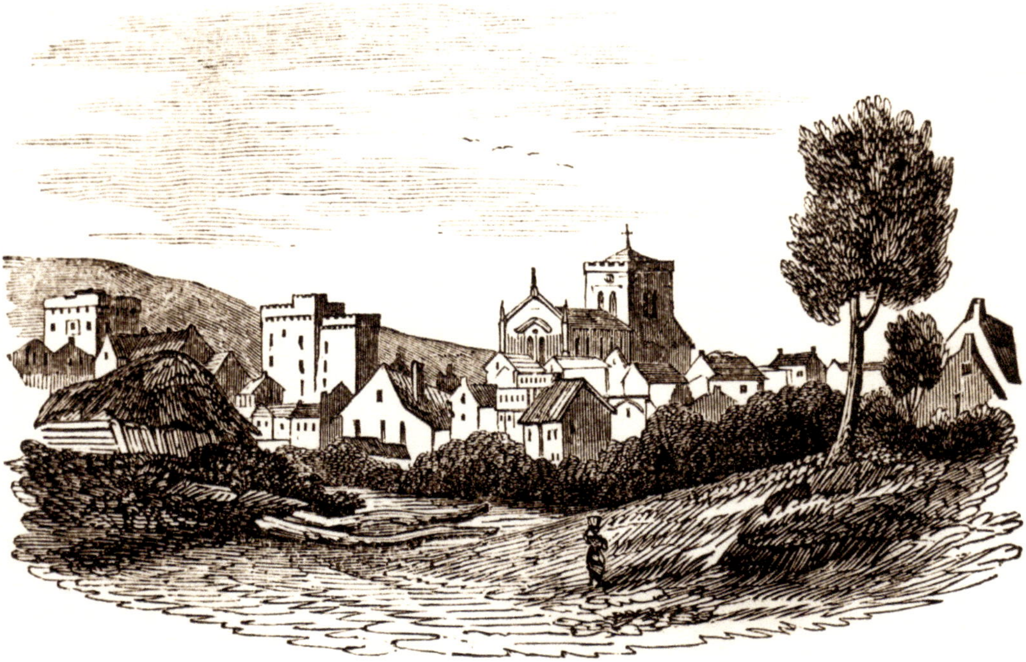

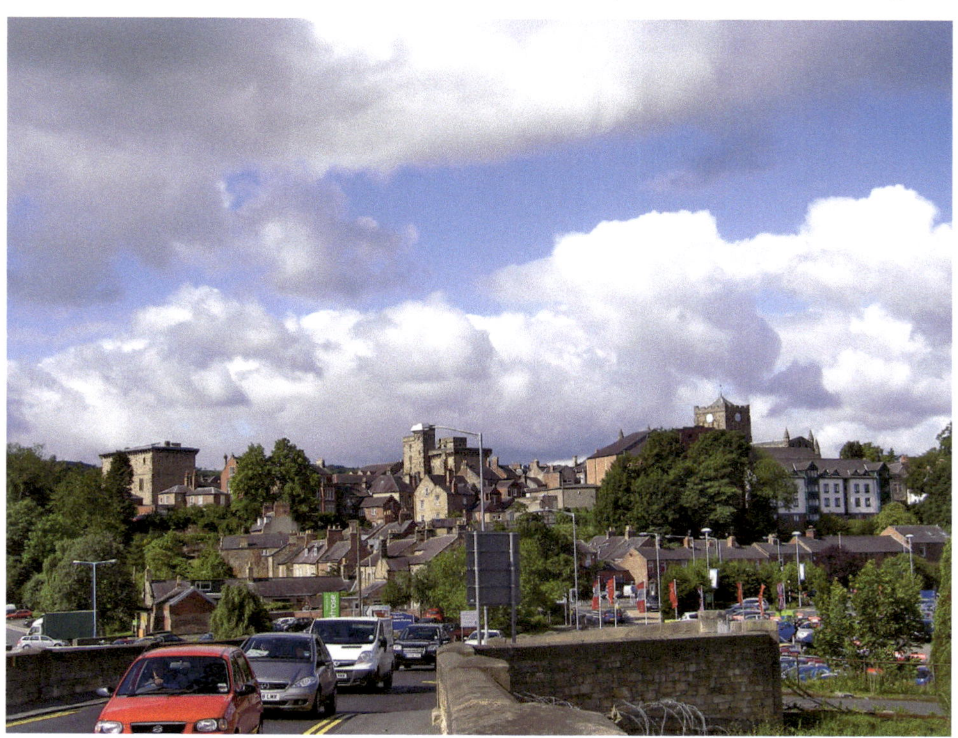

An old sketch of the town centre from the river and today's view from the rail bridge.

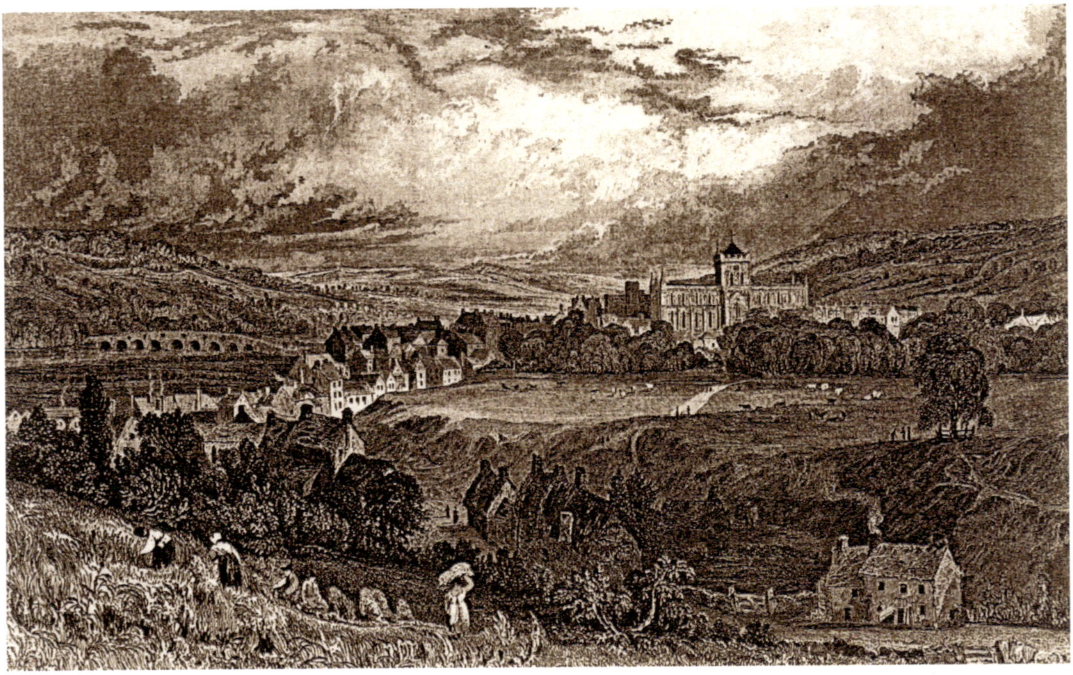

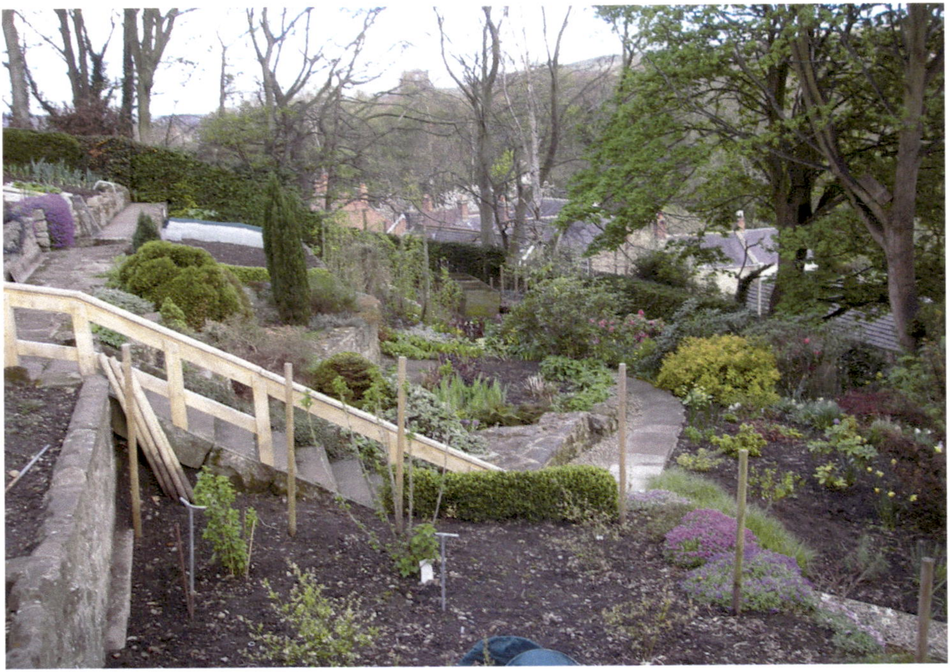

A view south across the Cockshaw Burn, a tributary of the Tyne, from Windmill Hill, where there used to be a mill for grinding bark used in the tanning industry. The slopes were a source of grain, which we see being cut in the mid-nineteenth century.

Today the sloping stream bank has houses and gardens built over it.

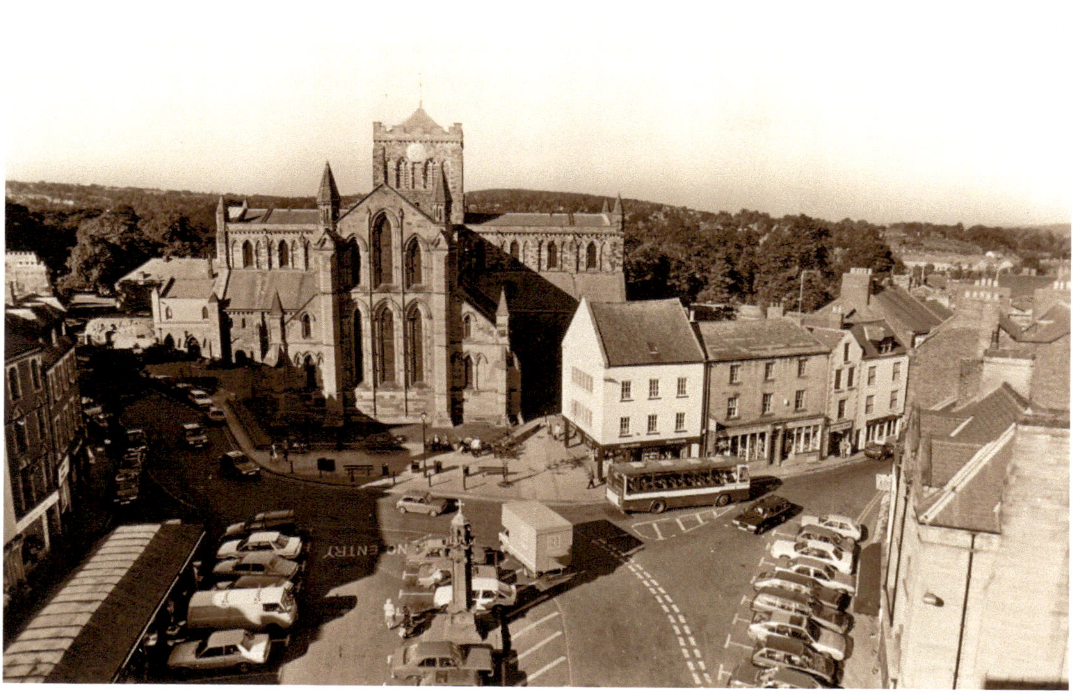

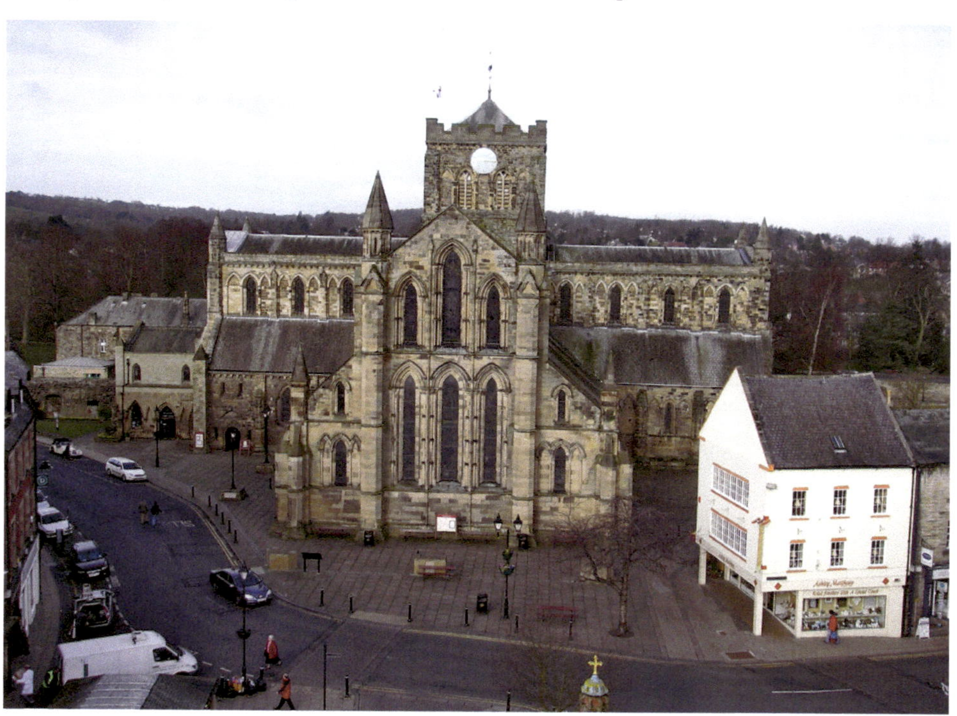

Abbey II

After an excavation around the east and south of the Abbey, sandstone paving was laid, sealing in many medieval graves. The view is from the top of the Moothall.

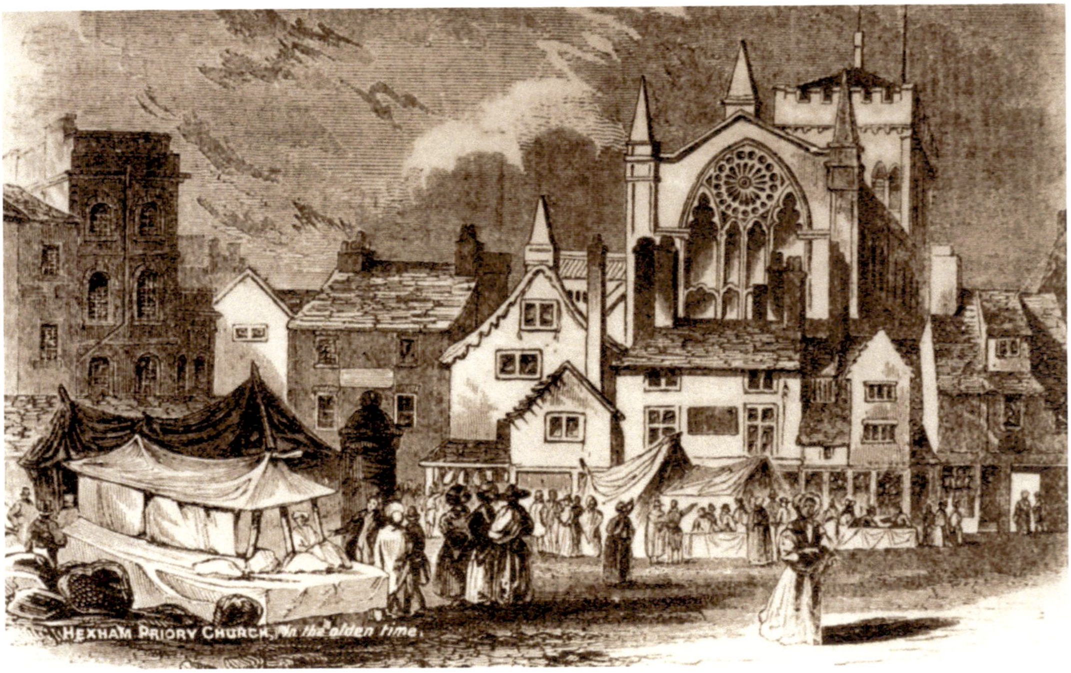

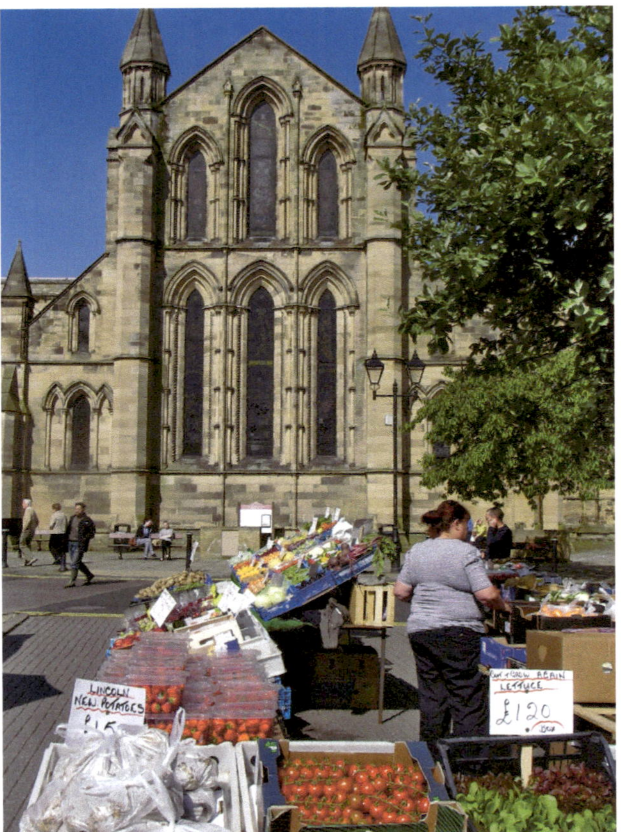

Market Place I

The Market Place was once covered with vertically-set sandstone blocks. The old drawing shows the west market, when buildings were crowded against the Abbey. Below, the Market Place today.

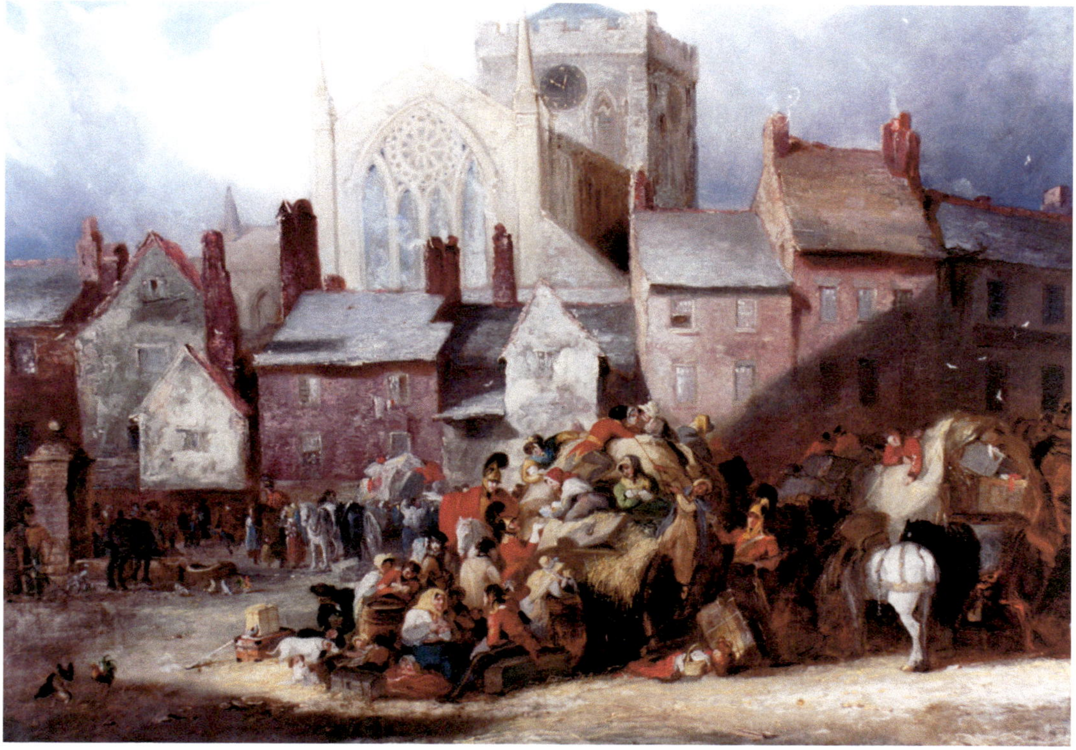

Unsanitary Hexham

A painting by Henry Perlee Parker in the
1820s has the same group of soldiers as
the one outside St Nicholas' Cathedral
in Newcastle, but the background gives
a vivid picture clearly of what type of
buildings filled the space before they
were removed: sawmill, abattoir, and
pig sties included. Rawlinson's report on
Hexham in the 1850s drew attention to
overcrowded and insanitary conditions in
the town generally. This is a re-drawn plan
of that area then, used by Rawlinson to
illustrate his findings.

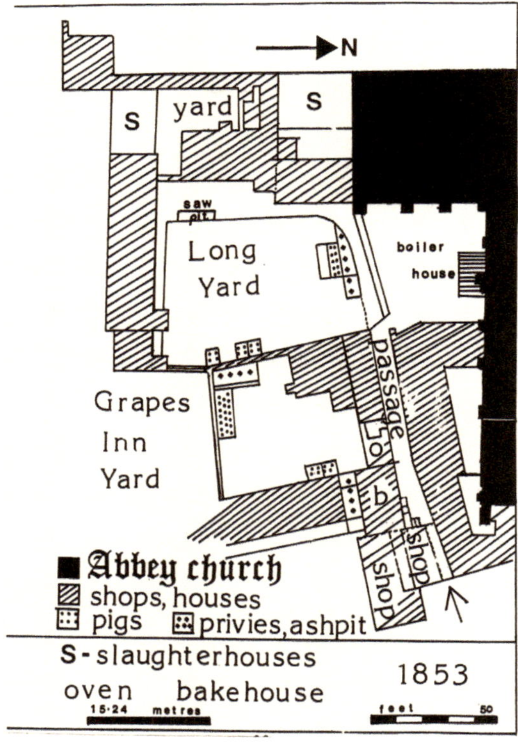

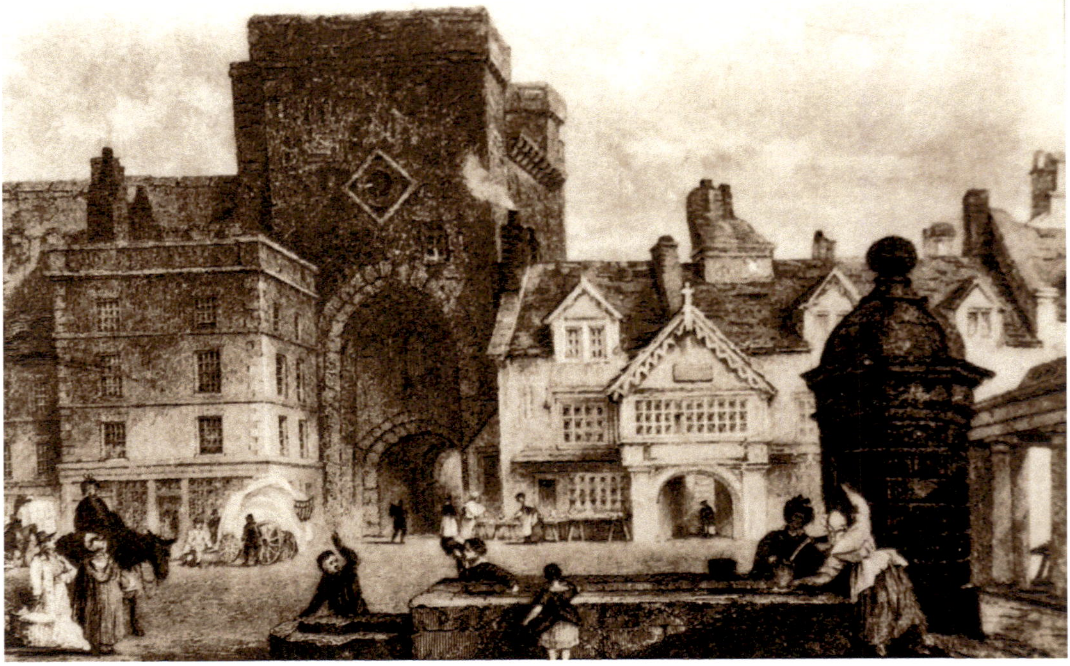

Market Place II

To the east, the Market Place was more open, with the attractive White Hart Inn still intact. The entrance to the civil administration area was through the Moothall tunnel. Its wall was used later as a prop for brick buildings. The recent picture shows the extent of changes since then.

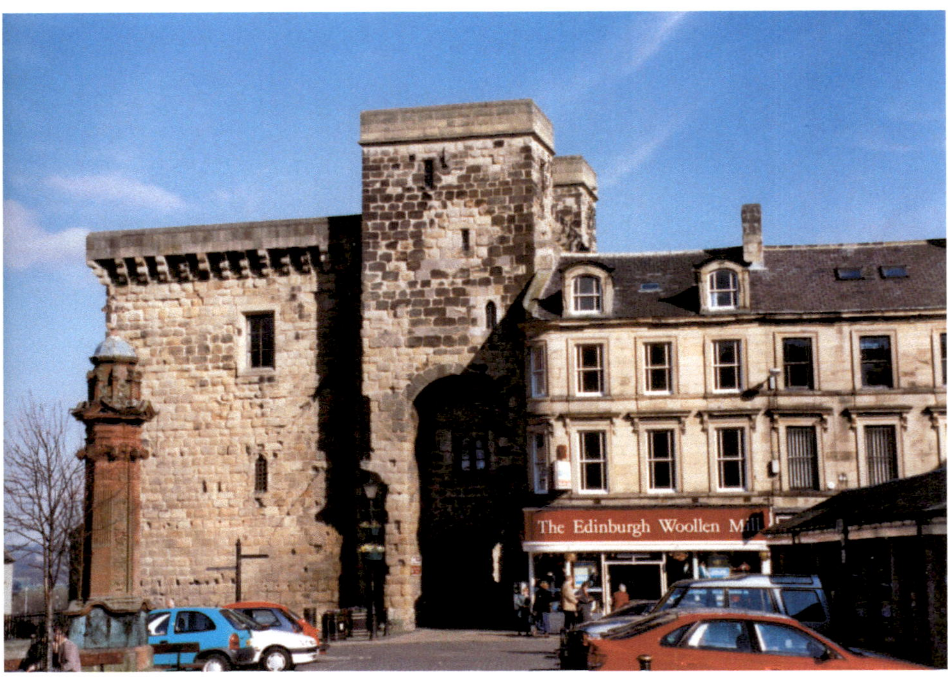

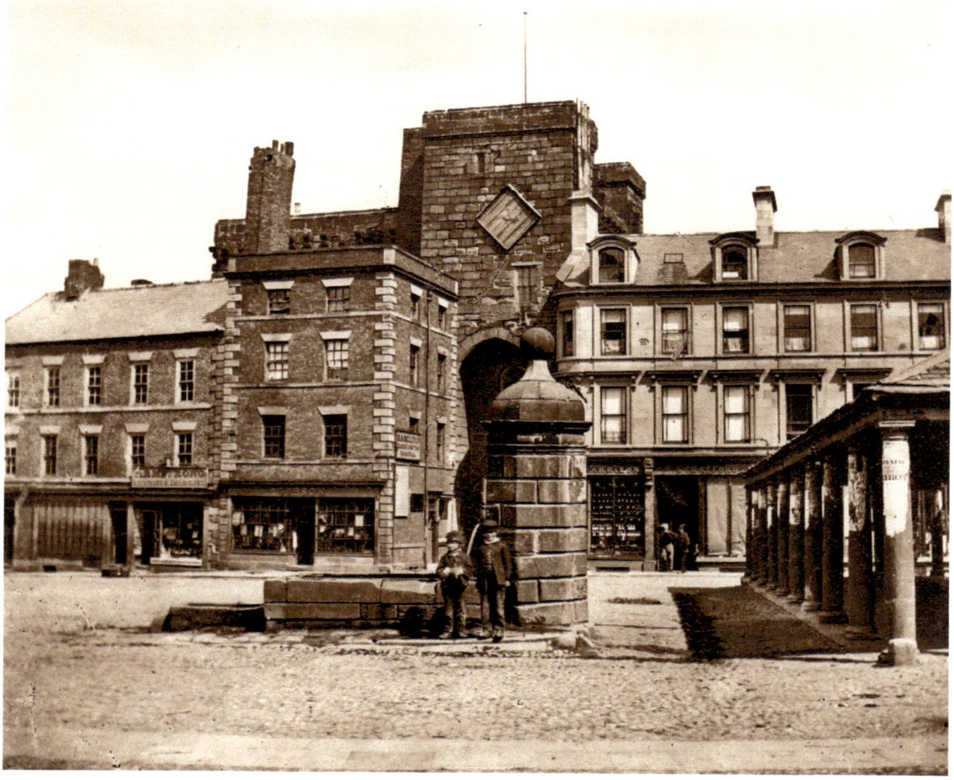

Market Place and Moothall

This more detailed picture of the White Horse Inn with the Shambles alongside shows what an attractive building has been lost. Changing styles of architecture and function of buildings are a common theme in history.

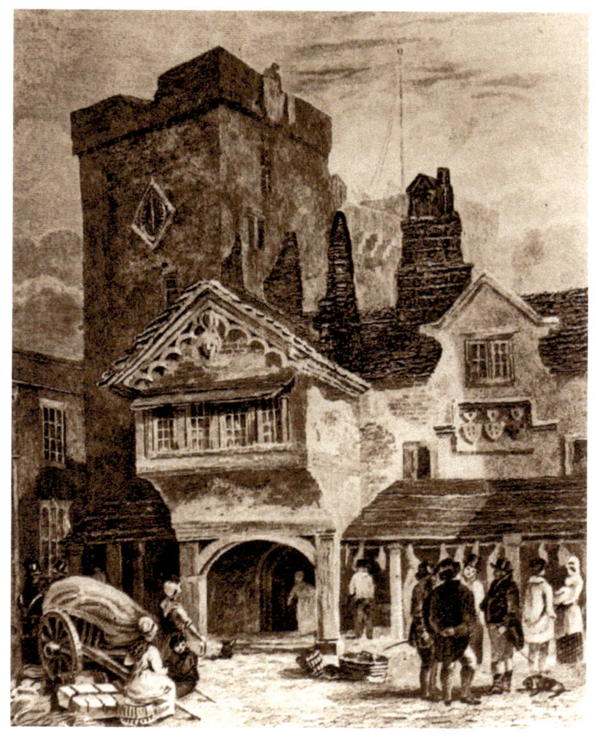

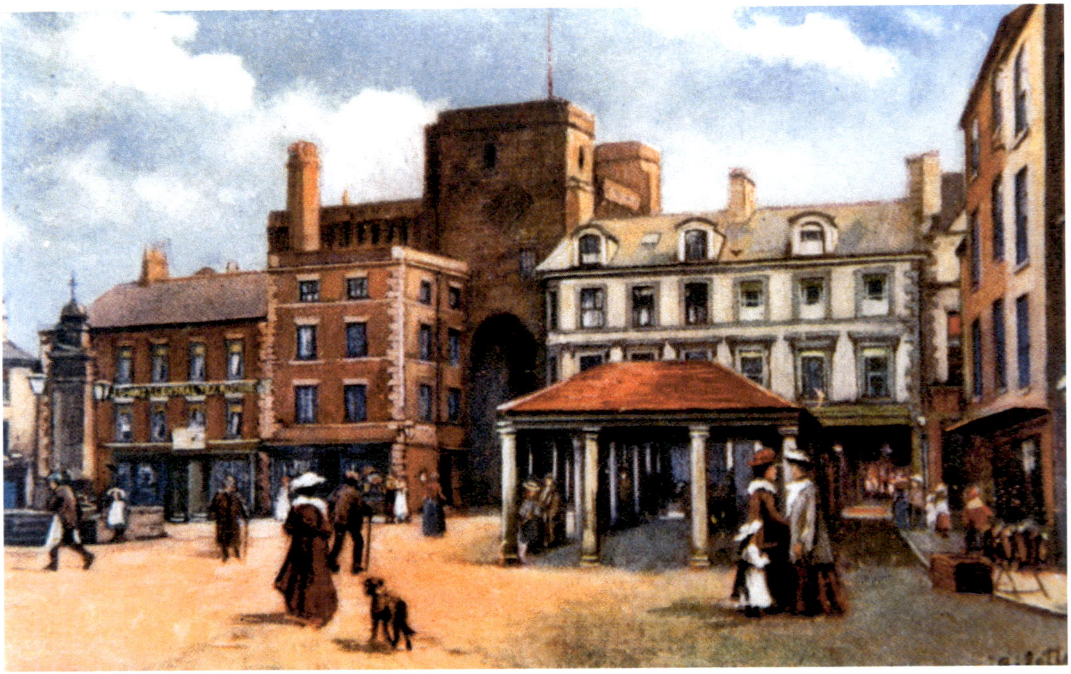

Market Place III

Postcards of the Market Place were popular, as well as place mats, and many survive from the twentieth century. They are often hand-painted photographs. The present fountain with its poem by local poet, Wilfrid Gibson. The modern Christmas Market has a nice touch of humour on one of its stalls.

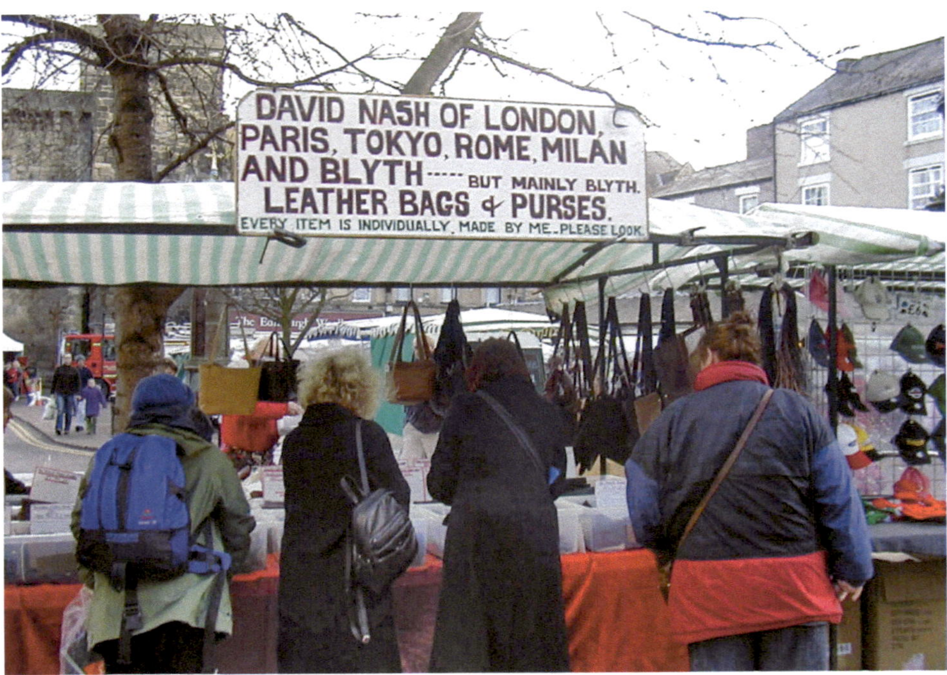

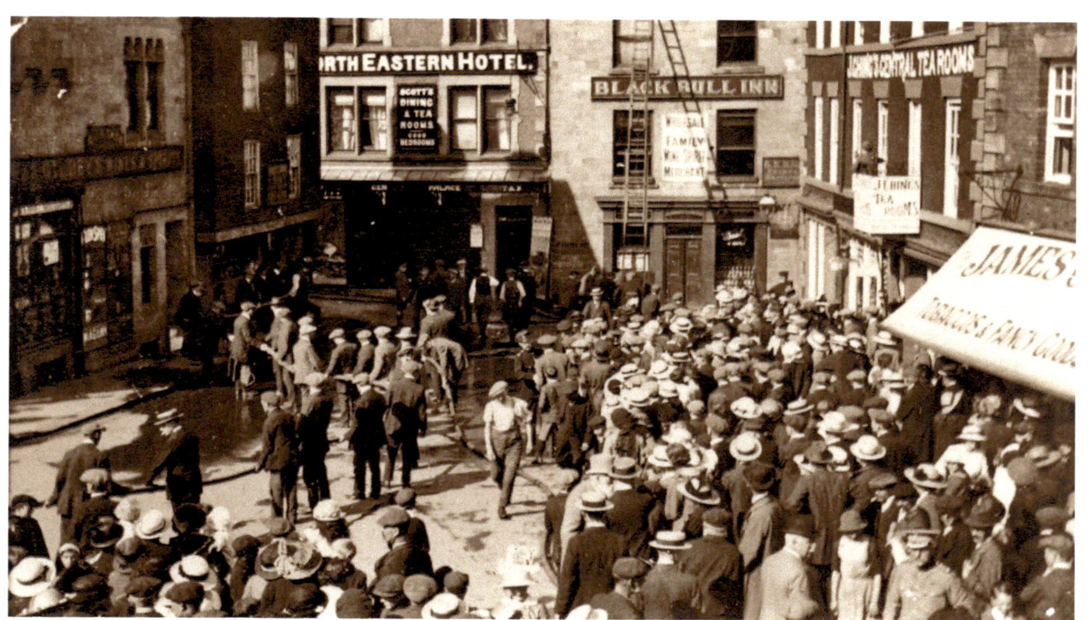

Forum Cinema

In the 1960s there was a fire in what is now the Forum Cinema area. The Black Bull inn gave its name to Black Bull Bank, leading down to Haugh Lane, but is now called Hallstile Bank. The North Eastern Hotel has gone and the Gem Palace is now the Forum. On the left is the Queen's Arms Inn.

Below, the same area today shows some of these changes. The top of the inn has been taken off and Wetherspoon's, and the Forum Cinema and a working men's club have taken over the top of the area.

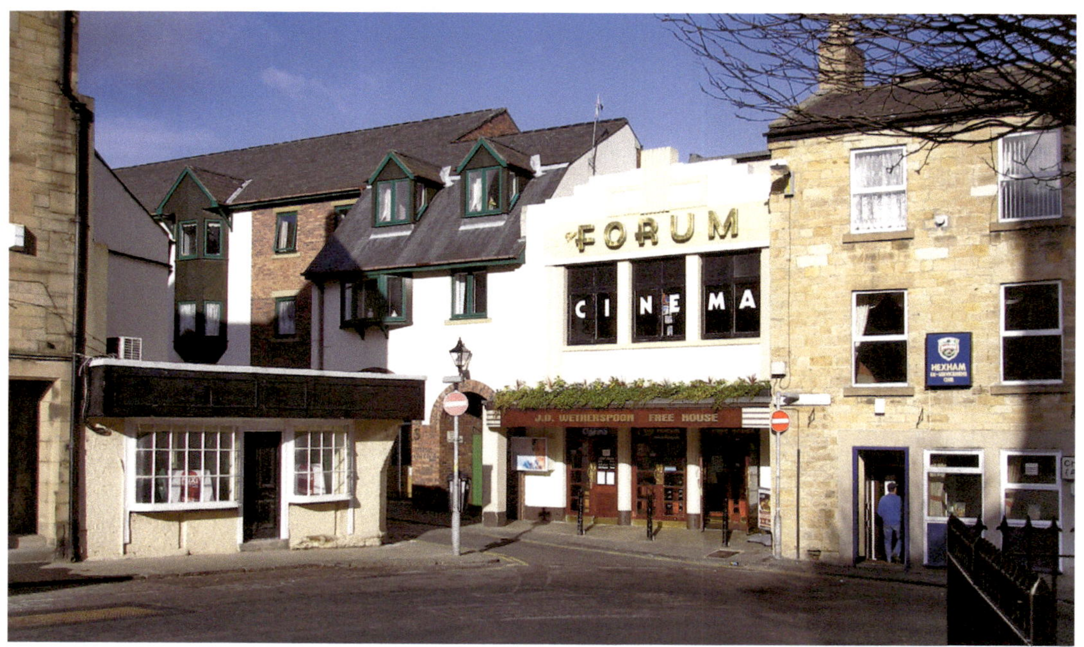

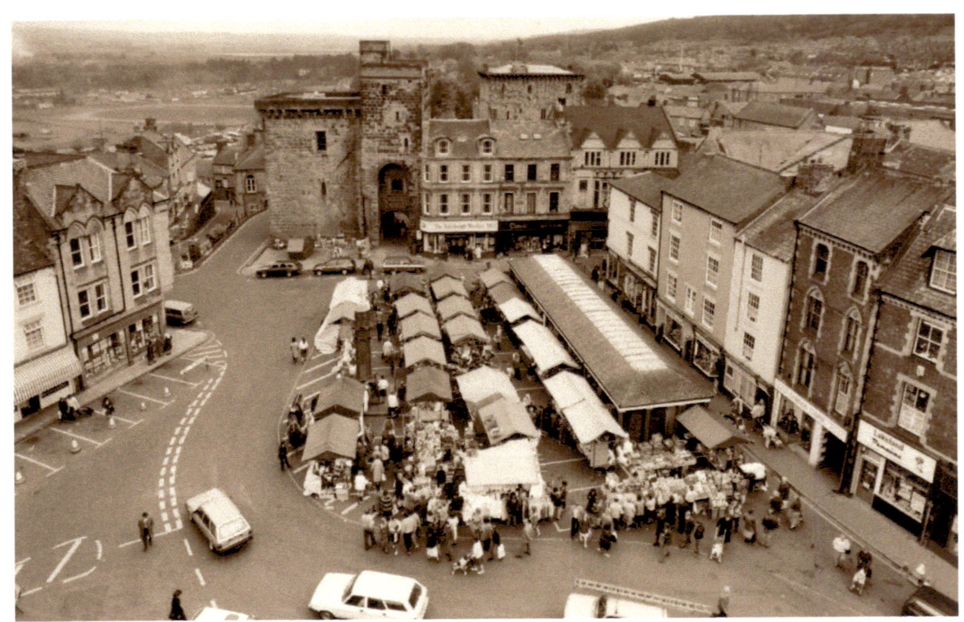

The Shambles – a rectangular building to the right – was built by Sir Walter Blackett, Lord of the Manor, as a covered market. The straight line of shops on the other side follows the shape of the rectangular medieval church, with the shops built into and from it.

The modern information board, recently made, is a good guide to what research has discovered about the possible appearance of the Market Place. The depiction of the old thirteenth-century church, which became derelict and was used as houses and workshops, has the line of its nave arches facing north and depicts the administrative enclosure that includes the Moothall and gaol.

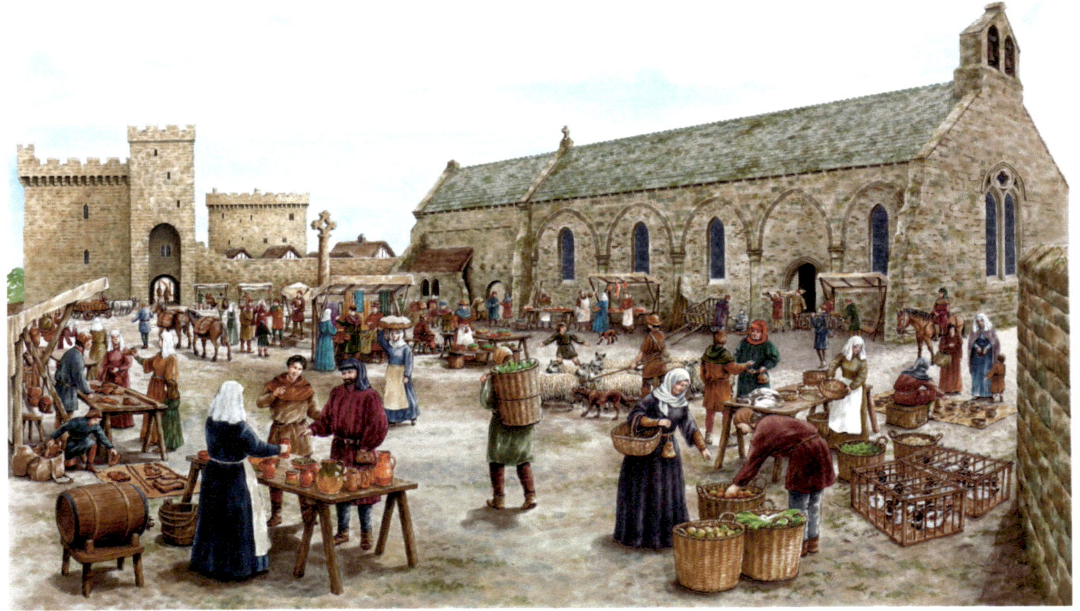

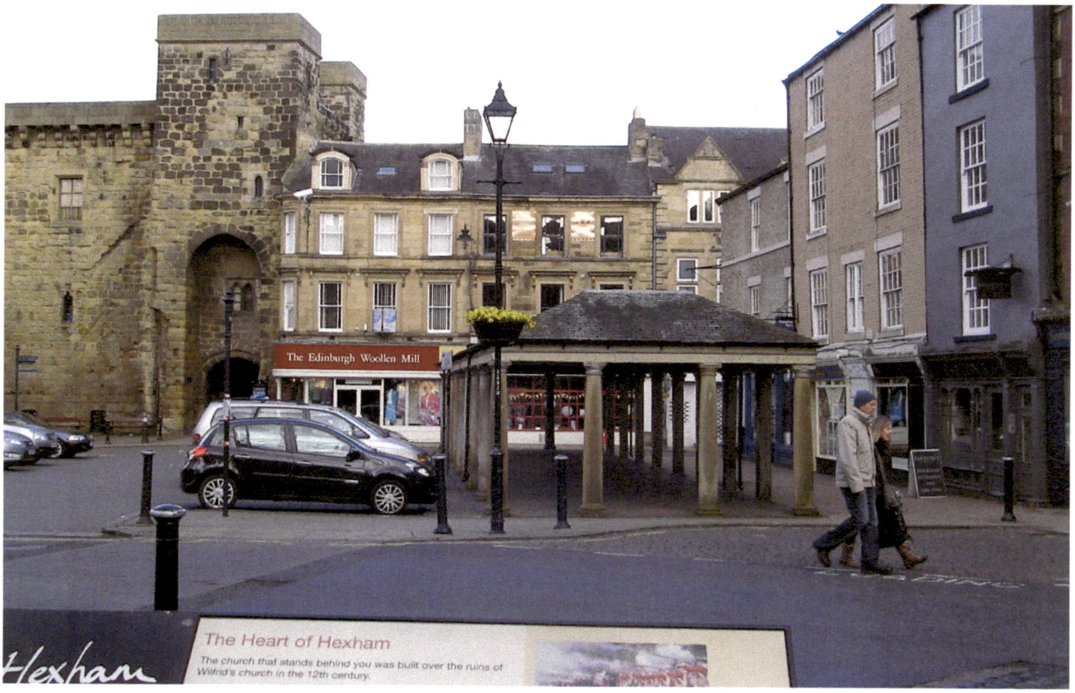

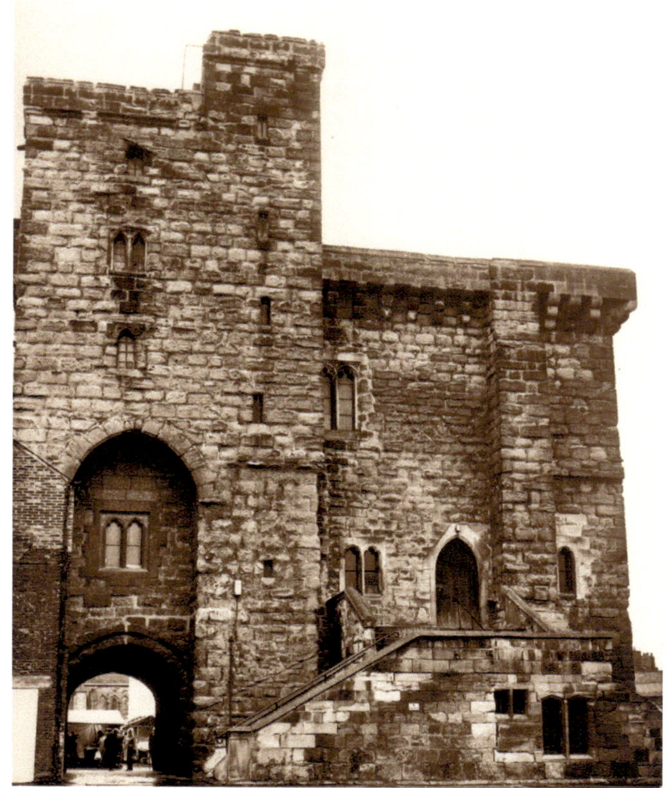

Market Today

Today we look over the notice board to see what has survived and what has been changed or added. A tunnel through the Moothall from the Market leads to the back of this old administrative building, only a little changed since this picture was taken.

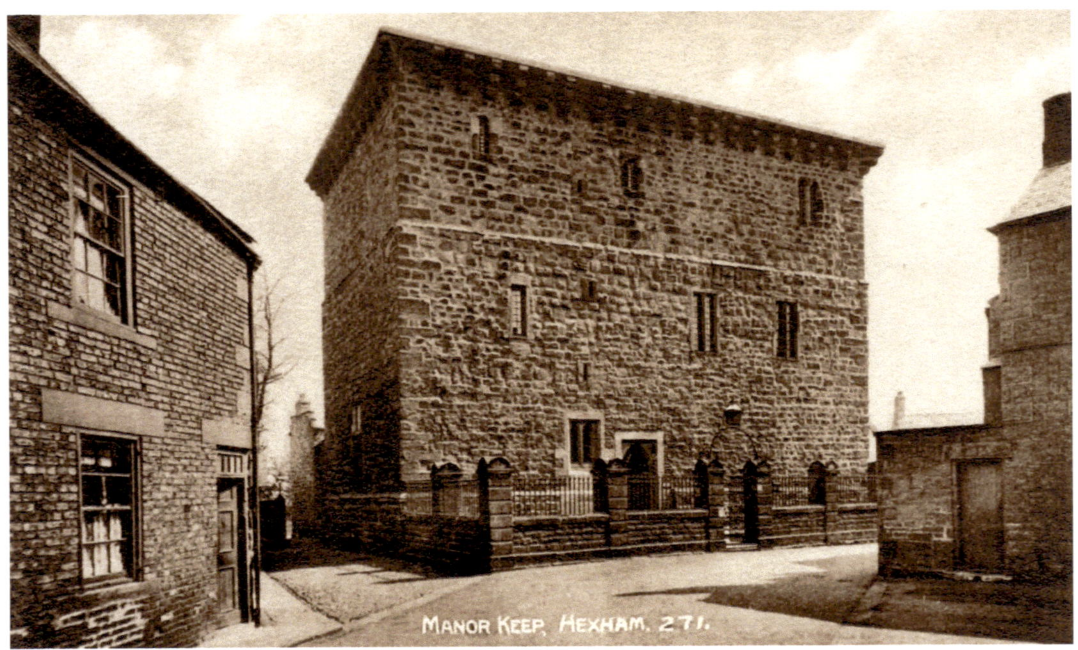

Old Gaol

The Old Gaol, later to become the Manor Office, was built by the Archbishop of York in 1330 on the site of an older prison. Today, this impressive sandstone block, with an added storey, is a museum and holds books and documents of Border history. It is fitted with a lift.

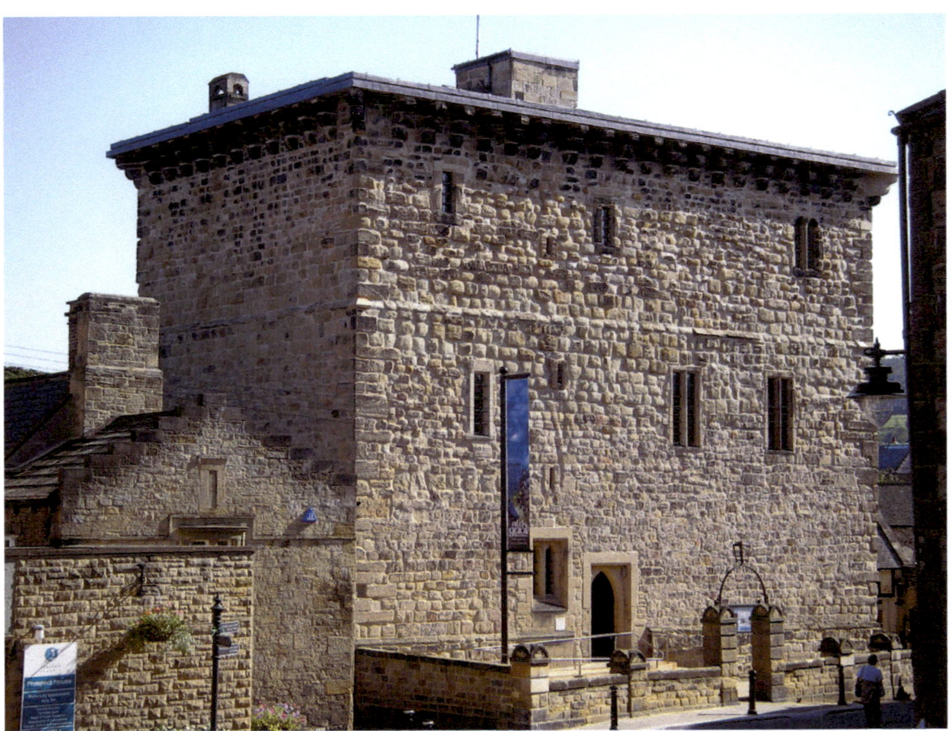

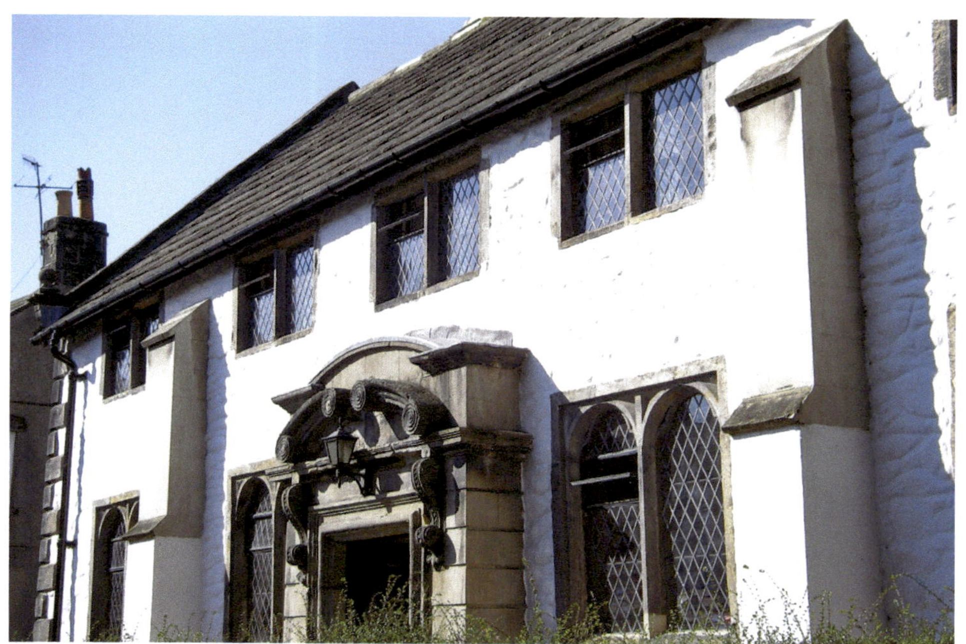

It has a relocated doorway, and is one of the four historic properties for sale since the formation of the Northumberland unitary authority, last occupied as a town planning office. Master and boys (boarders) are seen outside the school in the nineteenth century. It moved to a new site at Fellside where it is now the Middle School, then as a comprehensive school to the Hydro site.

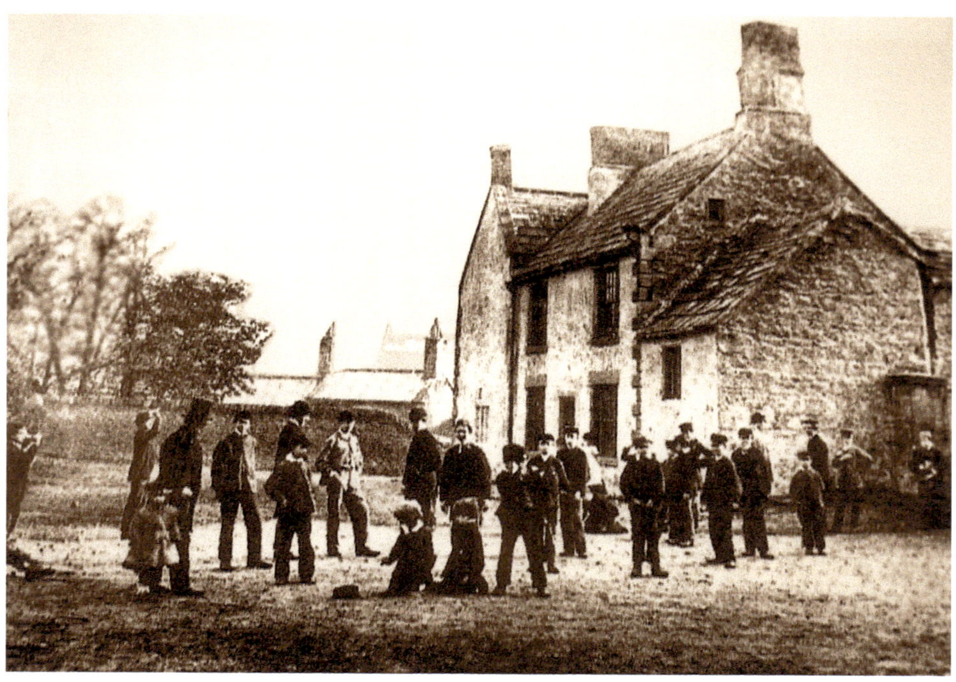

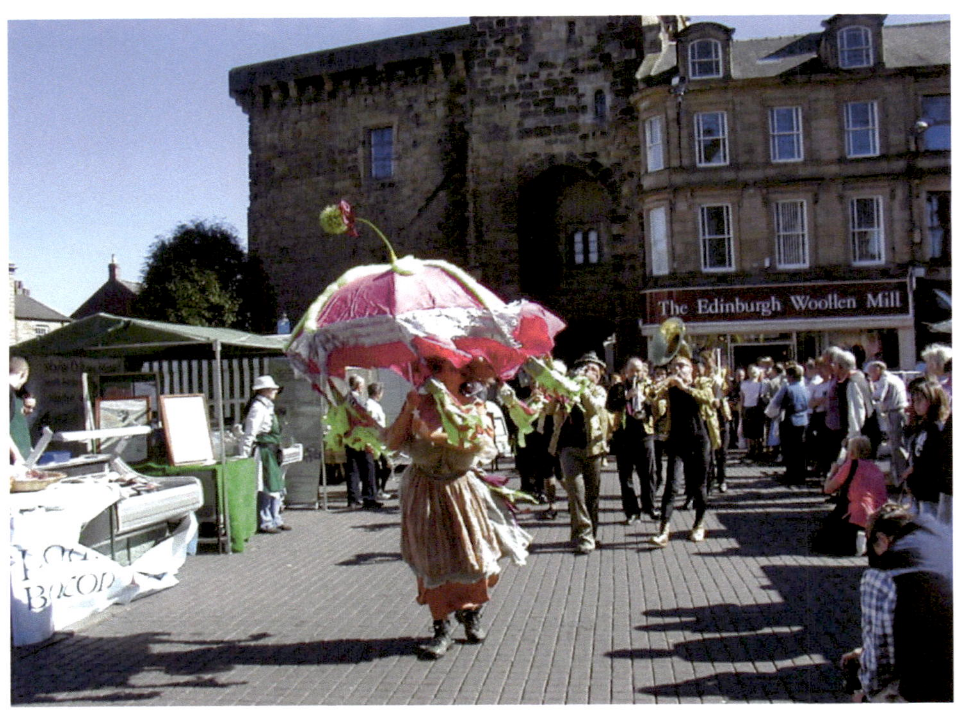

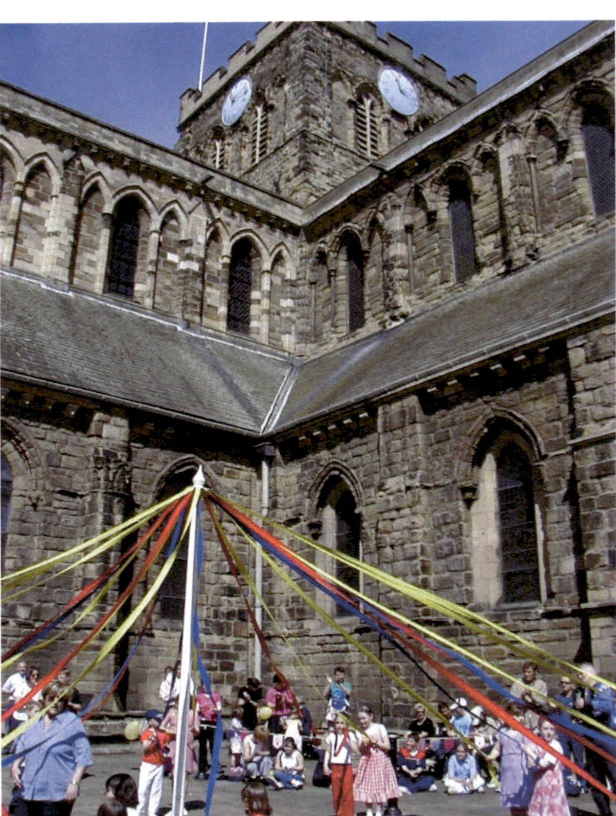

Market Place IV

The Market Place is a popular focus on festive occasions – in this case a jazz band in the Abbey festival. Other festivities spill over to the south of the Abbey, where a local First School has erected a maypole. Below, the flagstones on which they dance are the canon's graveyard.

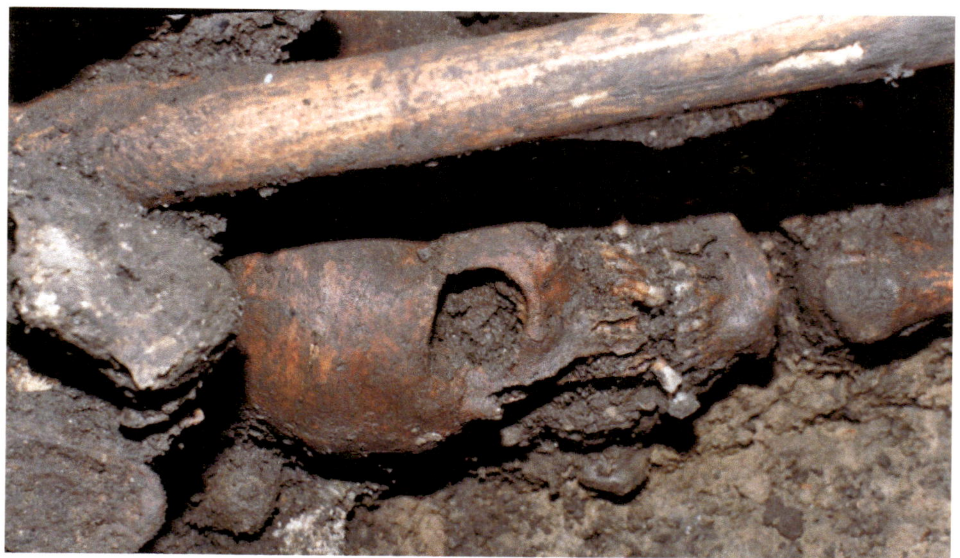

Abbey Excavations

In 1990, BT cable trenches unearthed skeletons by the Abbey pavement. The author cleaned up and recorded the trench. Loose bones were removed and examined by specialists, and those left in section were reburied without further disturbance. The lower bodies were buried on their sides with their faces to the south, and were probably Anglo-Saxon. Later burials above were on their backs, their feet to the east. The disturbed bones in this trench were reburied under the north transept floor at a special service.

In 1990 the Newcastle University Archaeological Practice excavated the whole area in preparation for the laying of flagstones and again there was a special service of re-burial in the north transept. In addition to the burials of pre-Dissolution canons, the foundations of a lean-to chapel were unearthed. All areas below the surface in the town are potentially of archaeological interest.

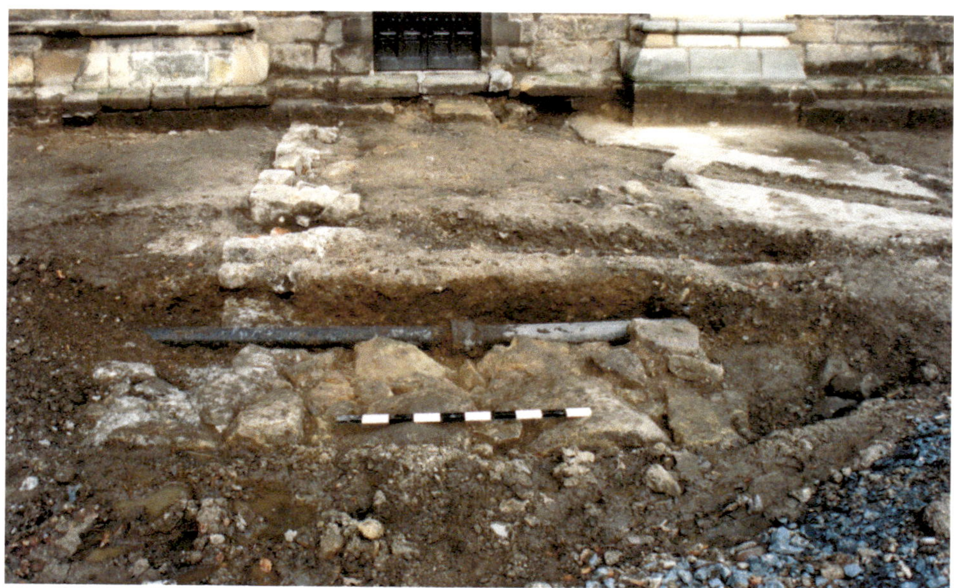

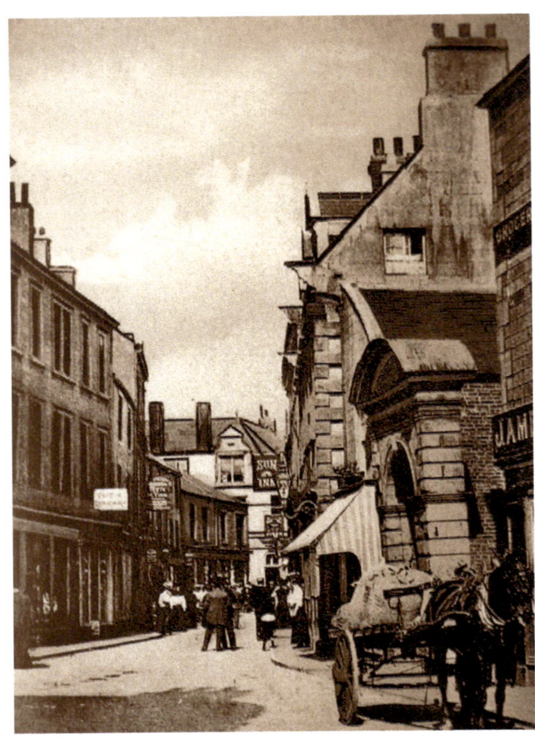

Fore Street I

Fore Street (Coastley Road) is a main route south from the Market. In the early twentieth century the archway ran to the White Hart Inn yard, and during the extension of Robbs' (now Beales') it became the entrance to the Abbey grounds as a war memorial. Below, the same view south in 2012.

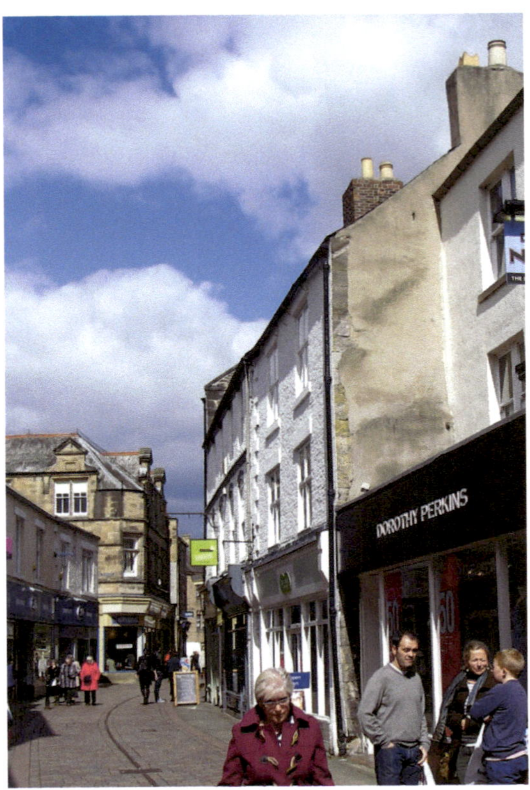

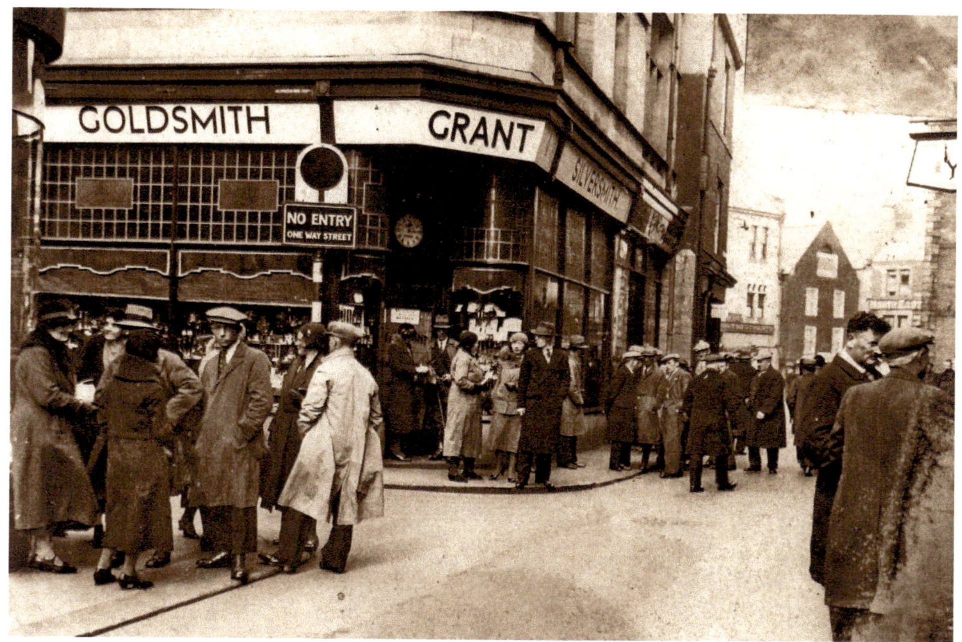

Fore Street II

A crowd gathers at the top of Fore Street outside what is now Greggs. An important survival is Gibson's pharmacy, the contents of which were recreated in London Science Museum for display in the 1960s, leaving the elaborate exterior intact in Hexham. The pharmacy had been opened in 1834. Because John Gibson became Freeman of the Worshipful Company of Spectacle Makers and a Freeman of London in 1908, this was commemorated by the coat of arms above the shop.

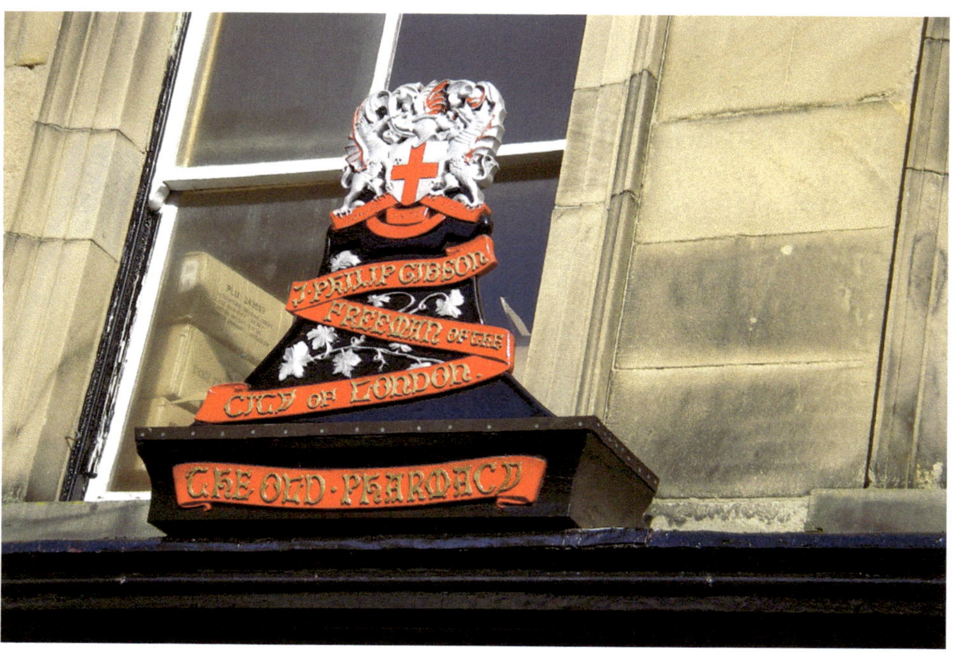

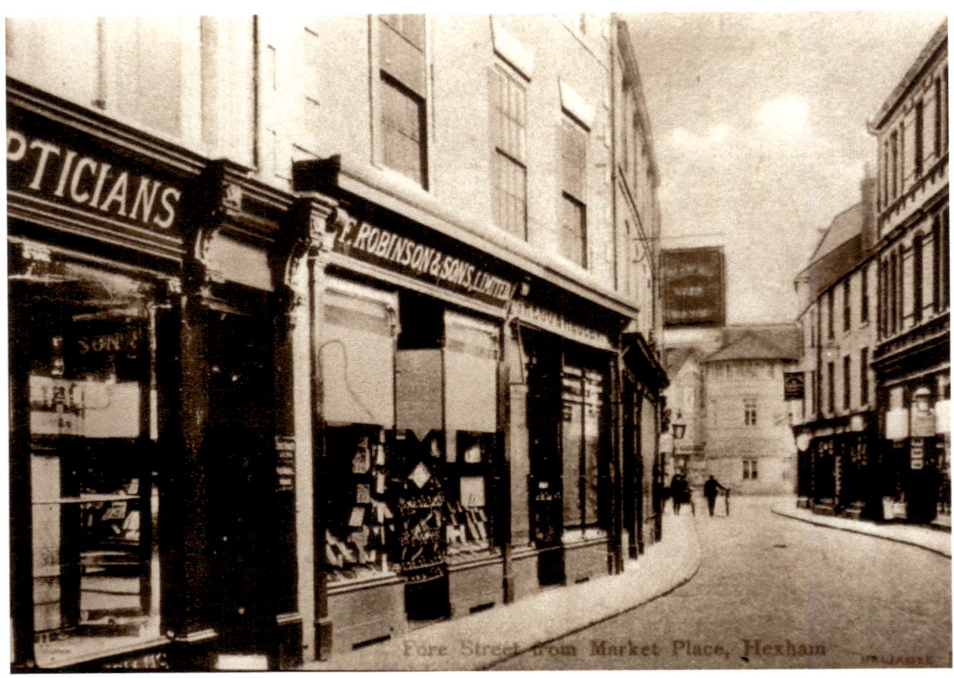

Fore Street from the South

This recent picture was taken from the top of the Moothall. The ruined medieval church of St Mary determines the shape of other buildings that face the market.

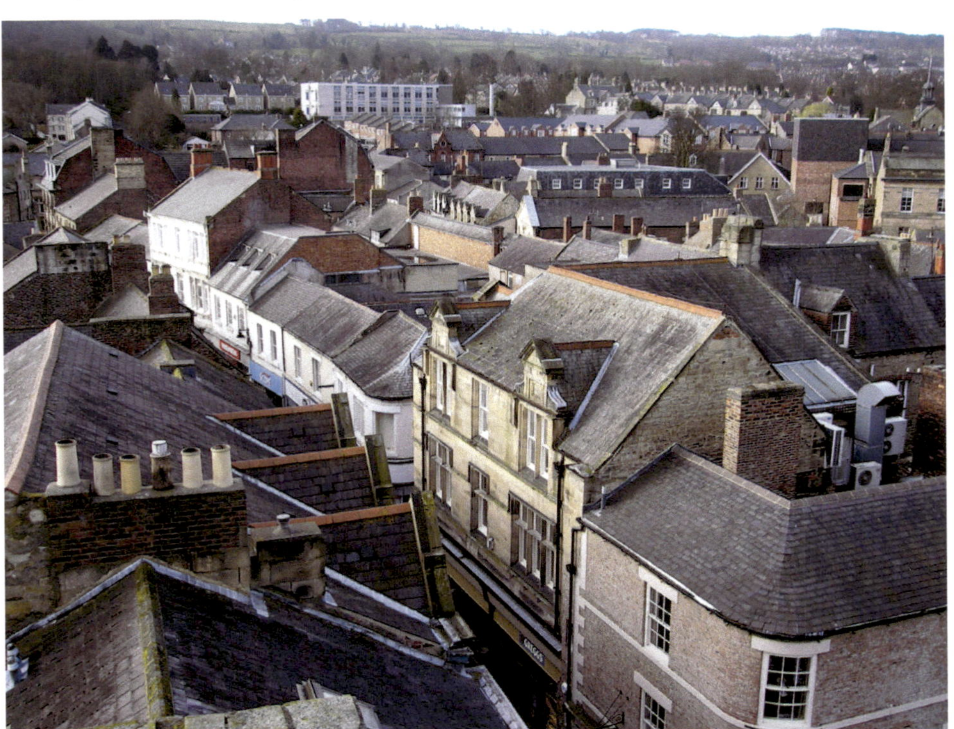

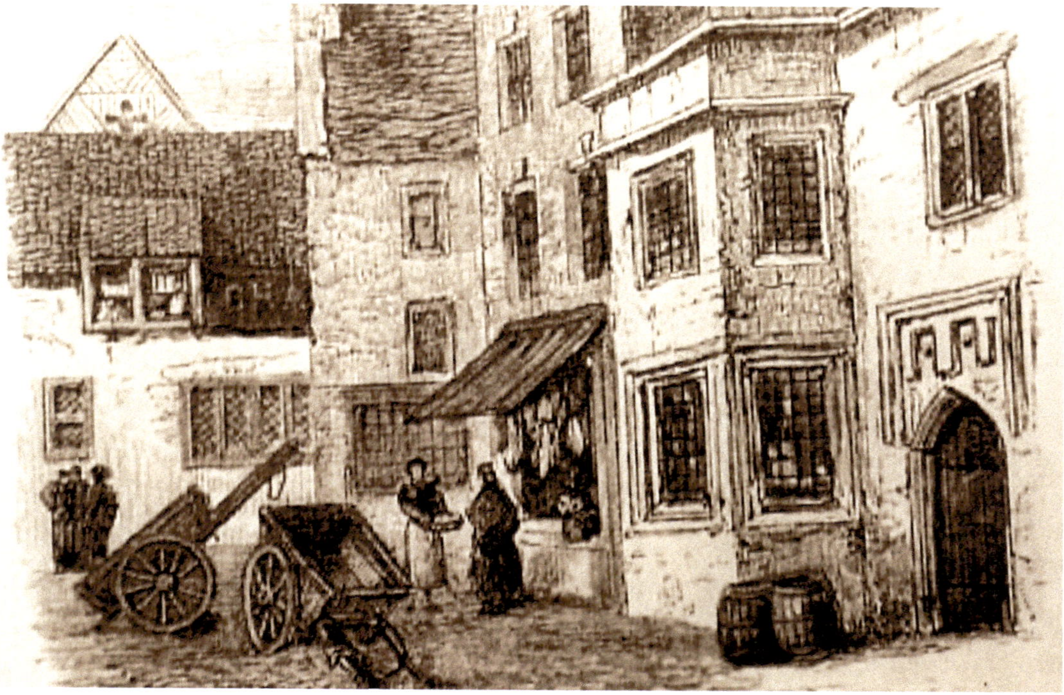

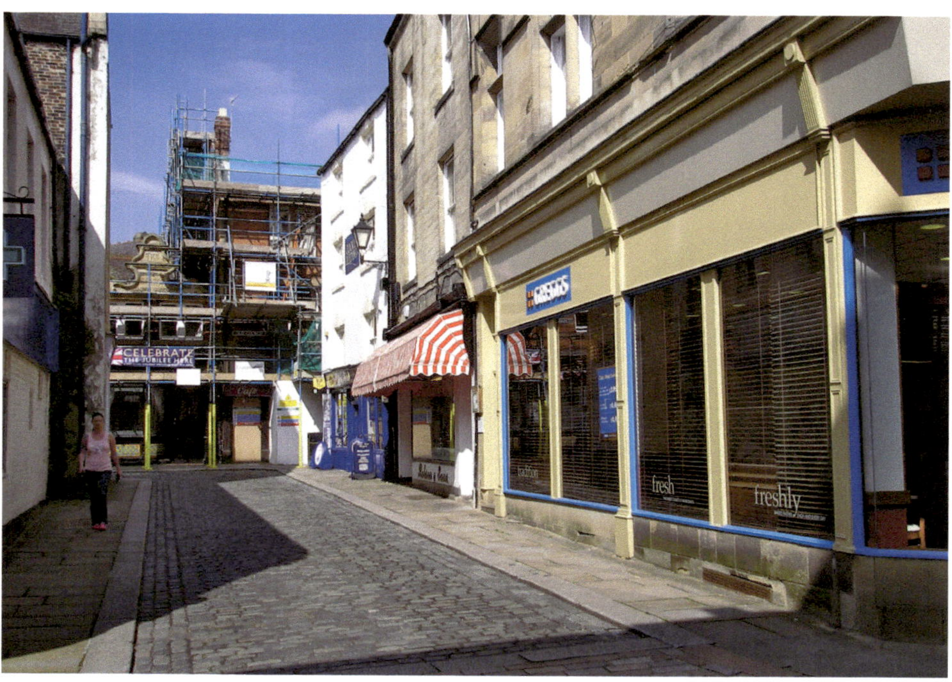

Meal Market I

The Meal Market had one of the oldest buildings demolished in 1883. On the site of the old church, the doorway survives by being built into a brick West End Terrace overlooking the Cockshaw Burn.

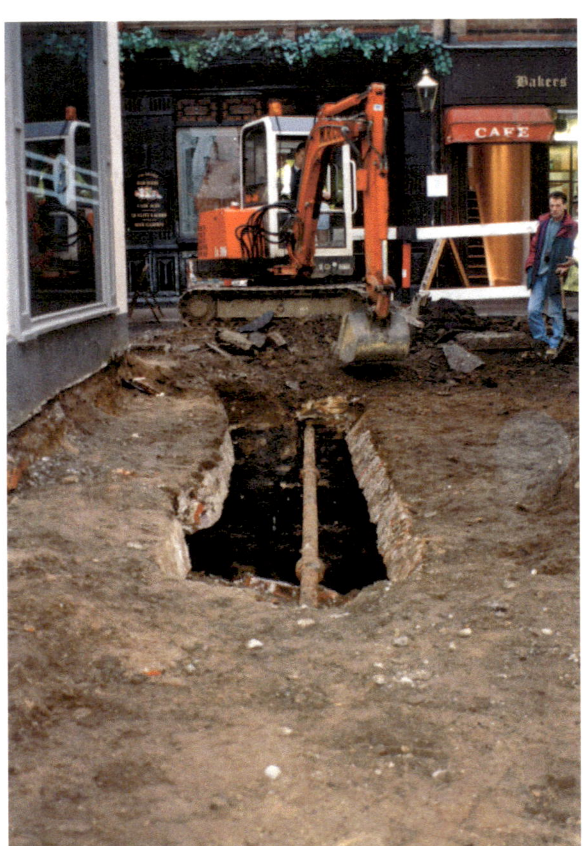

Meal Market II

In the 1990s the Meal Market road collapsed and revealed a cellar underneath where the department store preceding the present Boots Chemist stored crockery and glass. The cellars built in Hexham provided more space in a compact area, with an arched roof of brick and sandstone.

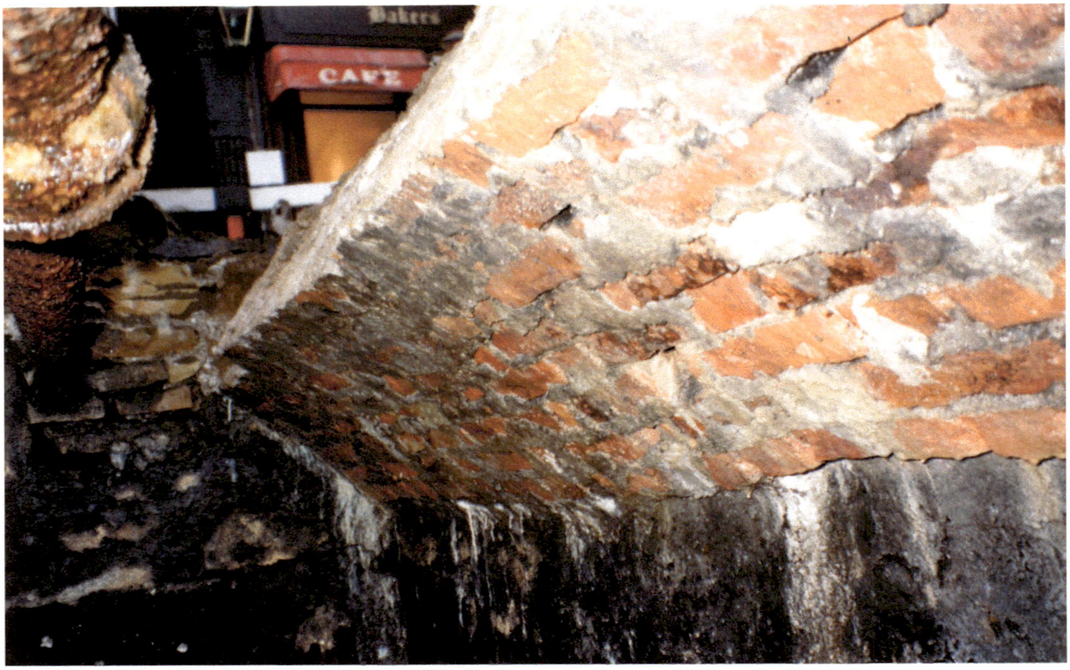

St Mary's Chare I

St Mary's Chare (a small street) or Back Street has strips of land on either side where houses, workshops rubbish tips and pig sties used to lie in a 'burgage' pattern. The old view is to the north and its access to the Market Place.

A modern view shows the modern Grapes Inn, with its lovely mixture of stone and decorated red brick, tiles and stained glass. Beyond that the development of Dickinson's furnishings continues.

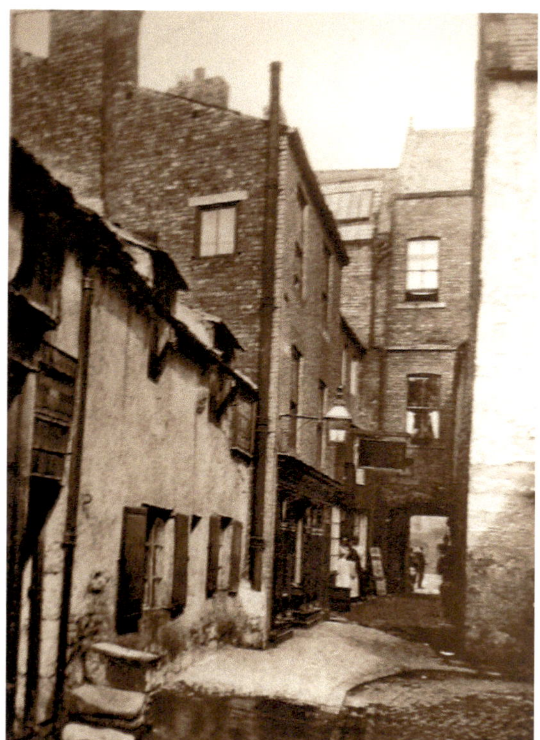

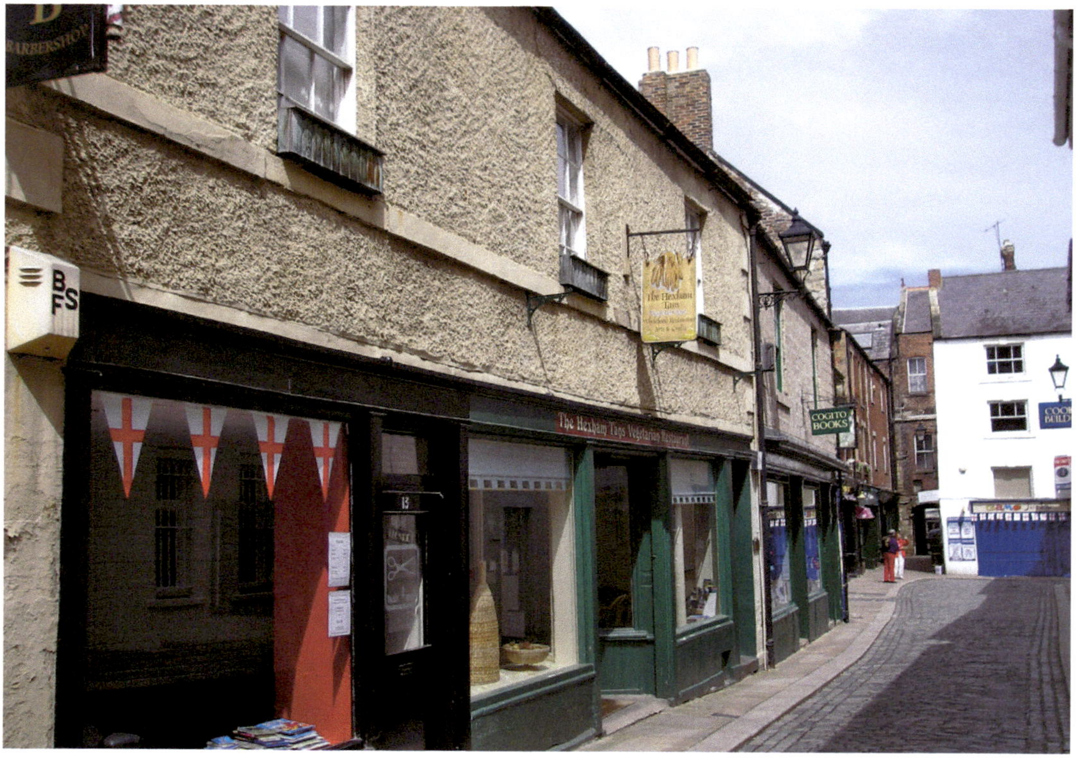

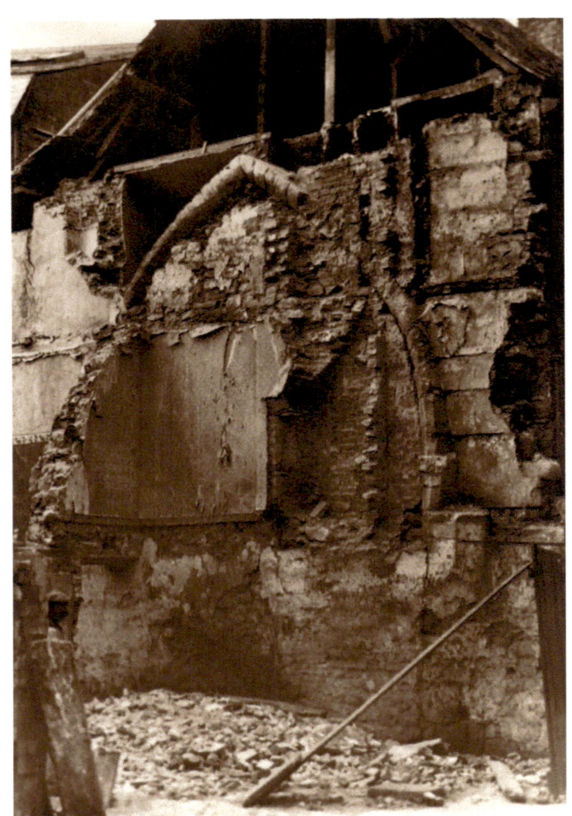

Dissolution

By the time of the Dissolution of Monasteries, the church of St Mary was already in disrepair, so much so that the Abbey church was left to be the parish church. This church, built in the thirteenth century, was rectangular, with parallel rows of Gothic arches. One of these arches is revealed in Dickinson's premises.

Other remains lie in cellars – especially that of Carris' shop; a shop and a bread oven was built into the church at Paxton's Fish restaurant (named by Peter Ryder as 'a plaice in history'). The most visible is in a small yard on the way to the market, where the Gothic arches are built into walls. The flat above the open archway has a thirteenth-century arch built into it, covered by wallpaper when I last saw it.

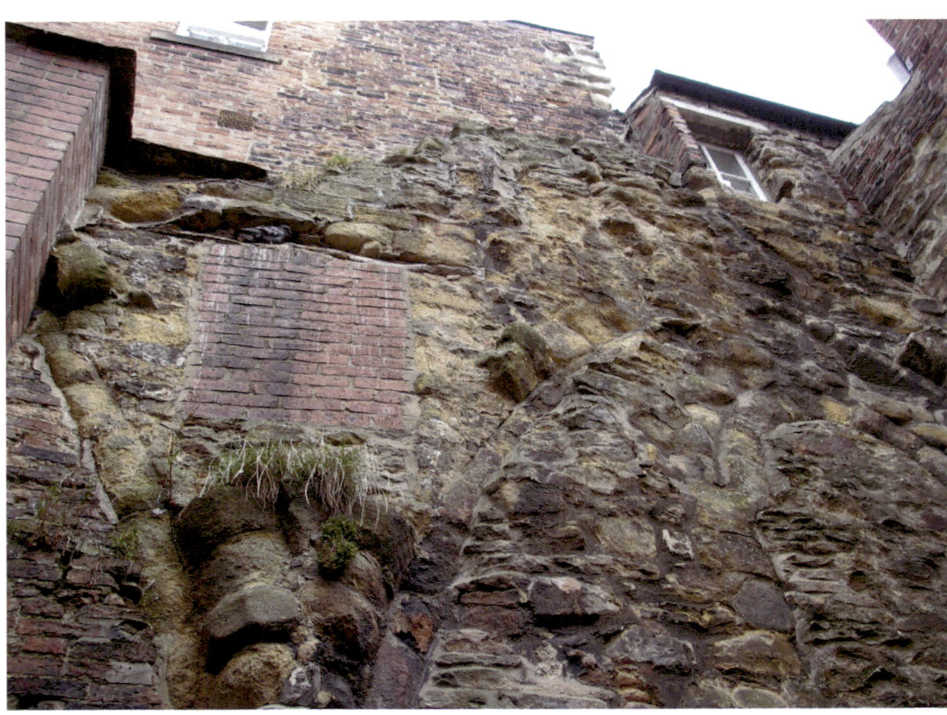

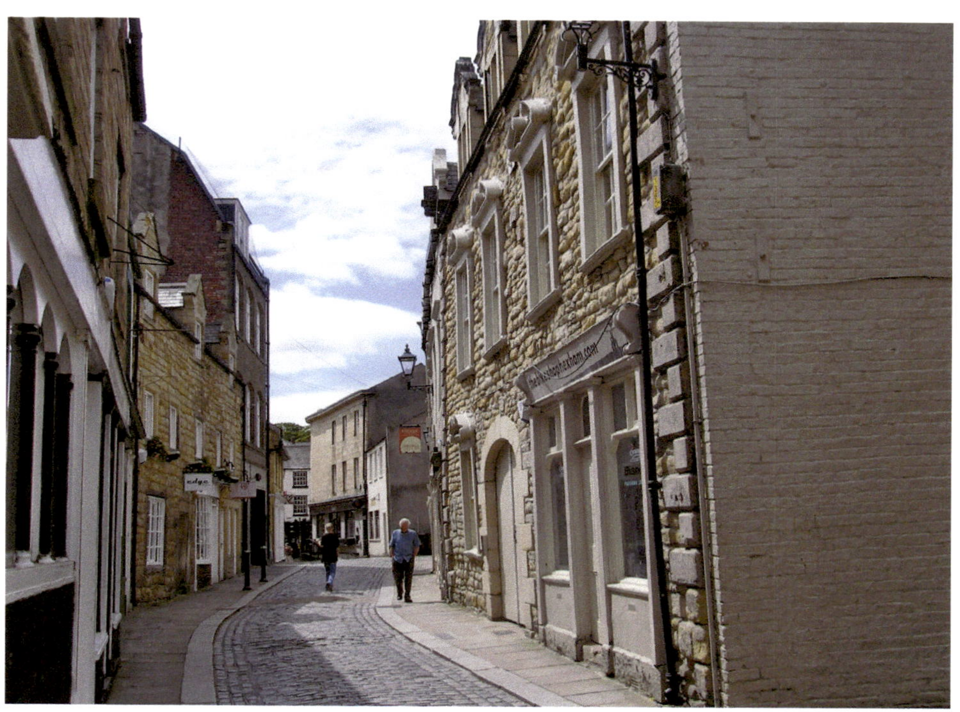

The Chare, Looking North

The front of the old George and Dragon was rendered until recently. Today, the original sandstone has been exposed and pointed.

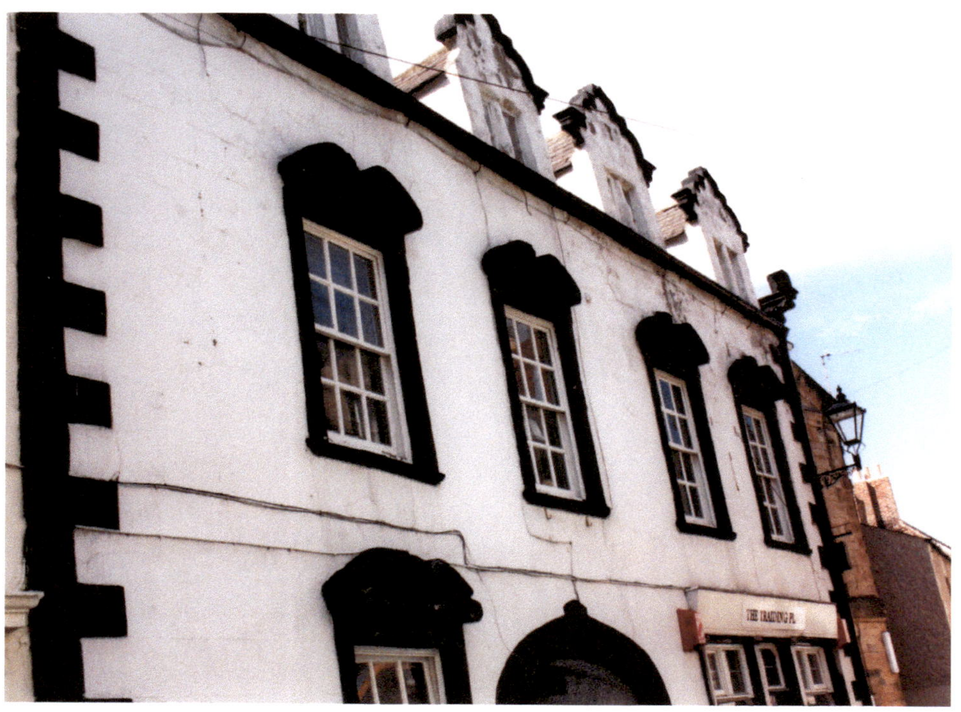

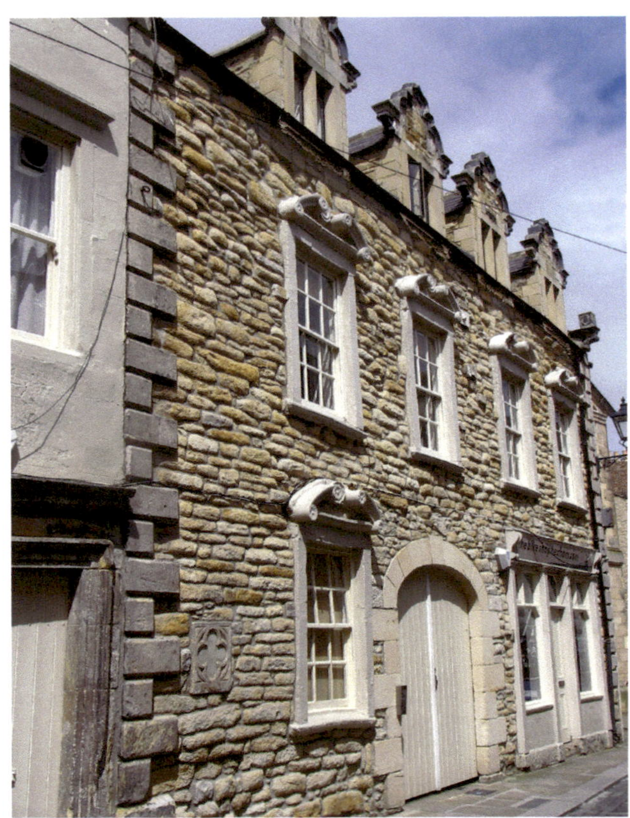

Coaching Inn 1

This courtyard coaching inn had more recent buildings removed. The quality of restoration is very high, and it is a great success.

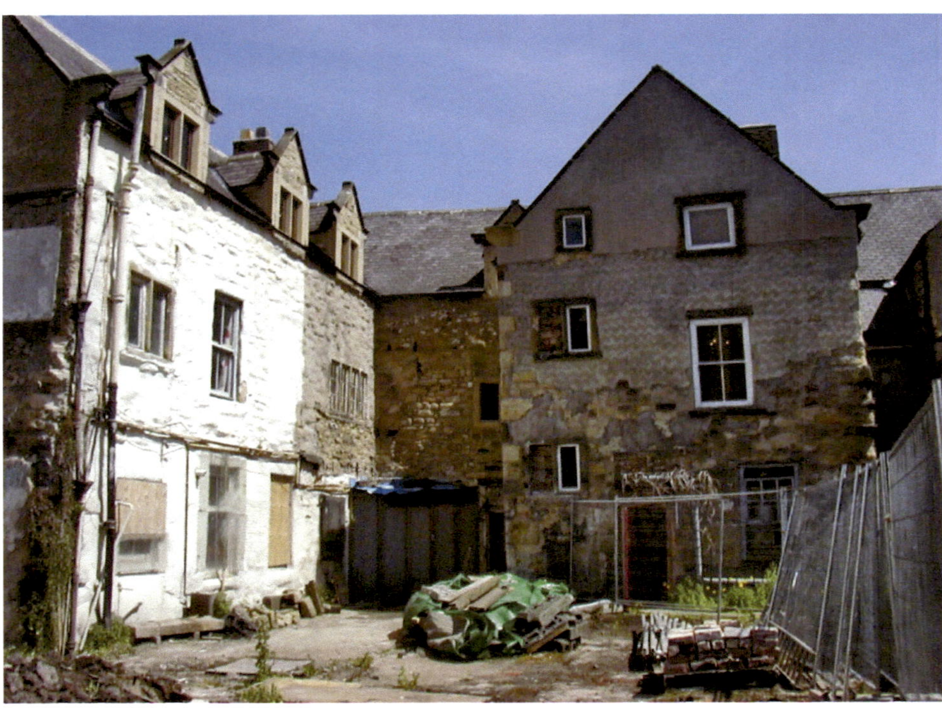

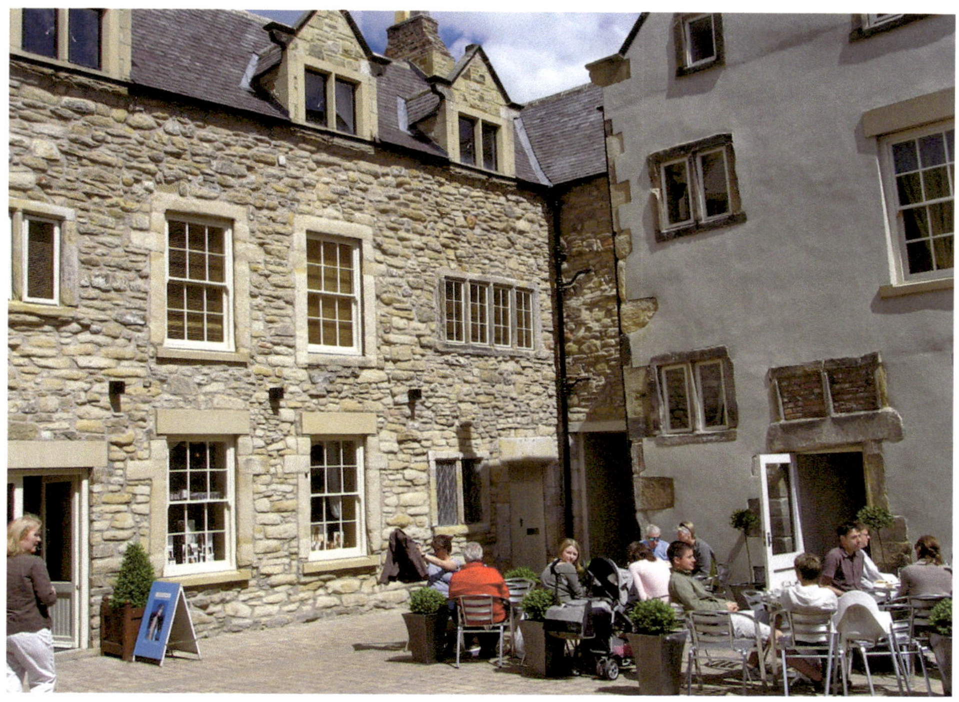

Coaching Inn II

The central court of the inn, where there was a circular well, with seventeenth-century features being preserved. The Priory wall has been preserved, and the outside is a good place to see it.

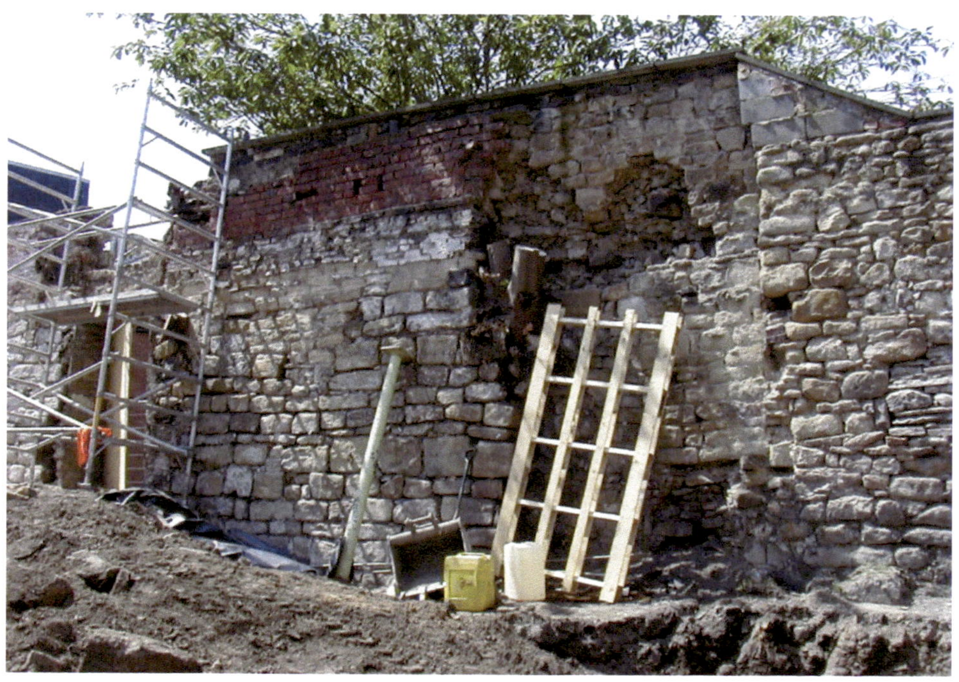

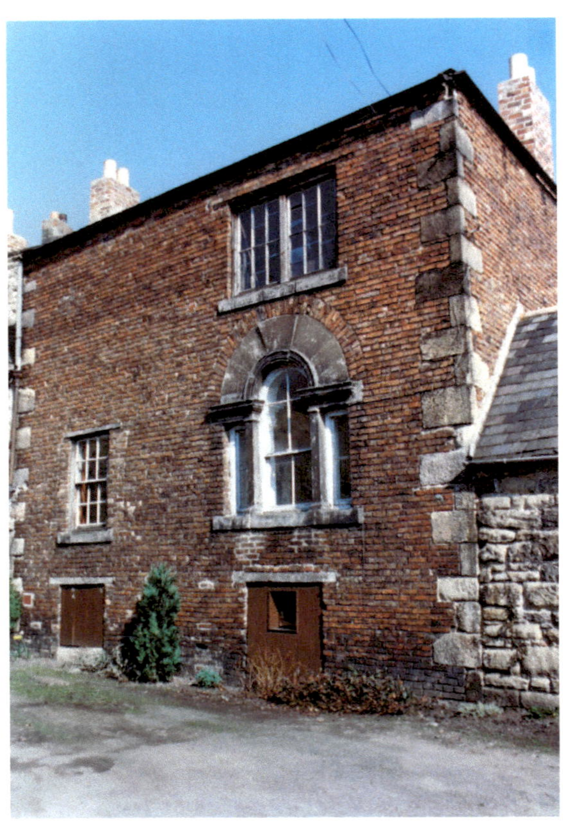

Priory Wall
Most of the wall which encircled the Priory grounds has gone. Behind the Chare a more recent building has cut through it, and here we see fine brickwork and a Venetian window.

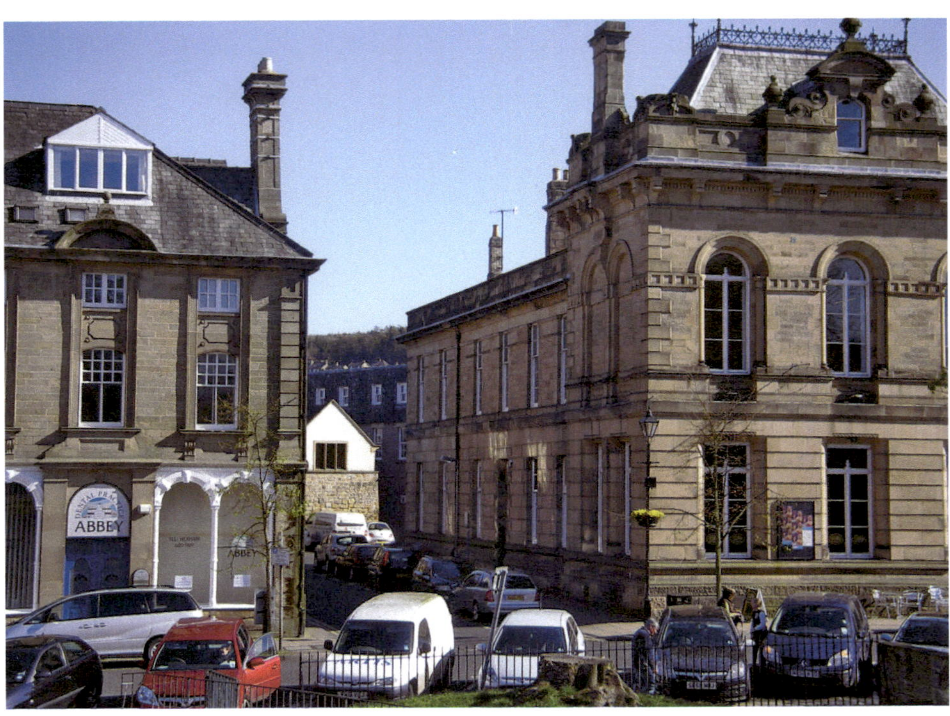

Beaumont Street I

A major change to the town was the building of Beaumont Street, from the market to Battle Hill. In the 1860s this area was being cleared of trees to make way for the road. Among the fine sandstone buildings is the *Hexham Courant* office.

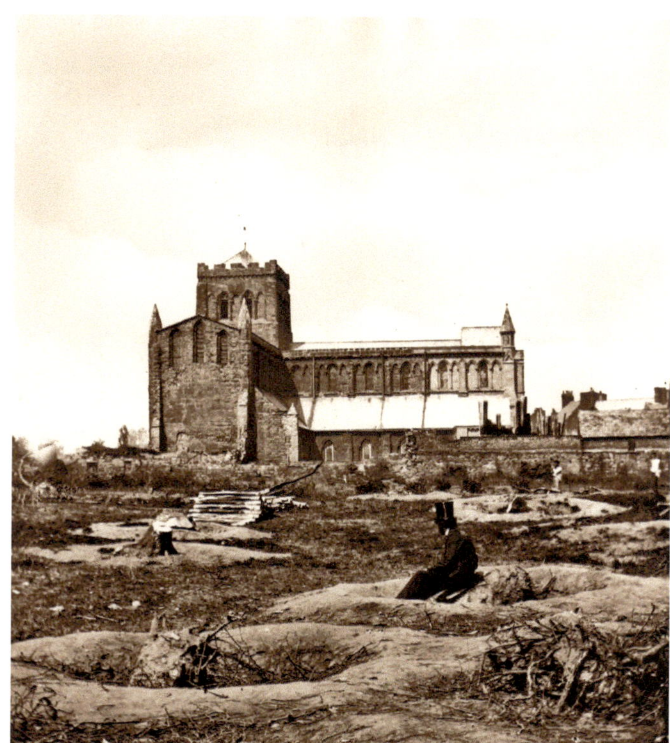

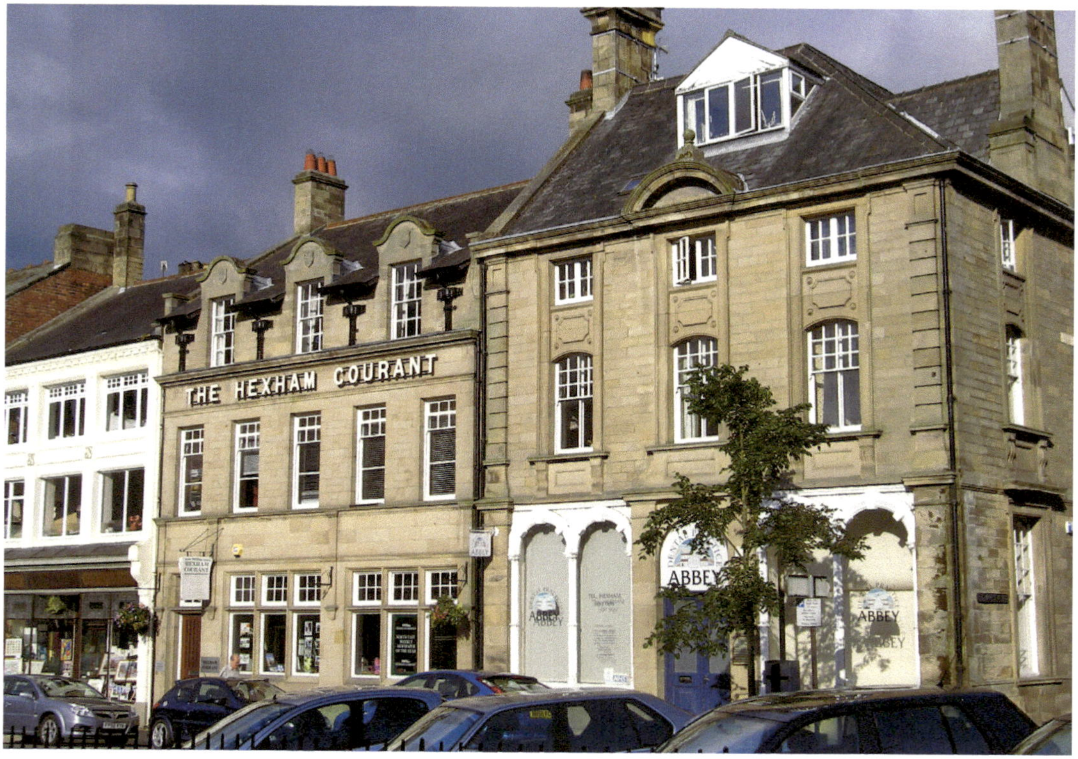

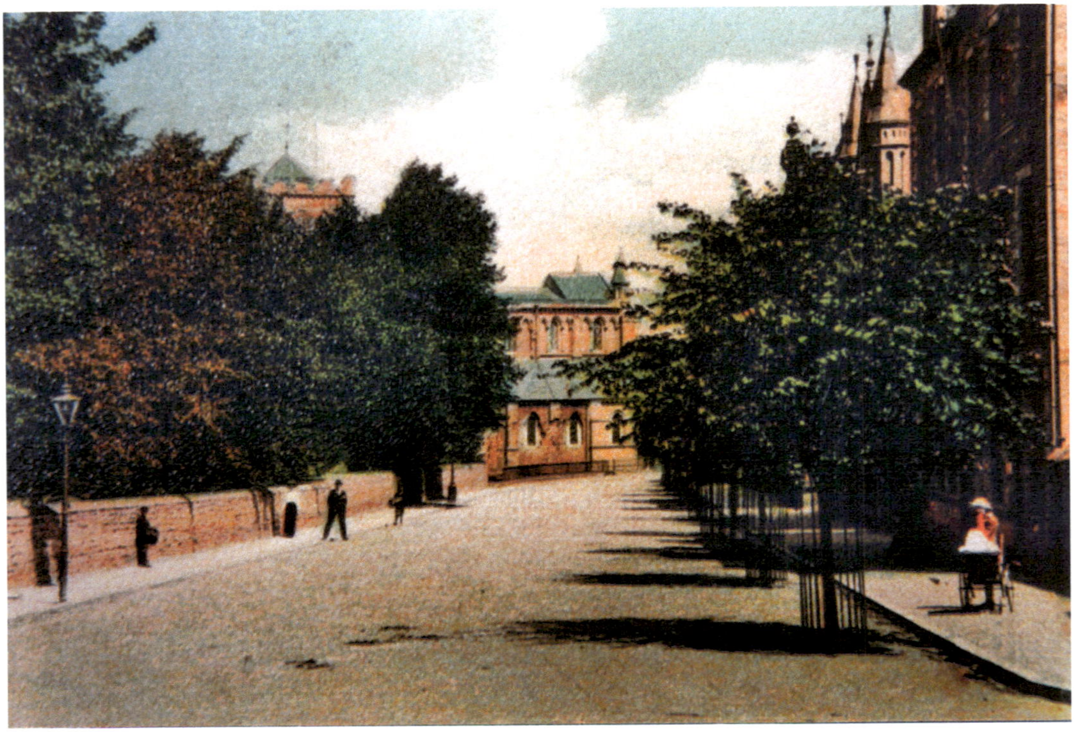

Beaumont Street II

This old postcard shows a fine growth of trees lining Beaumont Street. Some people were not happy about the parking of buses opposite the Queen's Hall and close to the Abbey.

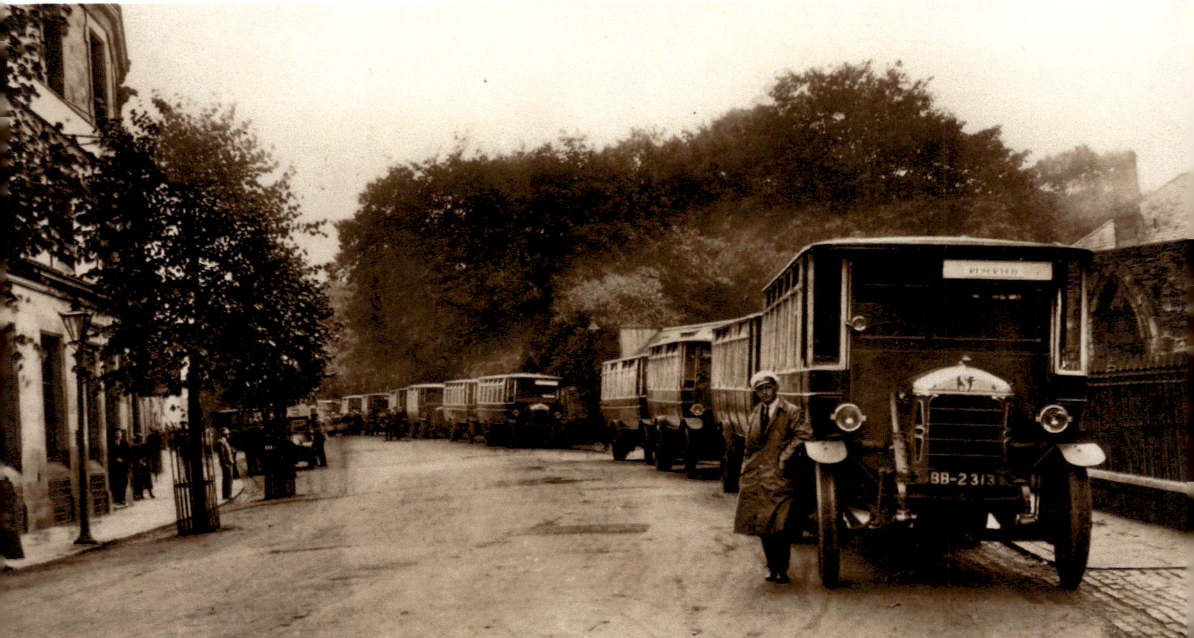

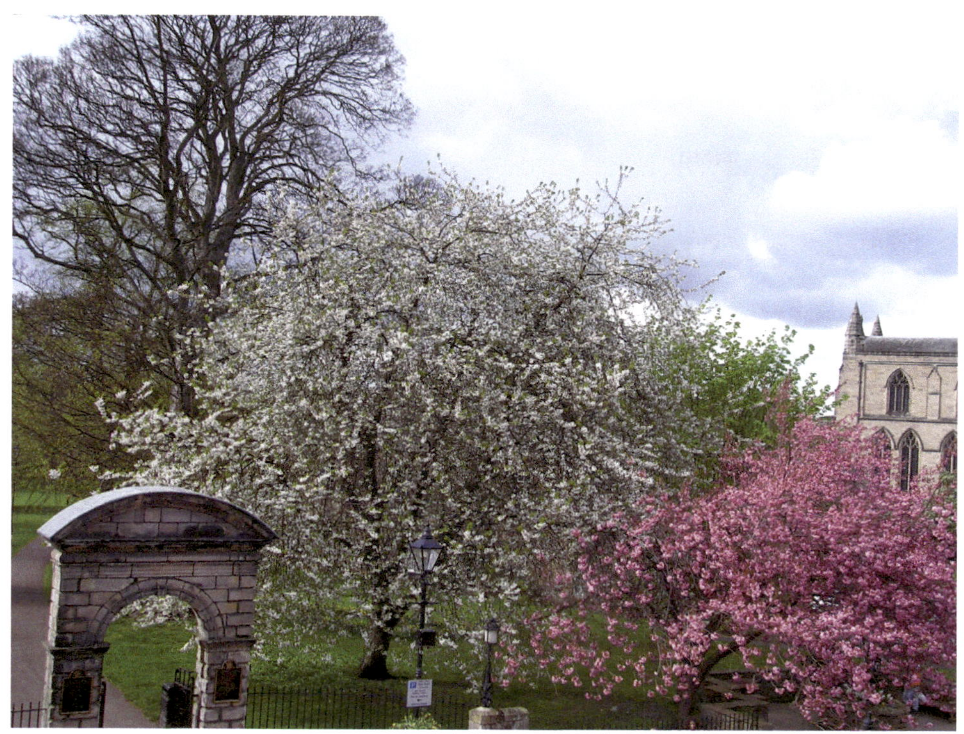

Abbey Entrance

The entrance to the Abbey grounds in spring, through the arch brought in from Fore Street. The Queen's Hall has not changed externally, but it has inside. For example, the present library was once a dance hall.

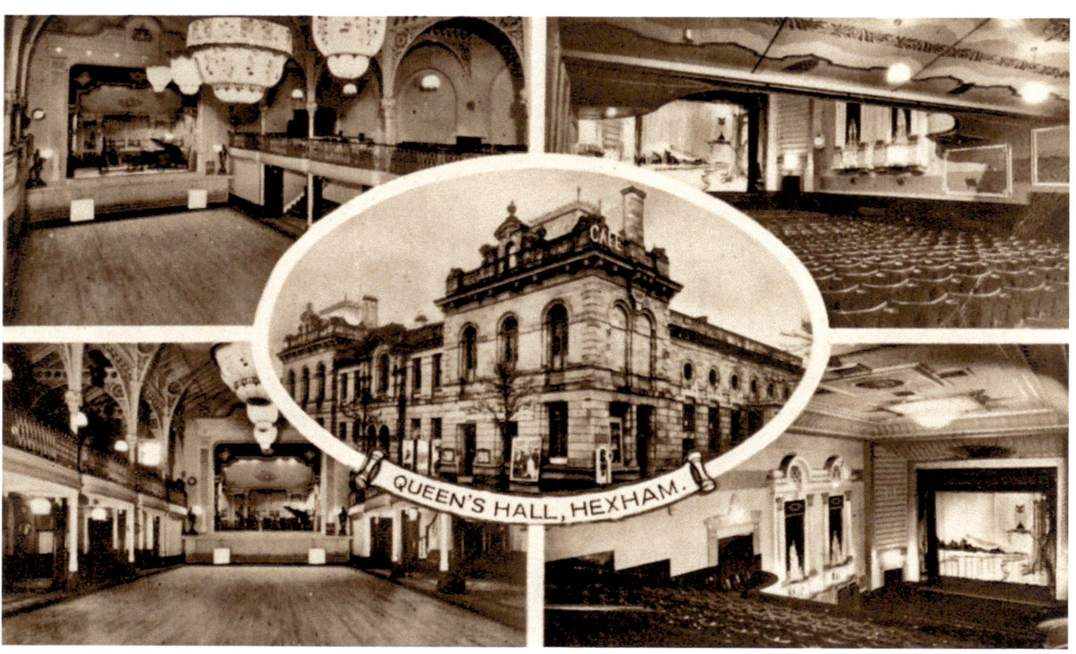

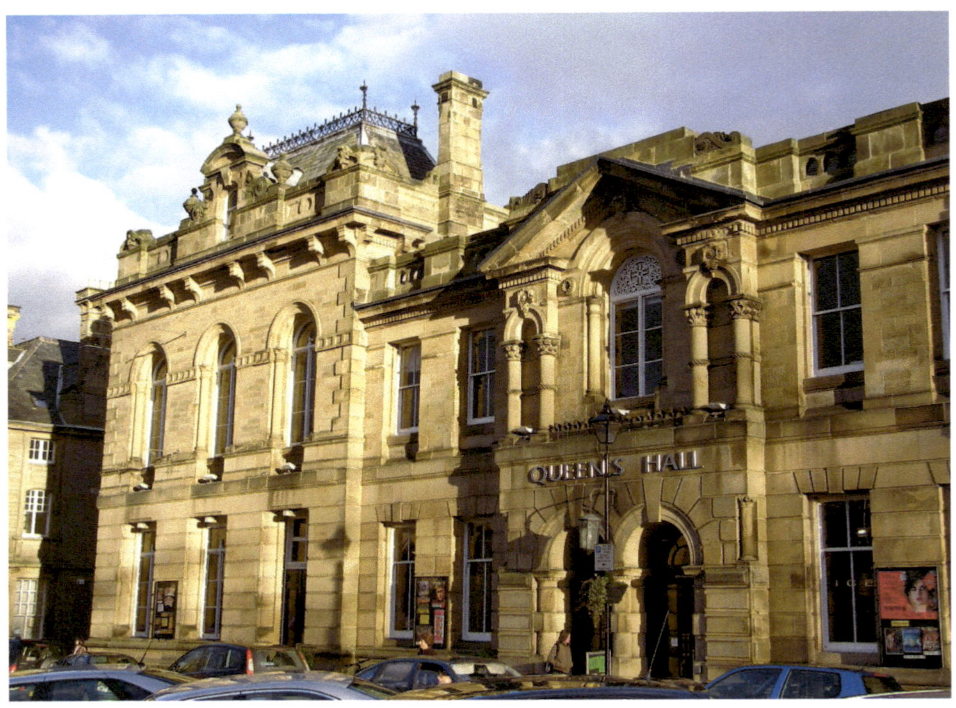

The Queen's Hall I

The Queen's Hall today is a great asset, and its sandstone is particularly attractive in strong sunshine. Further south is the Trinity Methodist church (formerly a Wesleyan Methodist church) and the Beaumont Hotel; the latter was formerly a temperance hotel (1902).

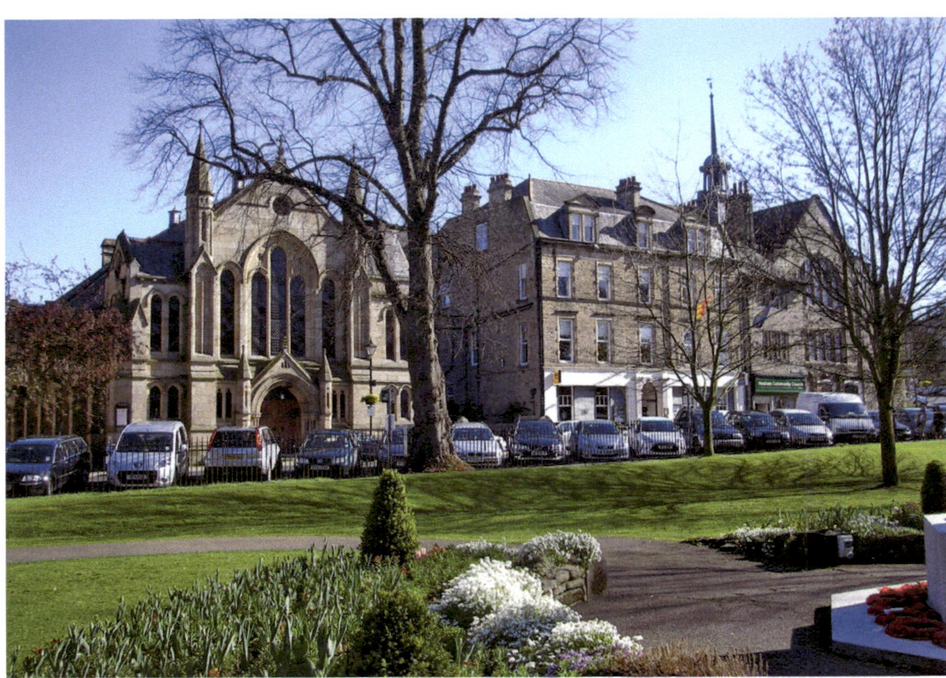

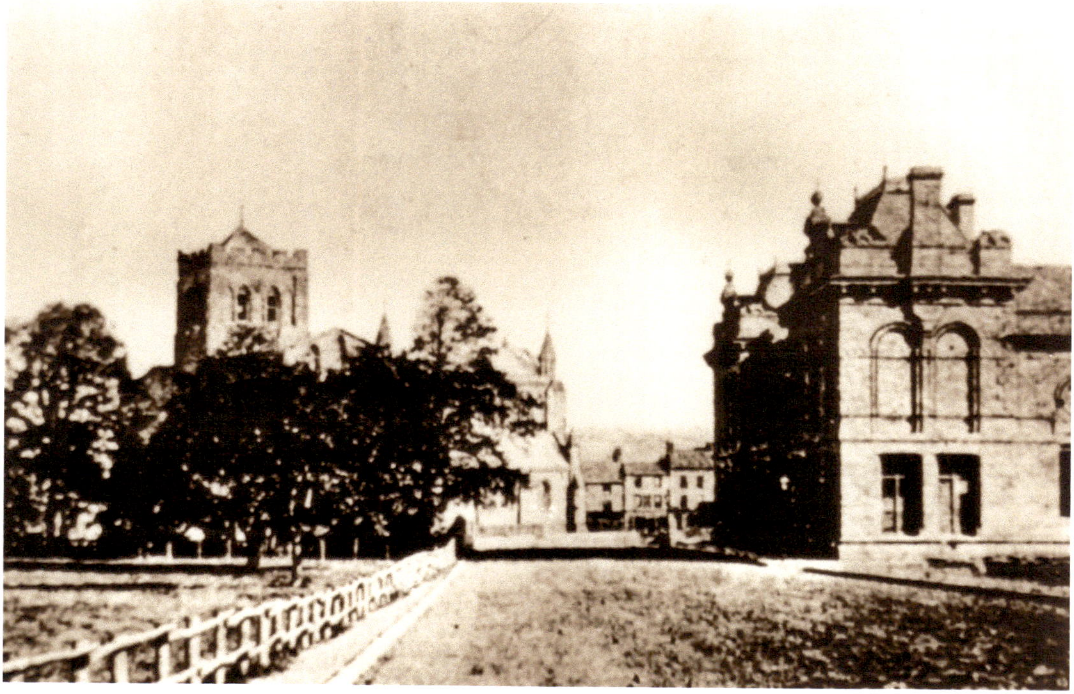

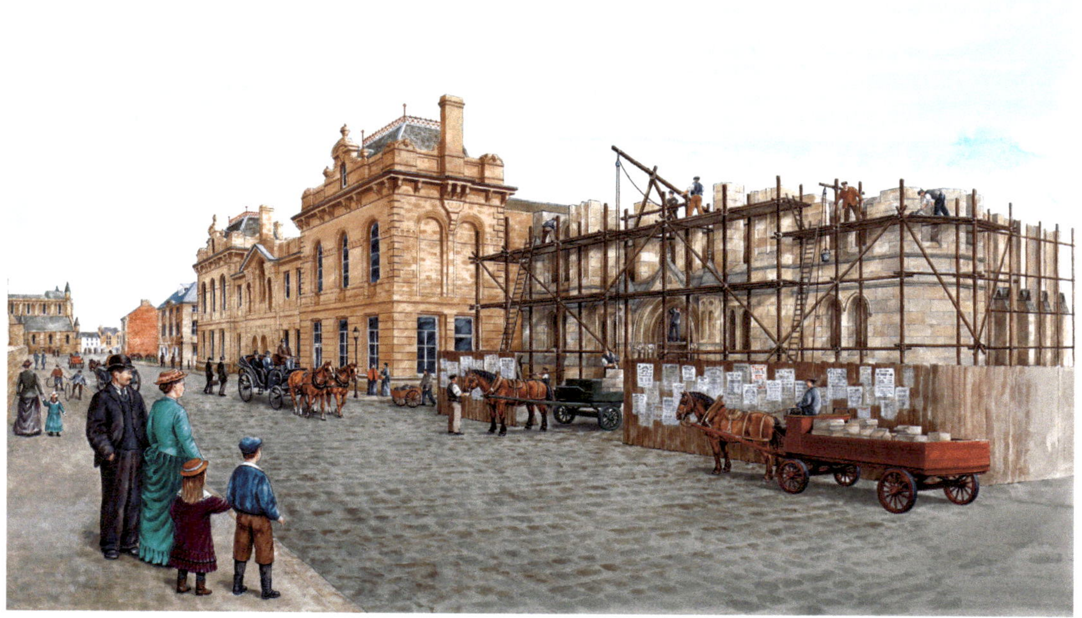

The Queen's Hall before Trinity Methodist church was built. The information panel reconstructs the building scene that continued to Battle Hill, culminating in the Presbyterian church (now the Community Church) in 1909.

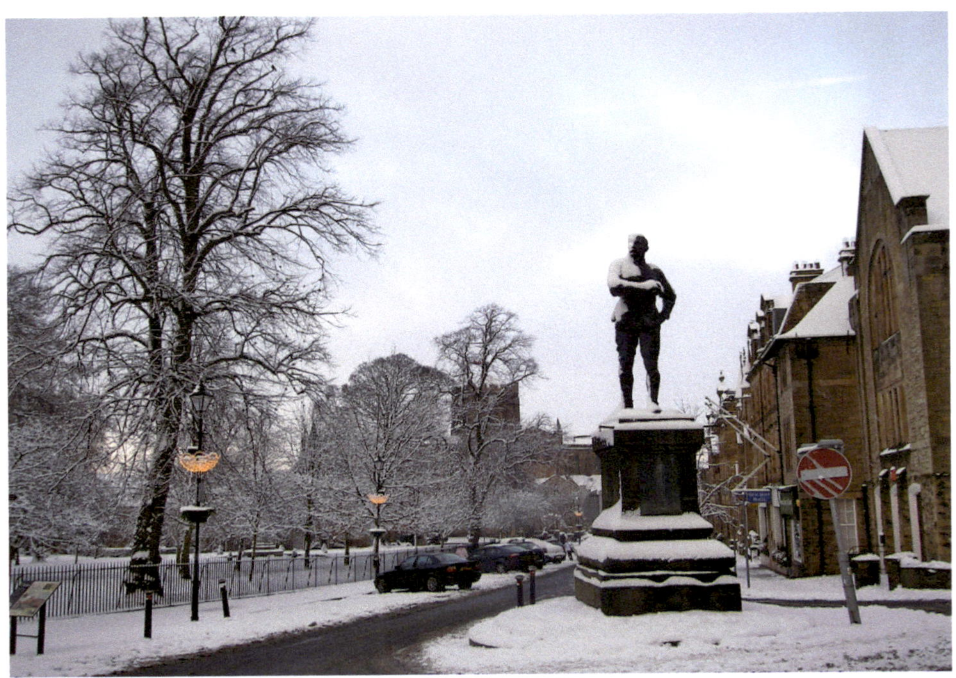

Colonel Benson

The statue of Colonel Benson, local Boer War hero, was erected in 1904. We must remember that hundreds of women and children died in concentration camps. Army Day in Beaumont Street, 2011, was where the Duchess of Northumberland awarded medals to soldiers who had served in Afghanistan.

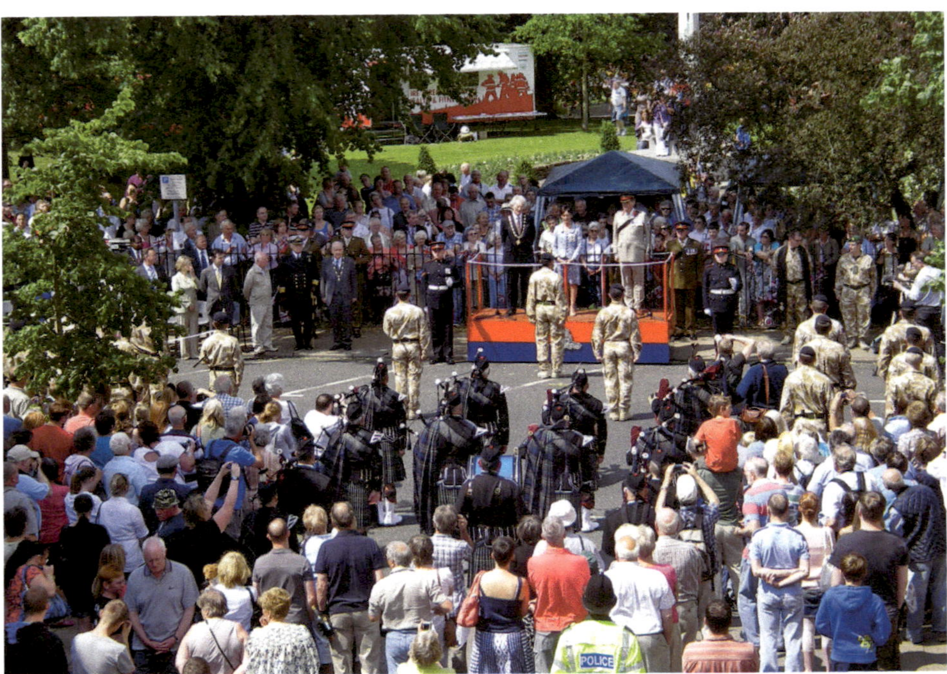

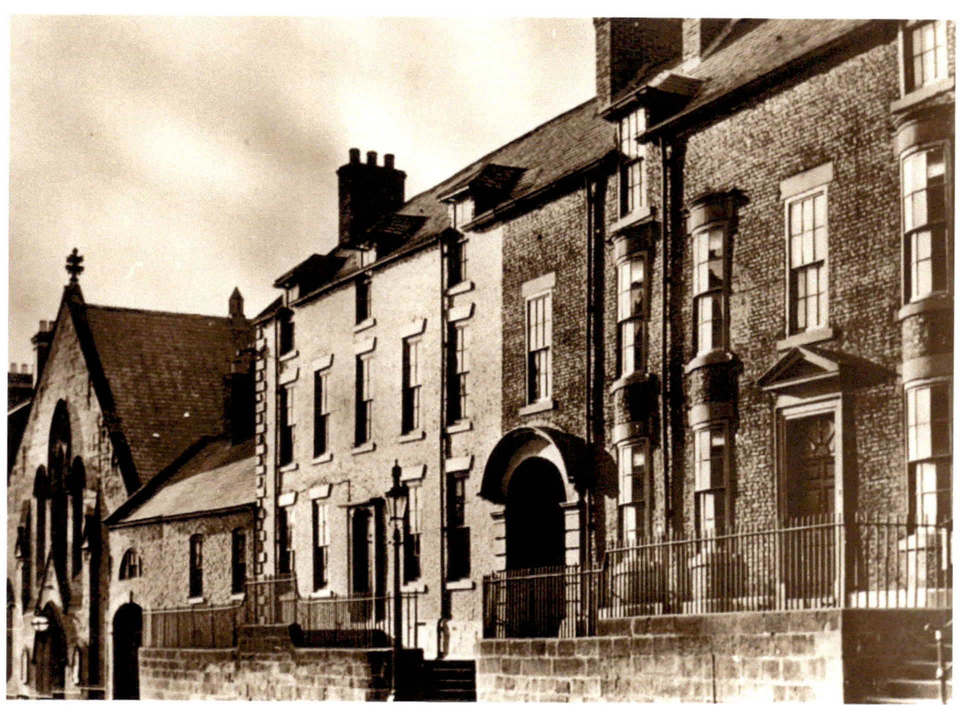

Battle Hill I

The top of Battle Hill in the late nineteenth century. 'Battle' probably derives from Old English 'botl', which means a building. Since then the changes have been profound.

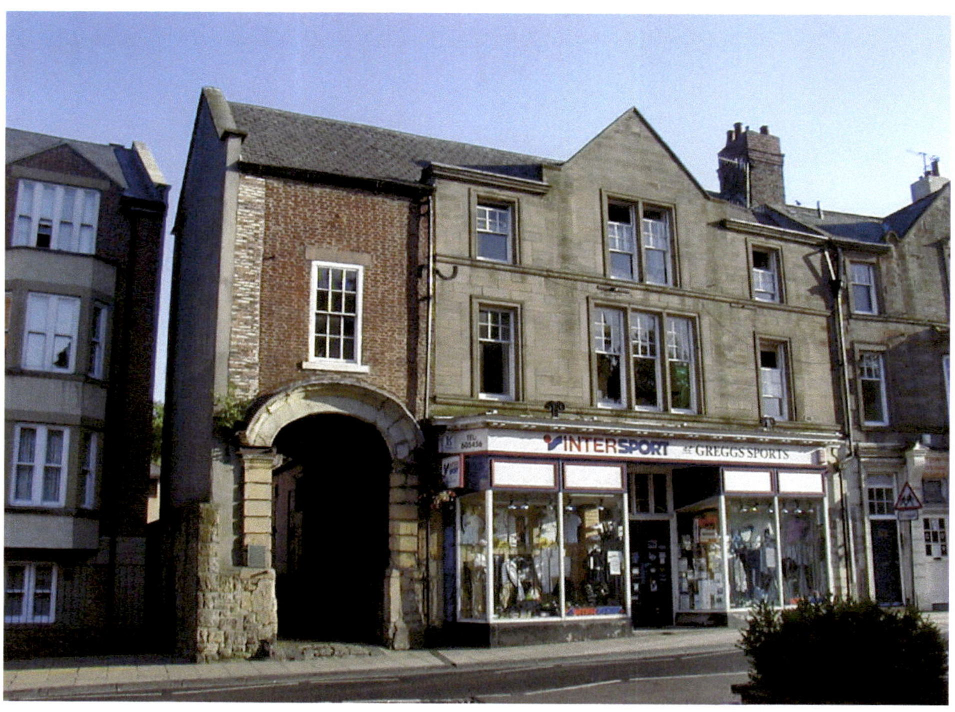

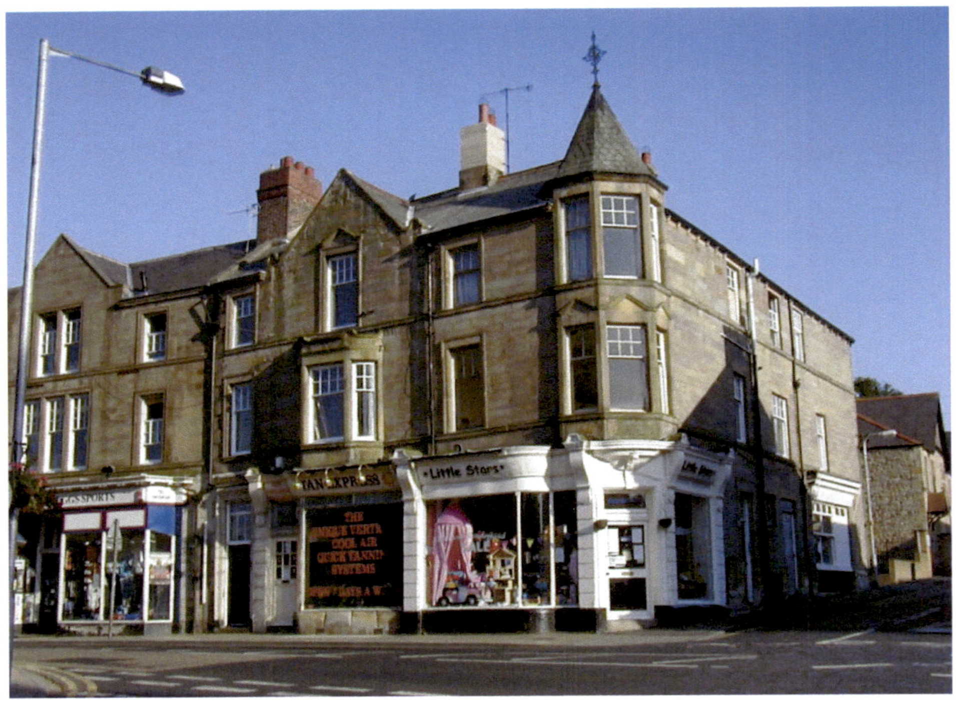

Battle Hill II

The buildings at the top of Battle Hill include the arch of the house in which the poet W. W. Gibson was born. The rest of the house was removed to make way for others. Most of the buildings below are very recent. The older style of building continues around the corner into Elvaston Road, which runs south.

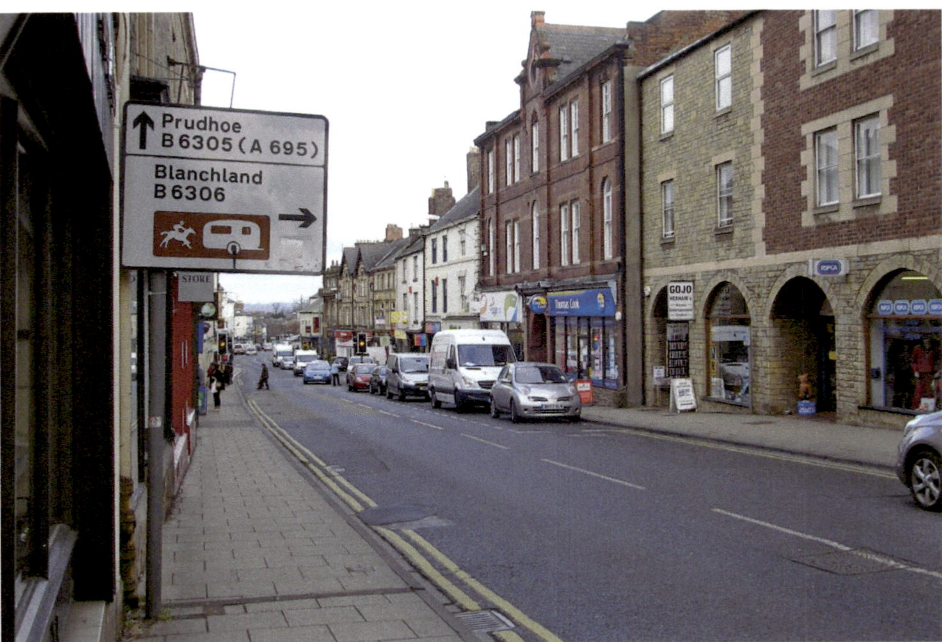

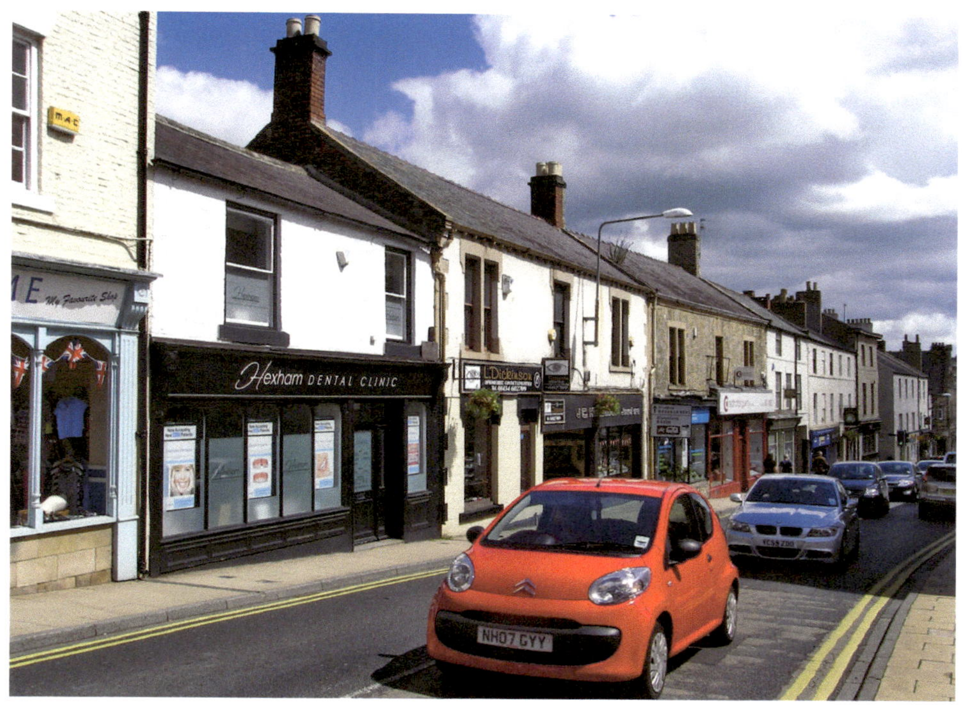

Battle Hill III
Battle Hill today, looking east. The Grey Bull is no longer an inn. 'Pyramids' means snooker.

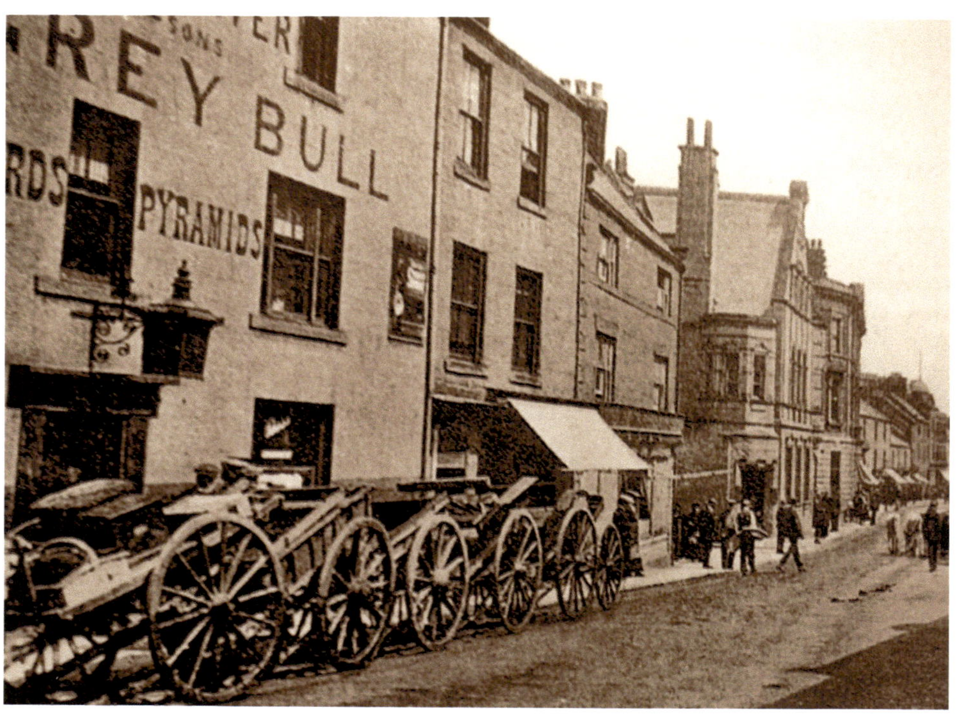

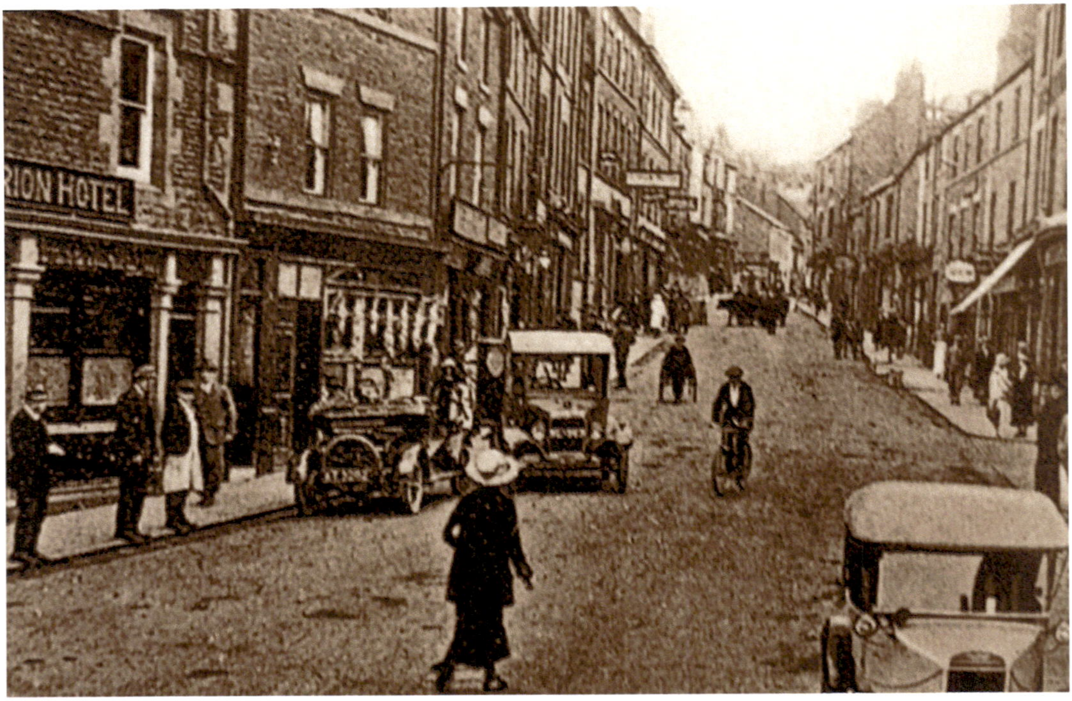

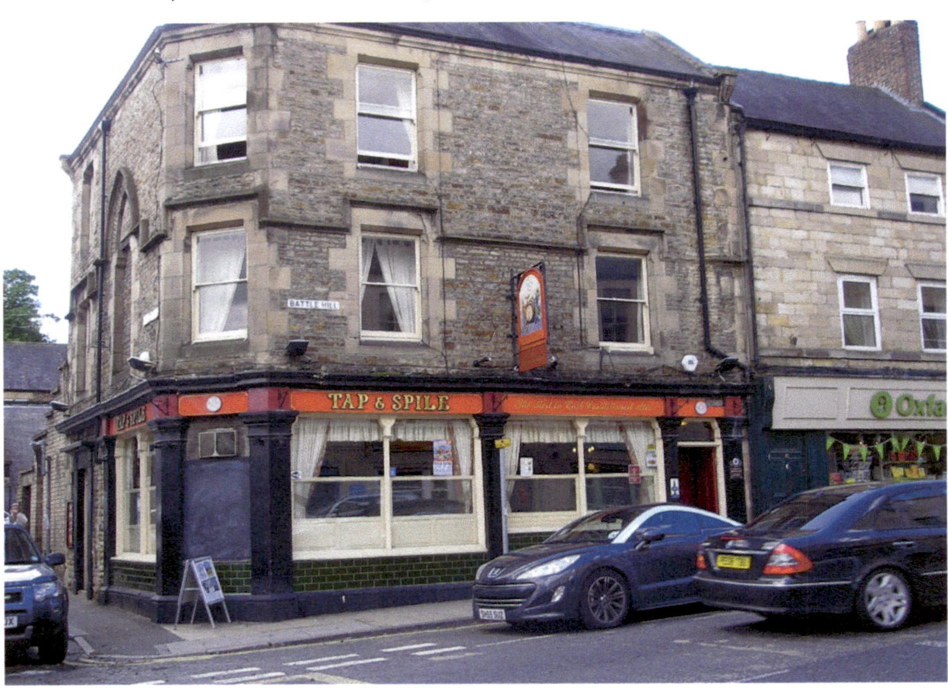

Cattle Market

Battle Hill becomes Cattle Market to the east, where we see the appearance of cars. To the left is the Criterion Inn, now the Tap & Spile. The same scene today shows modern traffic. Gone are the days when cattle were led past here to market.

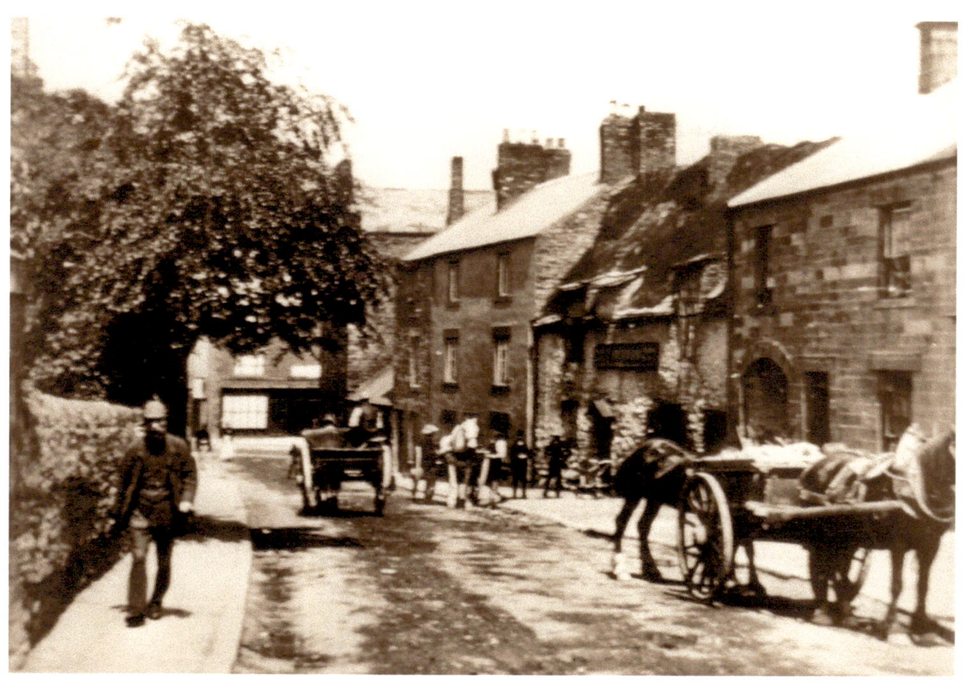

Eastgate

Eastgate runs south from the Cattle Market. We see the blacksmith's shop on the right. Today all the buildings have been refurbished and new ones built on the right-hand side, including a restaurant and a residential block. 'The Old Smithy' is a house.

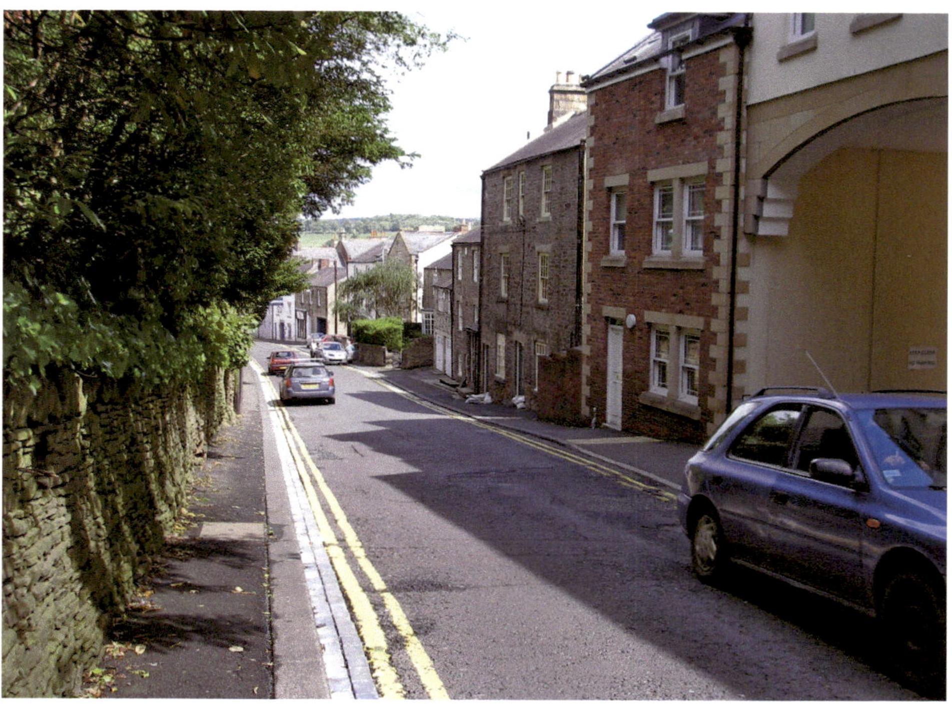

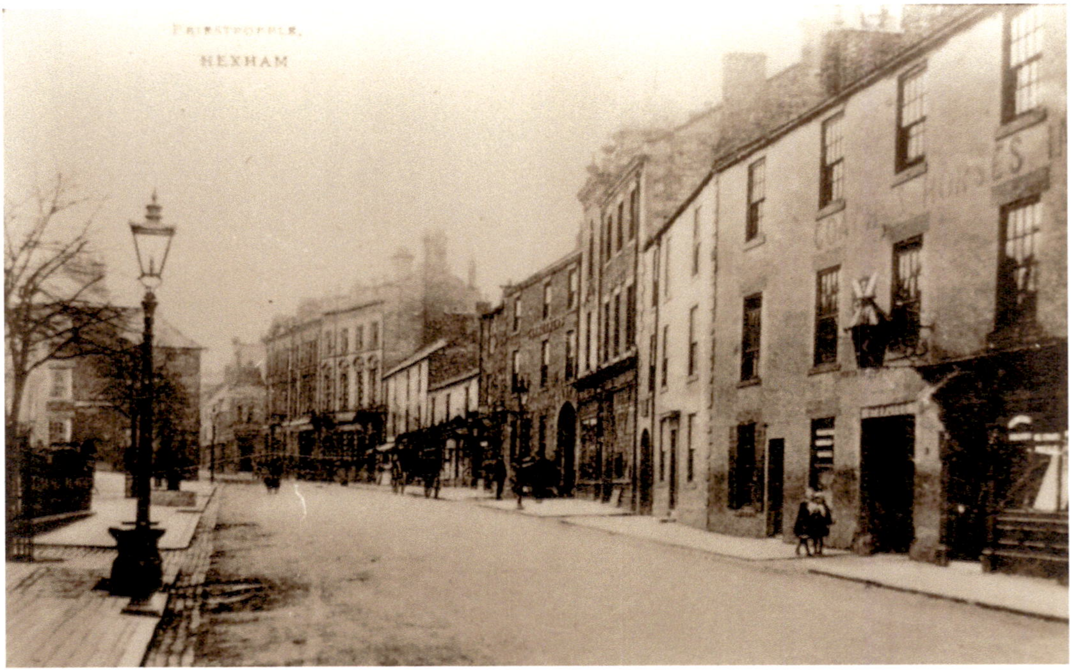

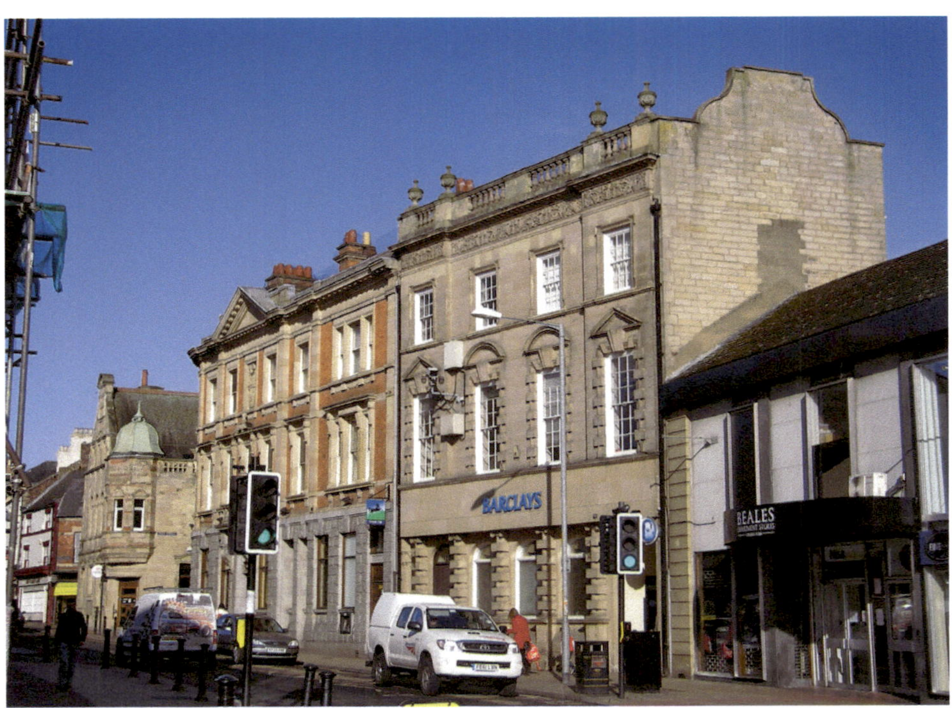

Priestpopple

Priestpopple continues east from the Cattle Market. It means small plots of land that belonged to priests. The site of Banks' is to the right. Lloyd's TSB and Barclay's banks are seen next to Beales' store (formerly Robbs').

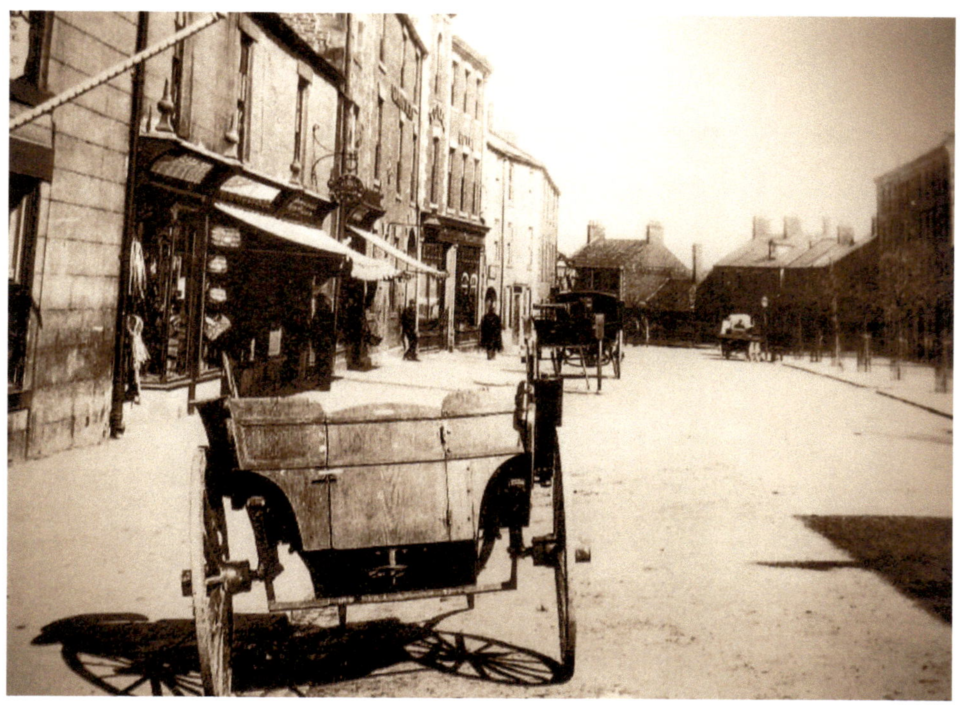

East Priestpopple

East Priestpopple is a wide road. Some of the buildings have been altered since this picture was taken. An unusual building is the Royal Oak with its gilded dome. The Coach and Horses remains.

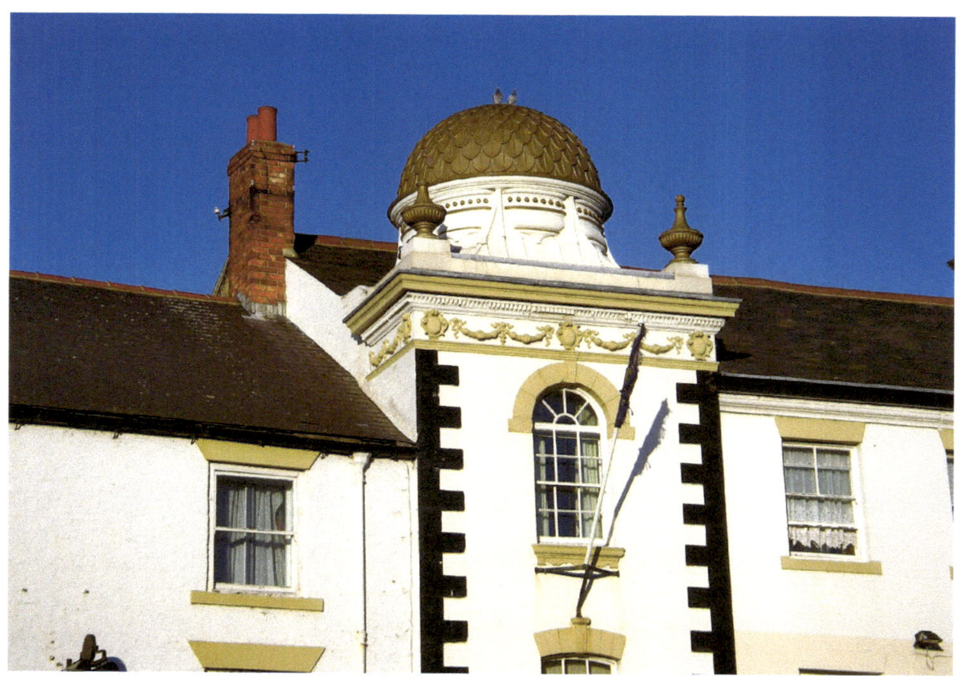

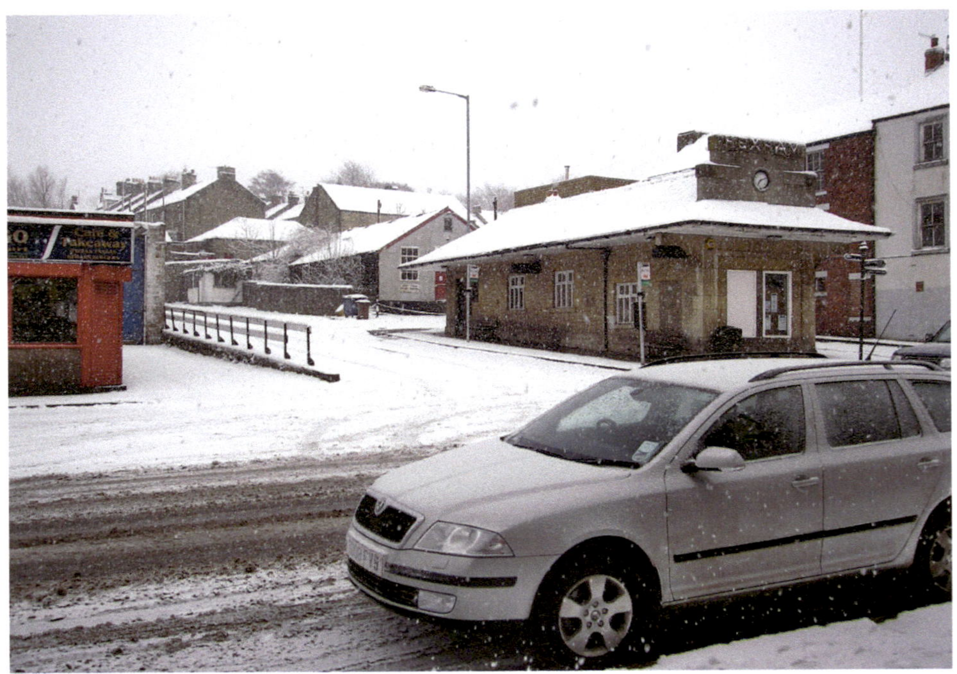

Priestpopple Bus Station

The present bus station in Priestpopple is inadequate for a modern town, and there is much dithering about how it should be replaced. Behind Priestpopple, to the south, there is an interesting survival of the past: a ropery. There used to be two. It is a long, low-roofed structure to which it is difficult to allocate a new function.

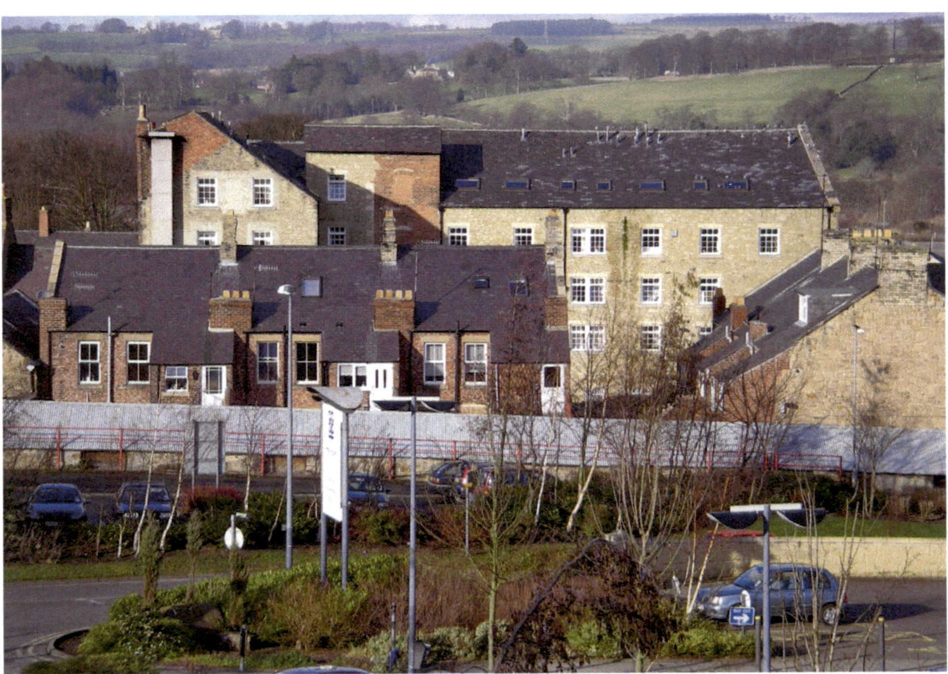

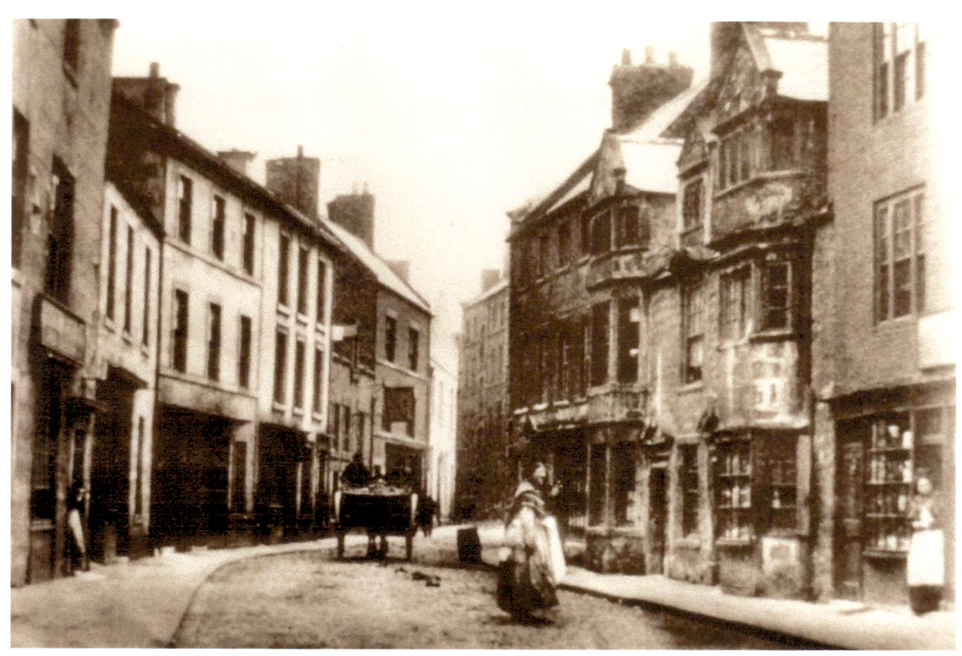

Market Street I

Another street running from the Market Place is Market Street, following the curve of the old priory wall. Today this street still has some seventeenth-century buildings, especially a hairdresser's on the right. There are many varied shops, an inn and the Salvation Army citadel.

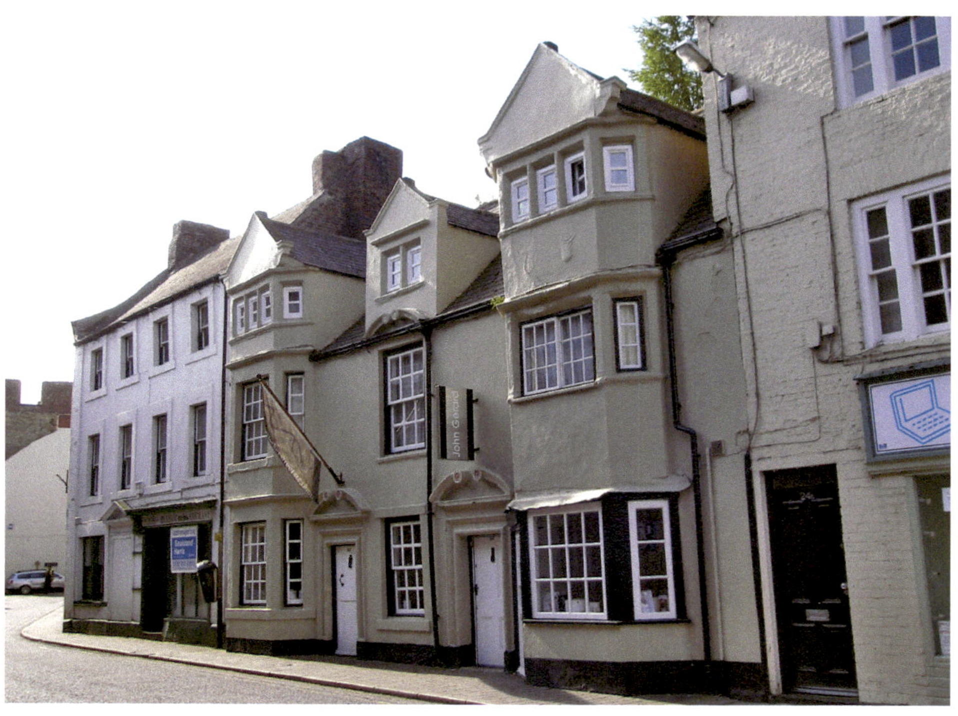

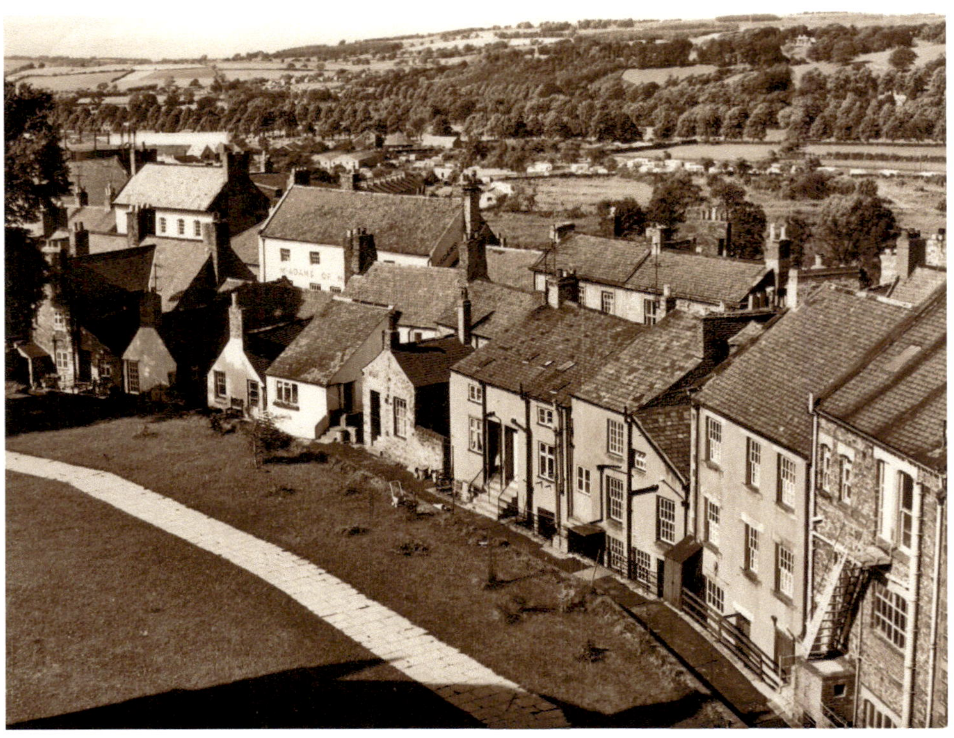

Market Street II

The scene behind the Market Street in the 1970s. Today the buildings behind Market Street premises adjoining the old graveyard have a variety of styles and materials.

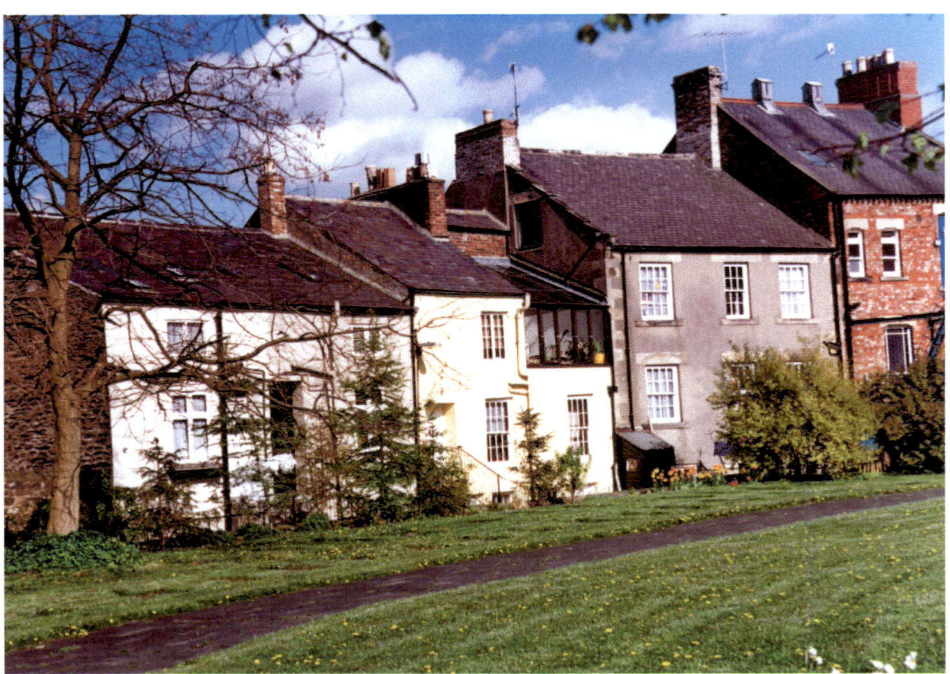

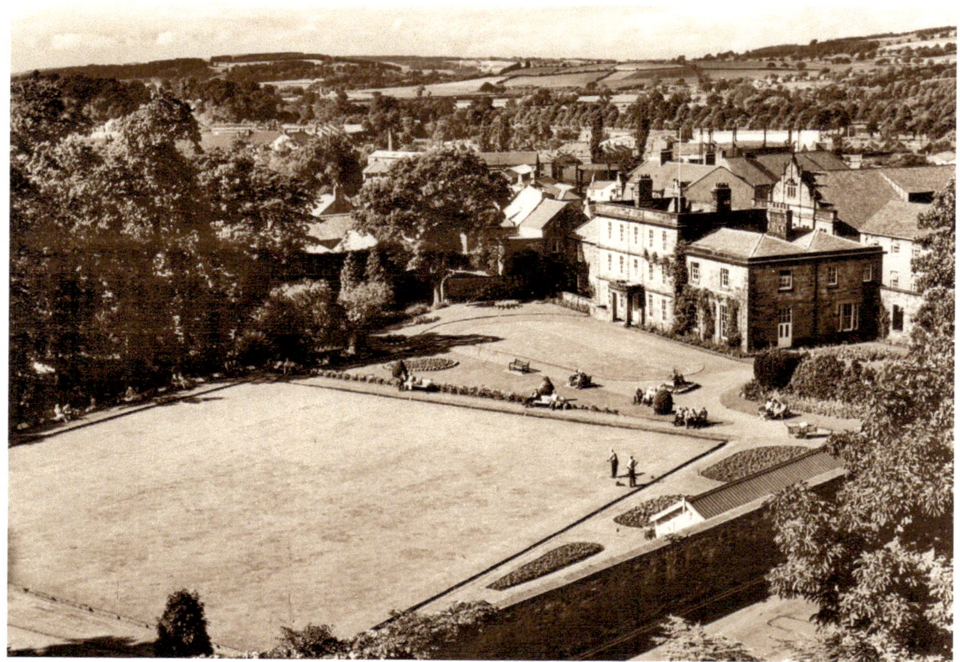

Priory Grounds

Within the Priory grounds an eighteenth-century rector was allowed to build a house and garden (1723); the latter now is the bowling green. One of the most attractive features of Hexham, the grounds here, give a splendid view of the Abbey, and have a constantly-varied floral display. The house has been for sale since the Northumberland Unitary Authority was formed, having been a school, public library and council offices.

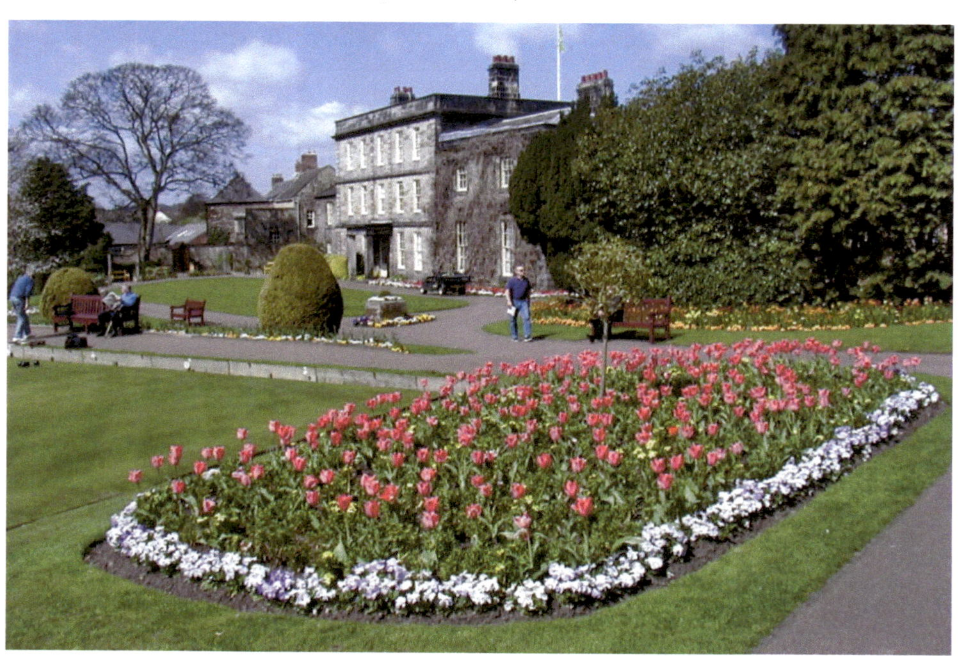

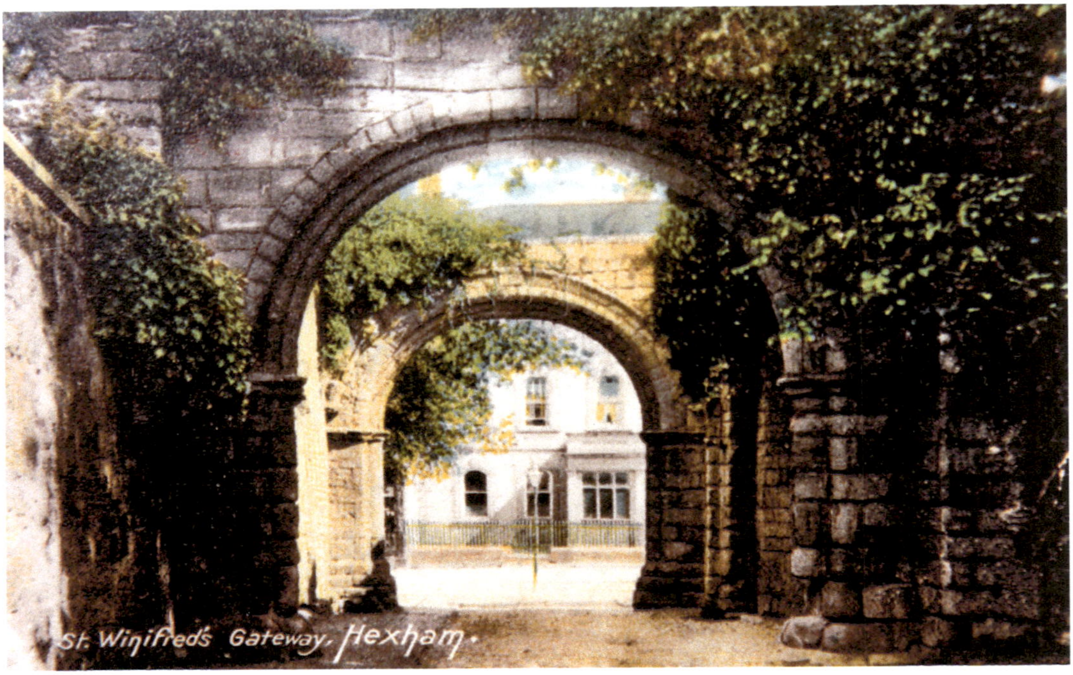

Priory Gateway

The Priory gateway is wrongly described as 'Wilfrid's' (often misspelt too) as it was in this postcard. It is a later structure. Today it has changed little, but seen through the arch into Market Street is the old post office, now town offices.

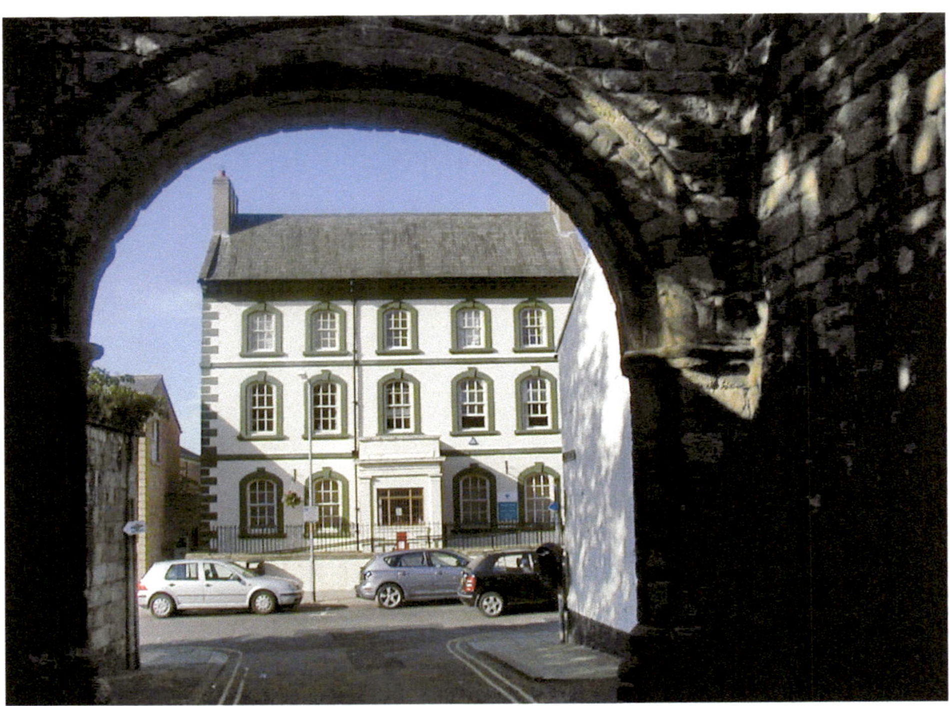

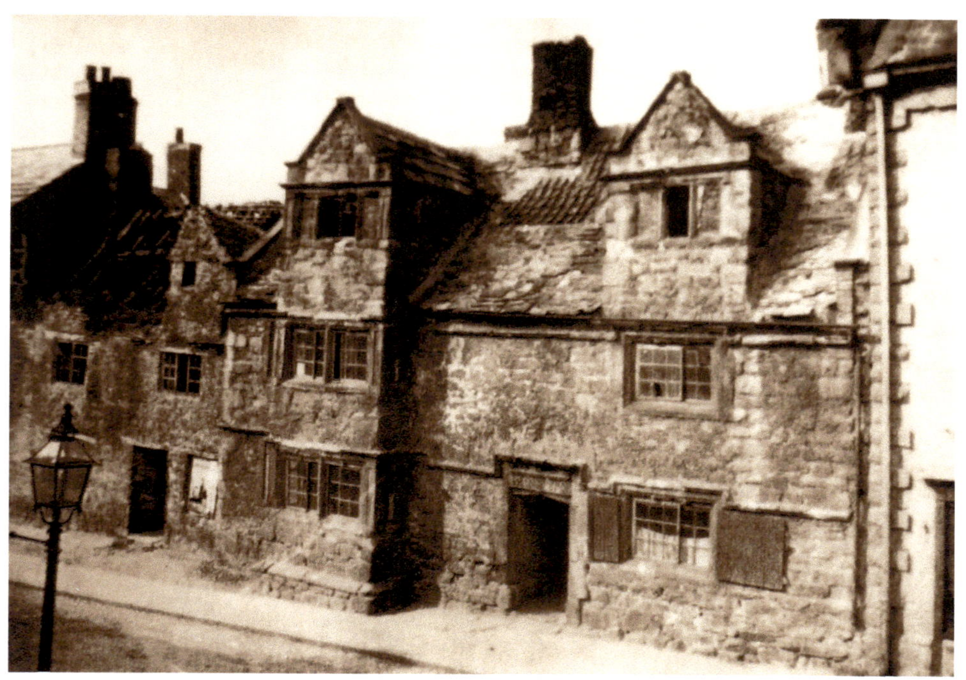

Wool Industry

Some fine seventeenth-century houses were already in decline when this picture was taken, and were pulled down to make way for the Wool Factory in 1885. It is a process that many towns have come to regret. The factory was built by Henry Bell, who also built the bandstand. The building retained its façade when it became the town's swimming pool. The pool itself was recently abandoned in favour of new one at the Wentworth centre.

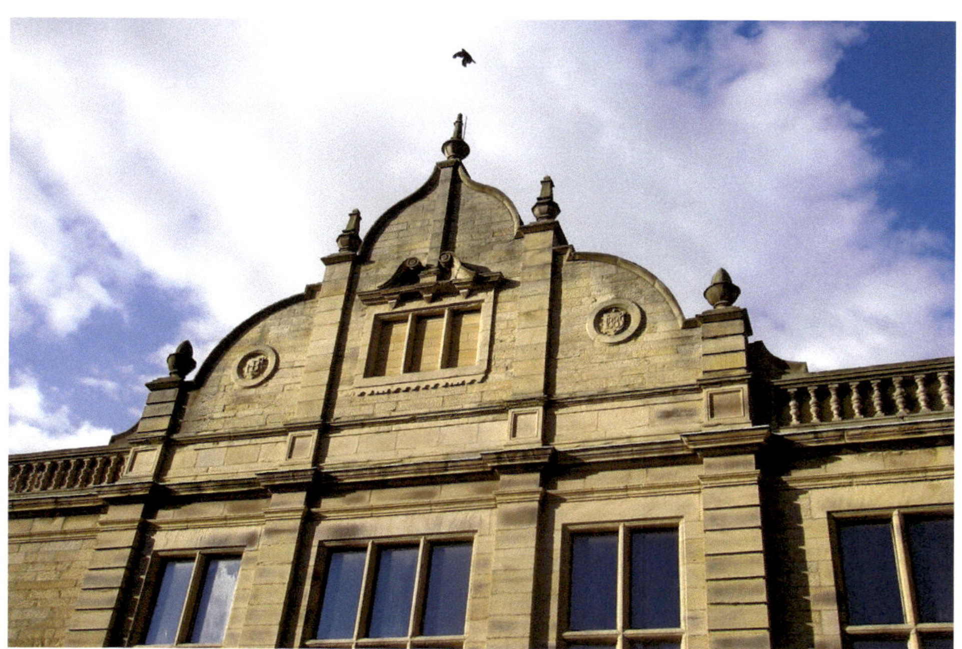

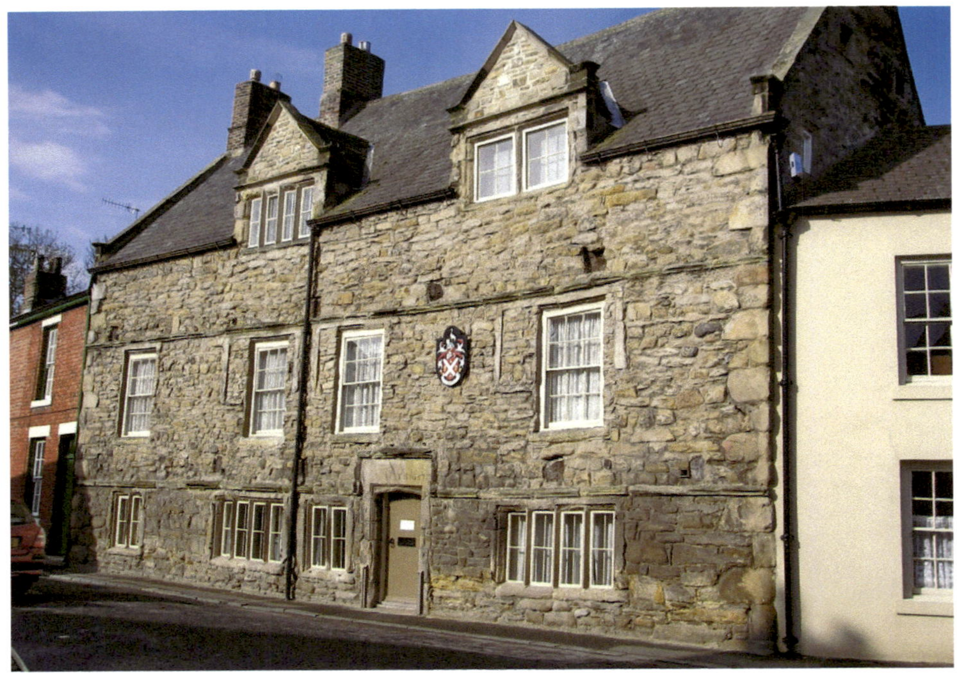

Holy Island I

Holy Island is so-called because of the number of religious establishments in and around it. Two culverted burns run on either side to form the 'island', originally crossed by small stone and brick bridges, now under the roads. Holy Island House, seen here, is a fine seventeenth-century building. Opposite, to the east, are some fine town houses, one here with one of the small shops that have closed and, in this case, has been erased.

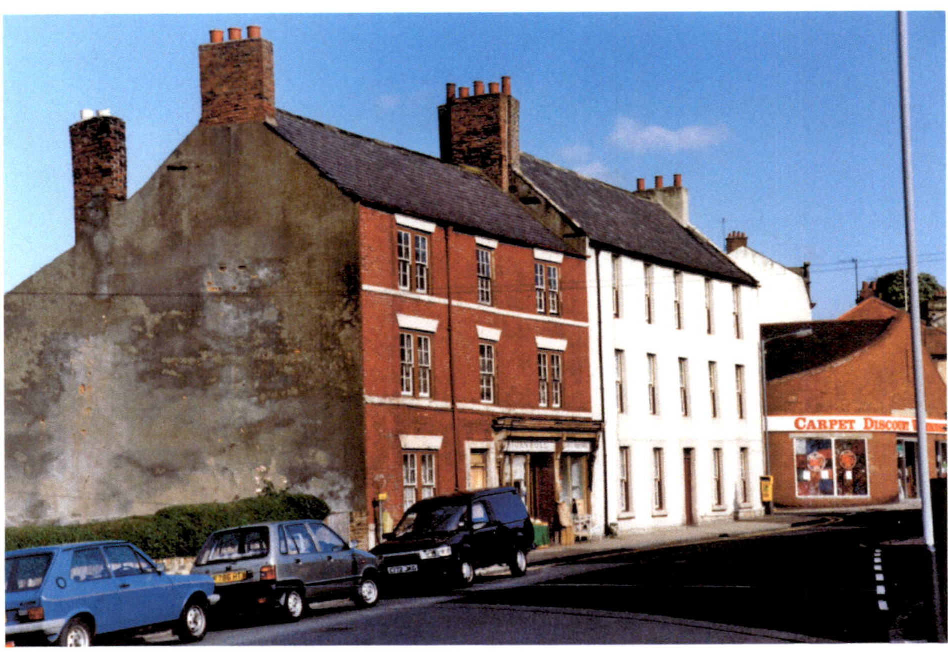

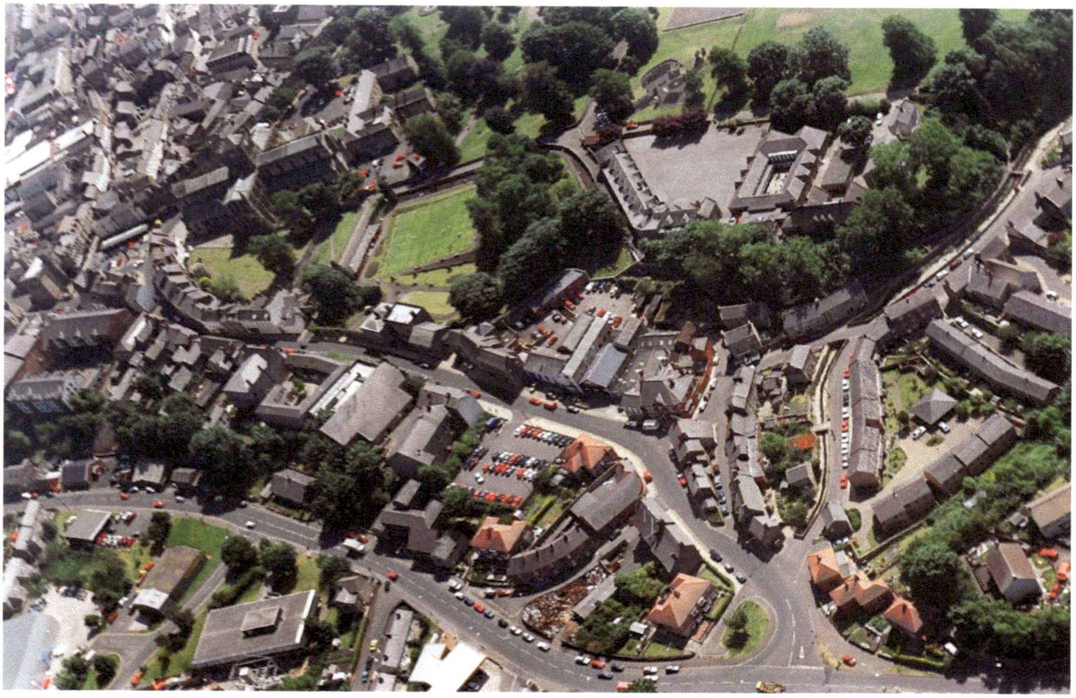

Market Street-Gilesgate & Cockshaw

Market Street-Gilesgate meets Cockshaw to form an island, bottom right. At the far right new housing covers part of the tanning industry. The mid-nineteenth-century map shows the location of tanning pits, none of which survive. They are at the bottom right-hand side of the picture.

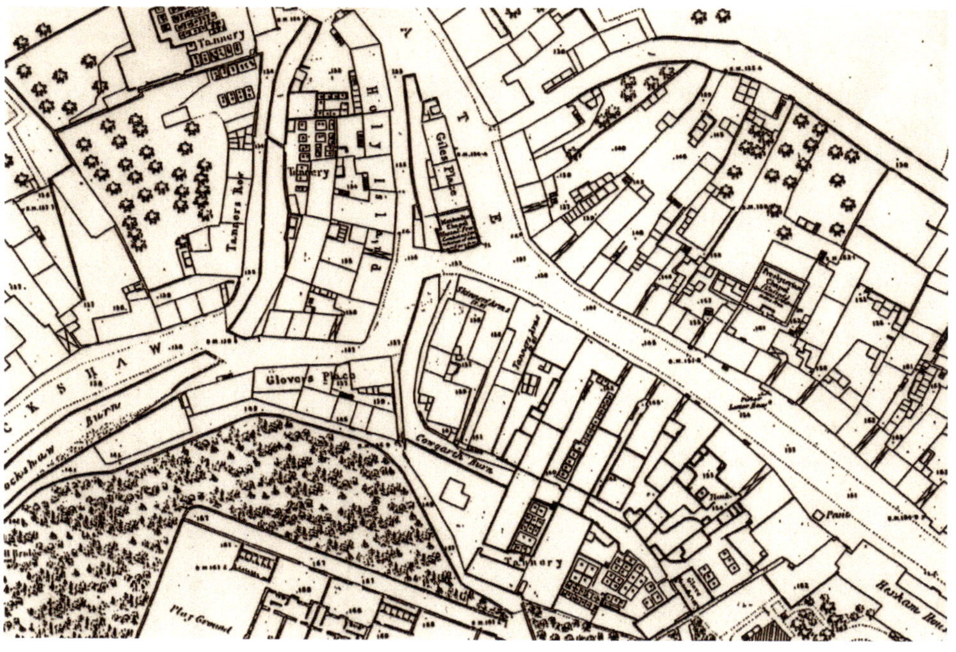

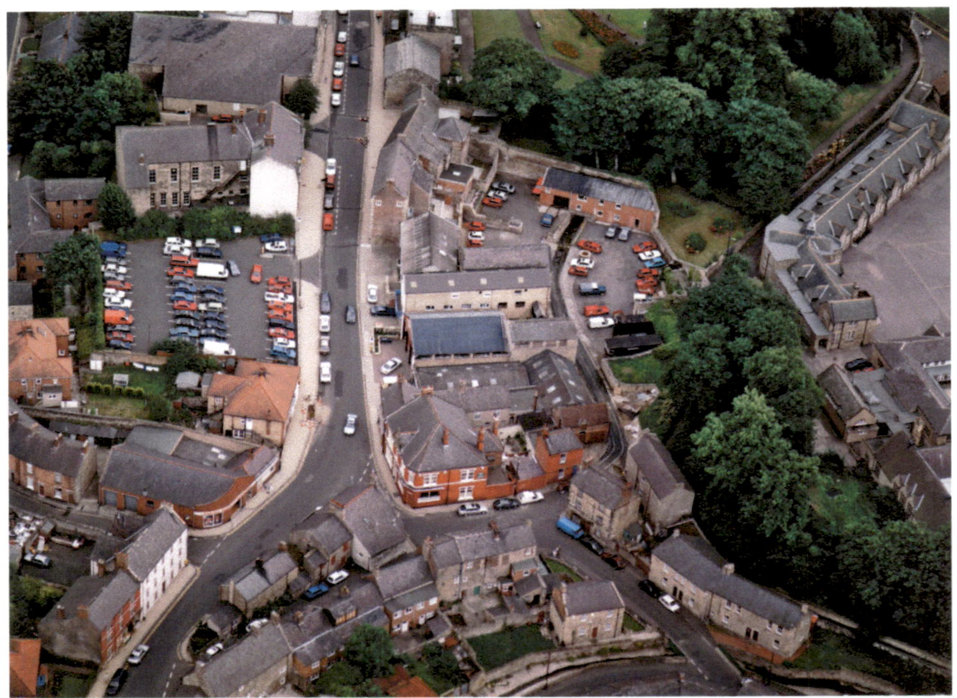

Holy Island II

A closer aerial photograph of Holy Island, central. The Halgut Burn (Cow Burn) flanks the 'island' on the right before disappearing into its culvert, flowing from the tree-covered parkland, above. Below is a rare picture of tanners at work at the small pits. The smell would have been appalling.

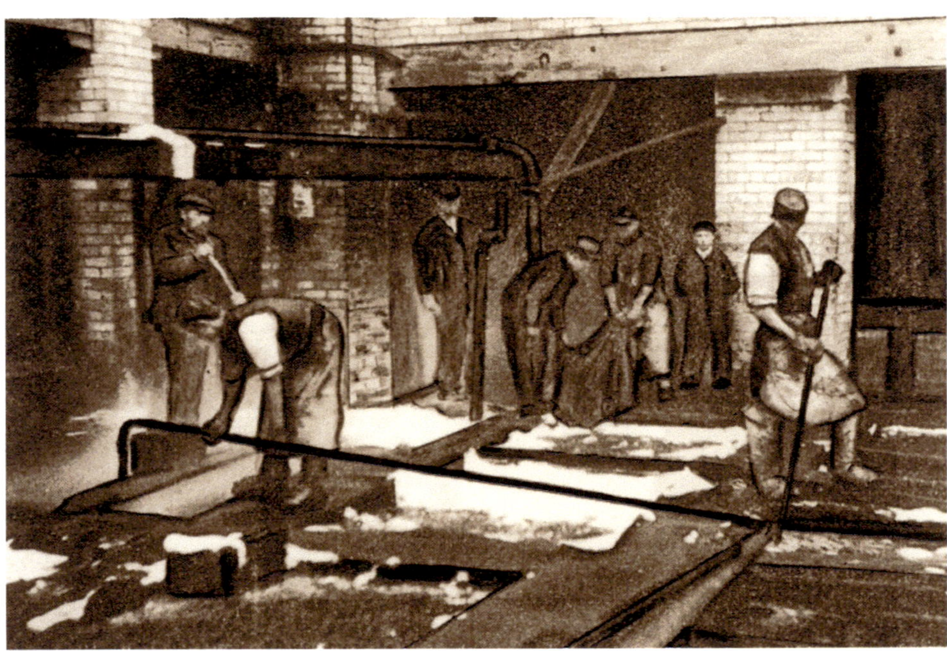

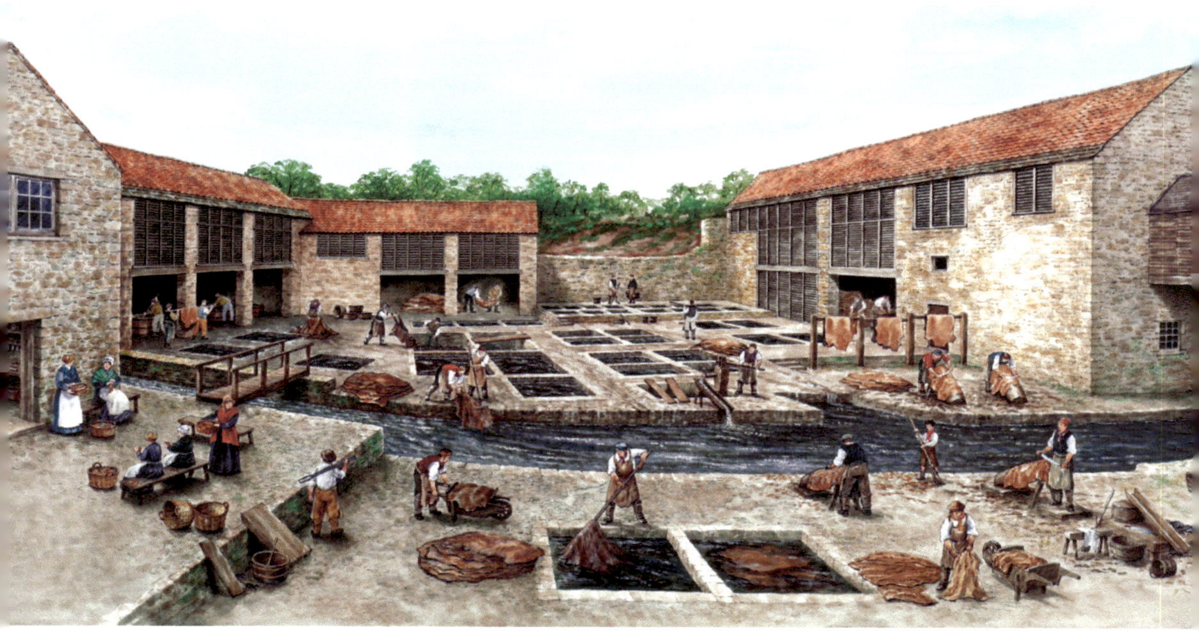

Tanning I

A reconstruction of what the tanning area would have looked like. The Halgut burn is central.

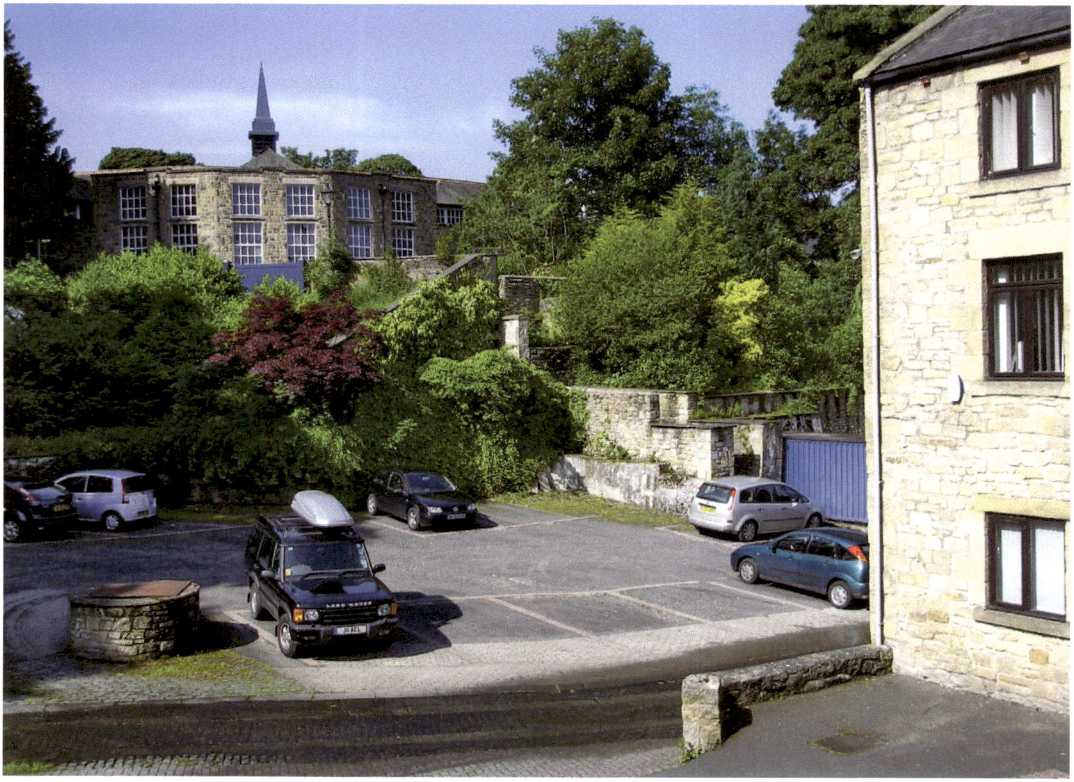

55

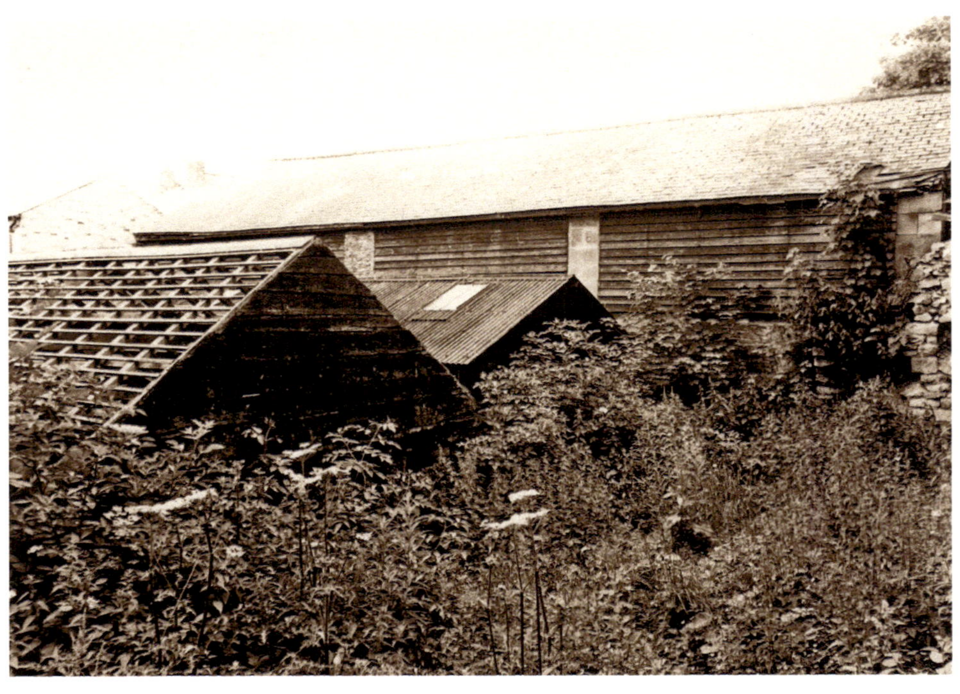

Tanning II

Fortunately Hylton Edgar recorded what was left on the site before it was partly demolished. Here we see some of the sheds. After dangerous structures were removed or saved, this is what is left today – to the credit of those responsible for preserving the past.

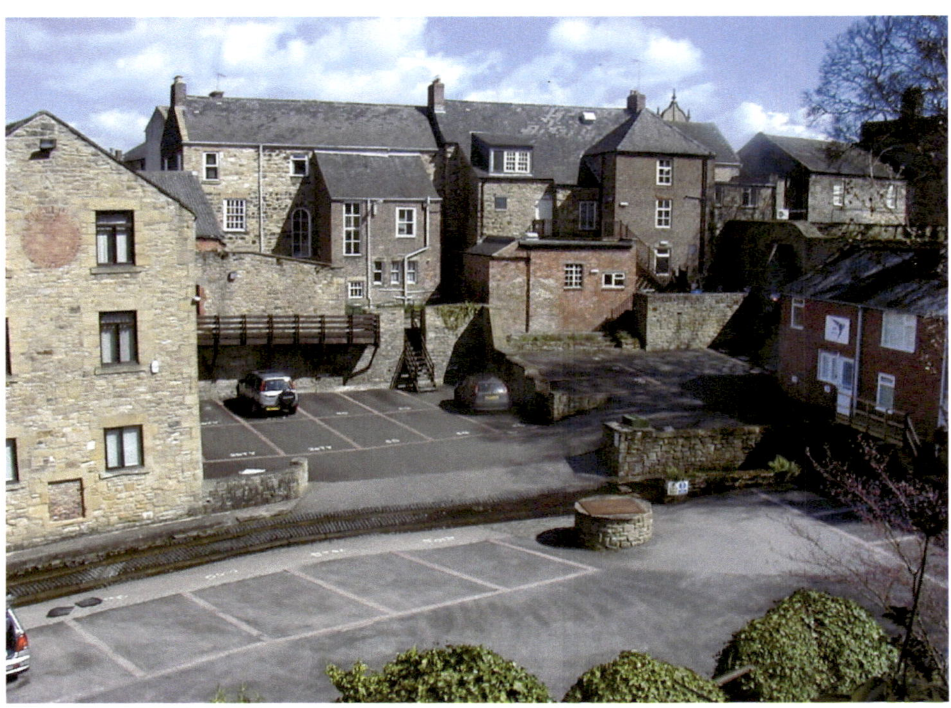

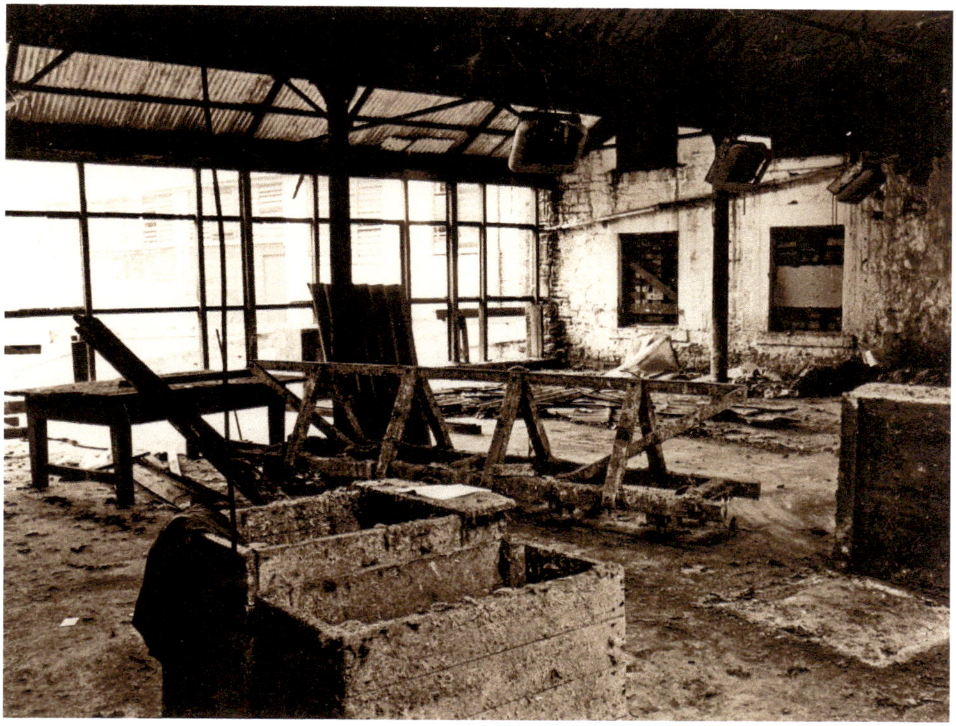

Tanning III

An inside view of the tannery before demolition. After the demolition, what we see today.

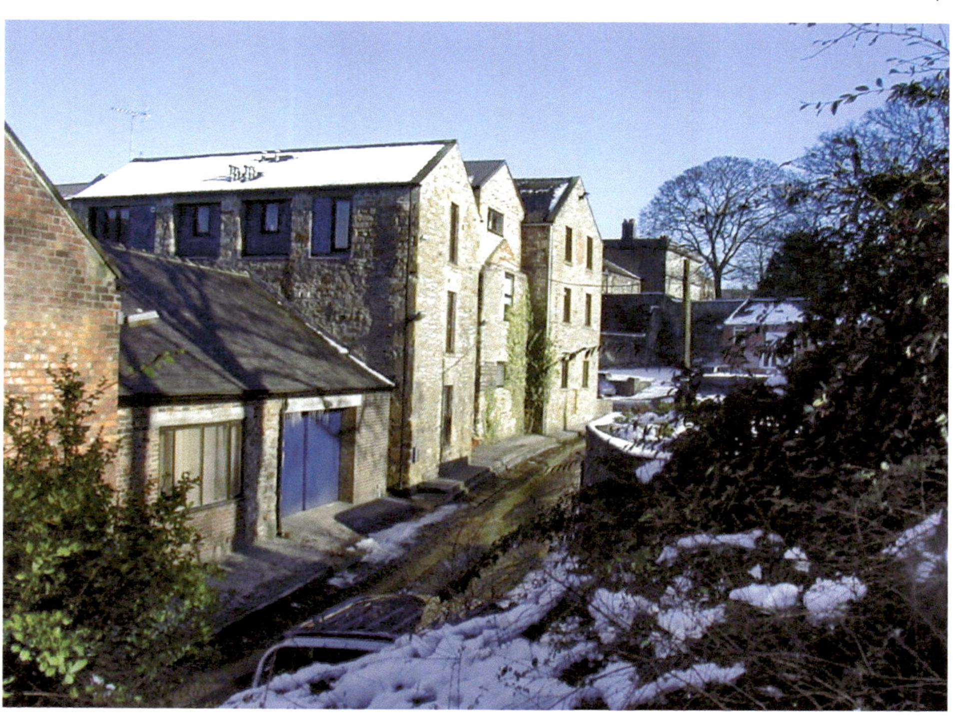

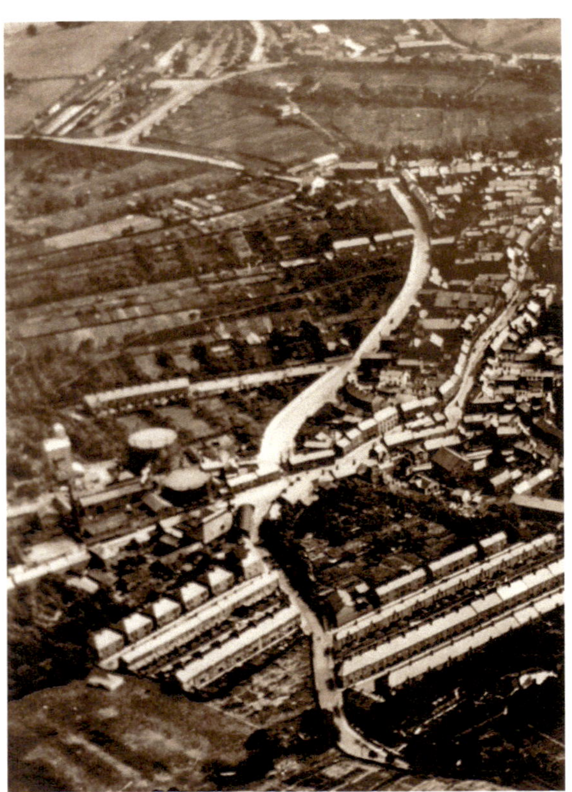

Hexham from the Air II

A rare old aerial photograph of the north of Hexham. There are many market gardens. Bottom left are two gasometers, now gone. Bottom right: terraces of houses, with one space left where a tan yard used to be. Haugh Lane runs into Eilansgate, bottom centre.

The focus of my modern shot is Gilesgate at the centre where roads meet. At the bottom is new housing at Cockshaw, Cockshaw Burn and Holy Island. New industries and retailers have spread towards the river.

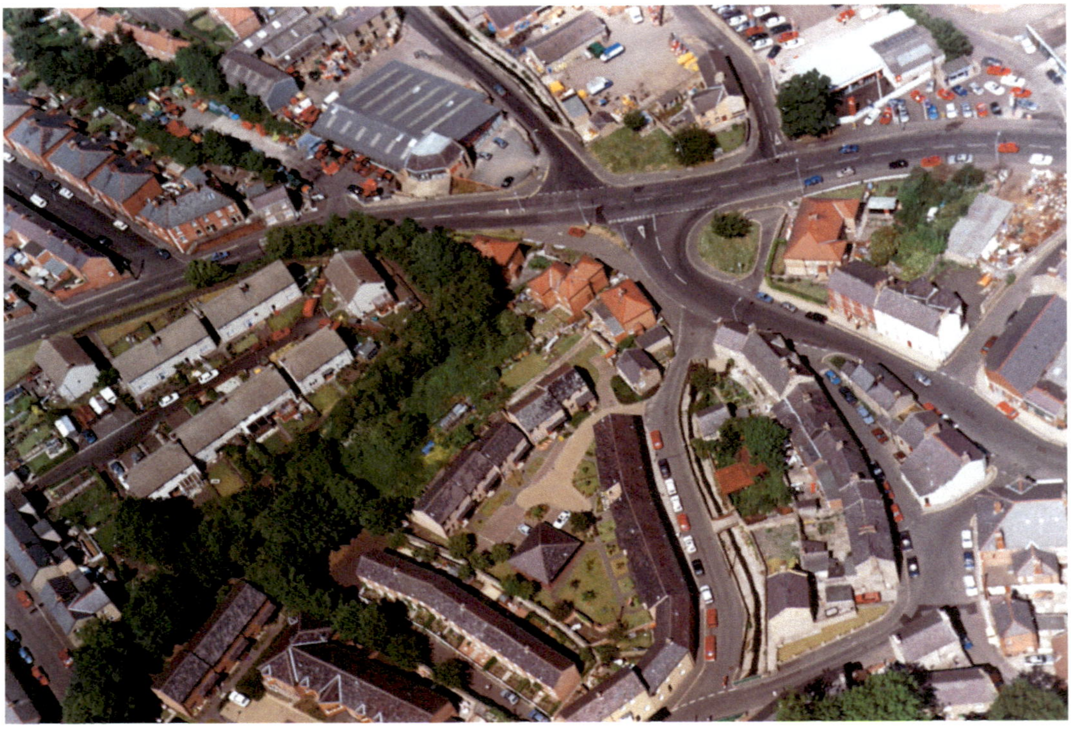

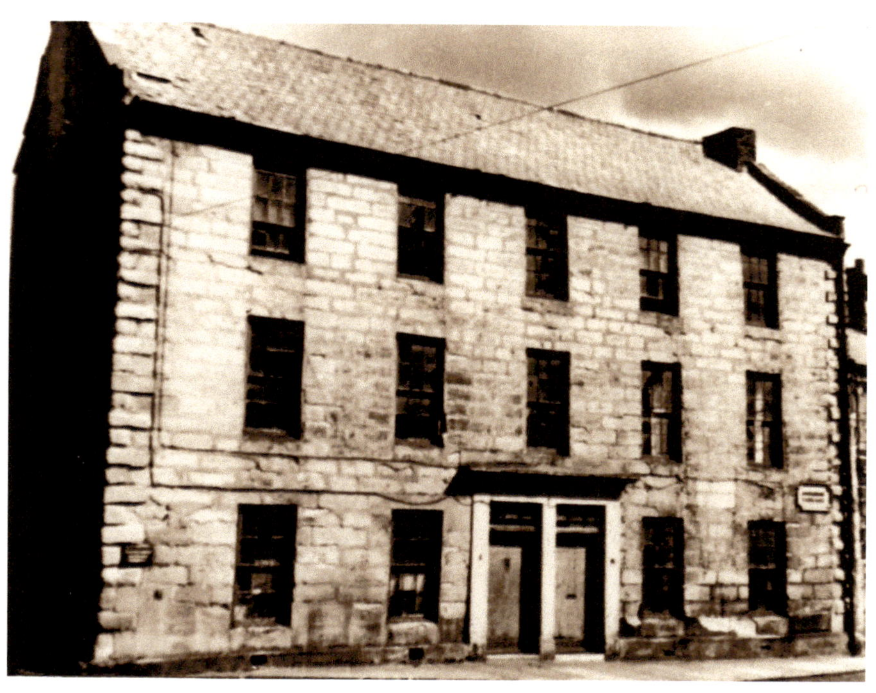

Cockshaw Terrace

Cockshaw Terrace was demolished in a big recent building programme. Here we see the demolition process.

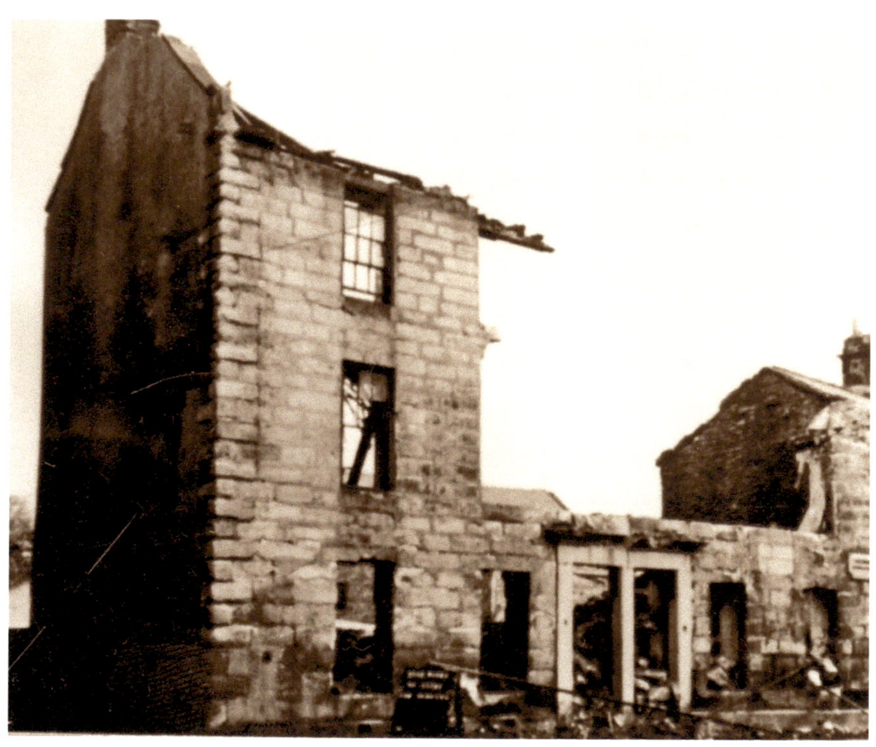

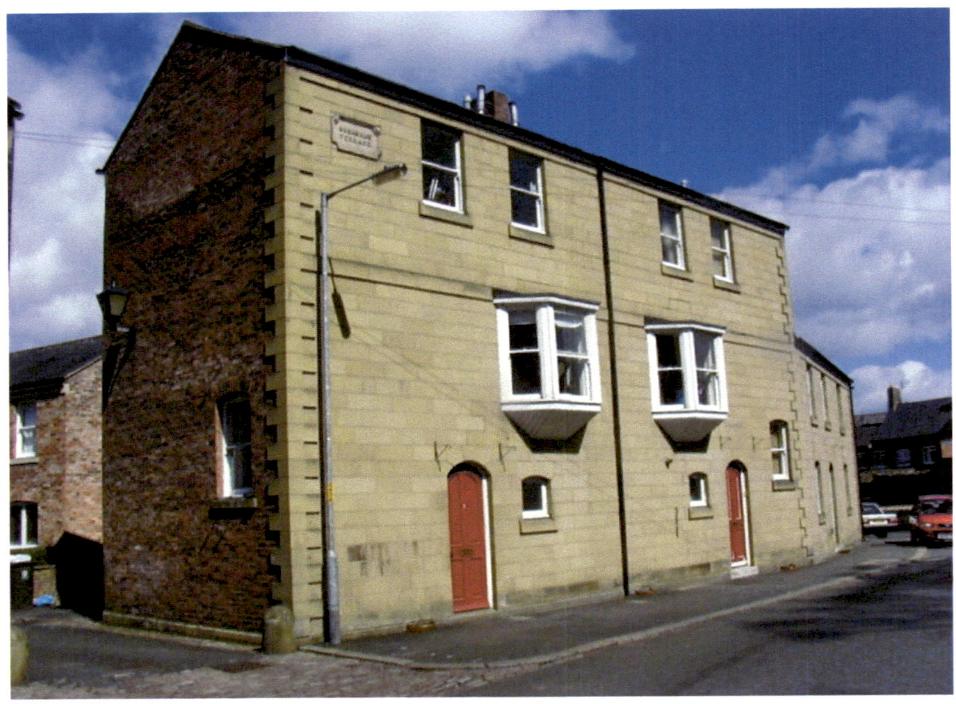

Cockshaw Terrace Today

Here is a row of old cottages on the right bank of the Cockshaw Burn. The house in the background was a chapel on Holy Island.

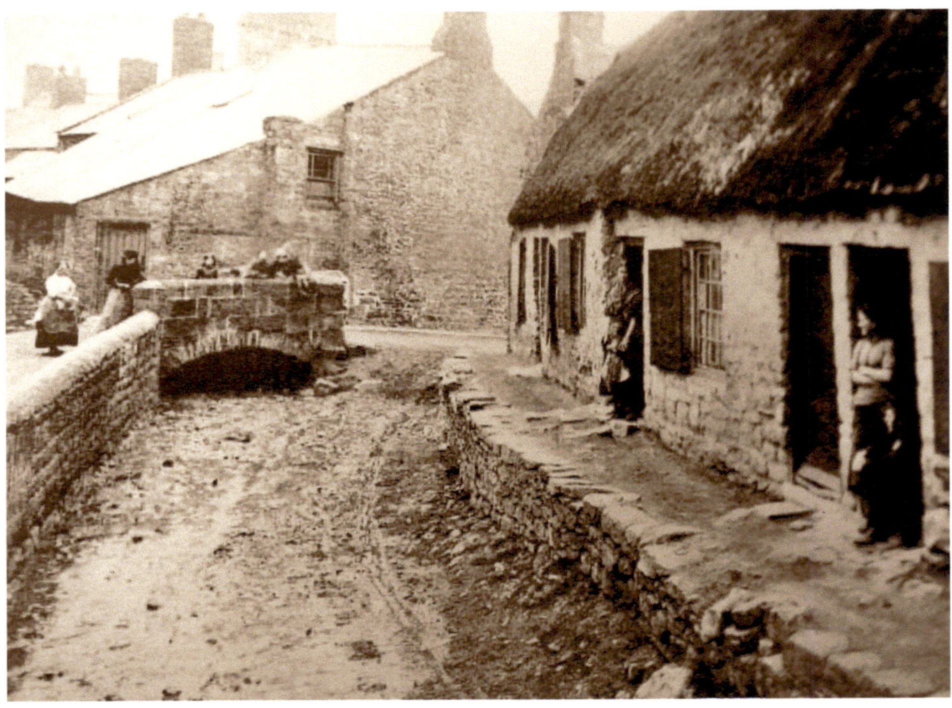

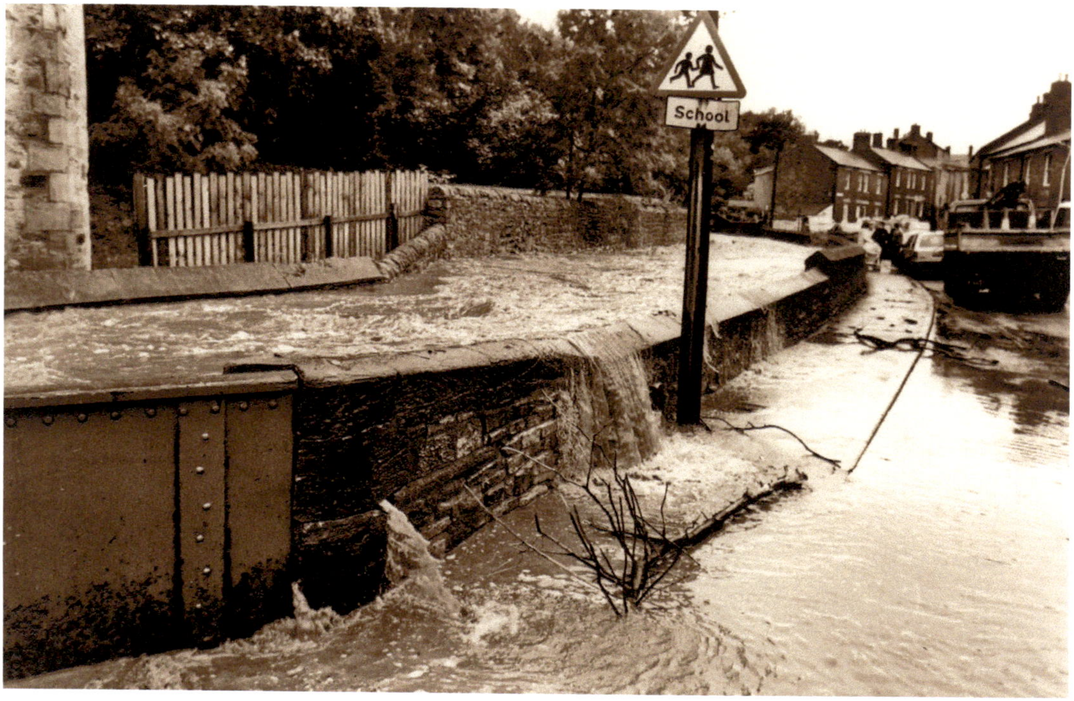

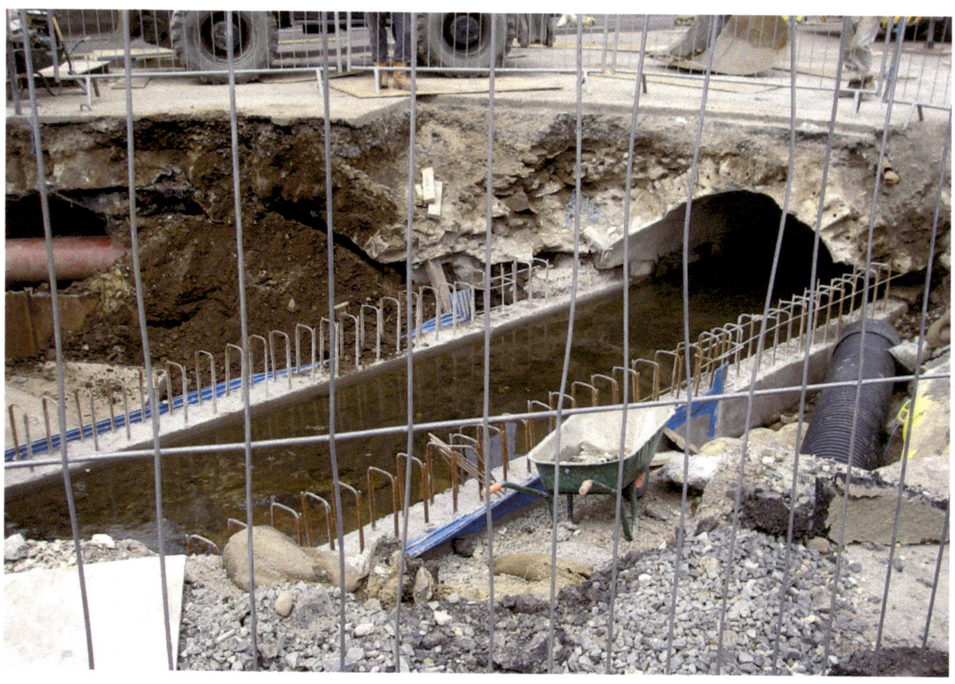

Cockshaw Burn II

The Cockshaw Burn area is prone to flooding, as we see here in the 1970s. The problem has been dealt with by work on the burn where it is still open and by culverting under the roads as it flows to the Tyne, north.

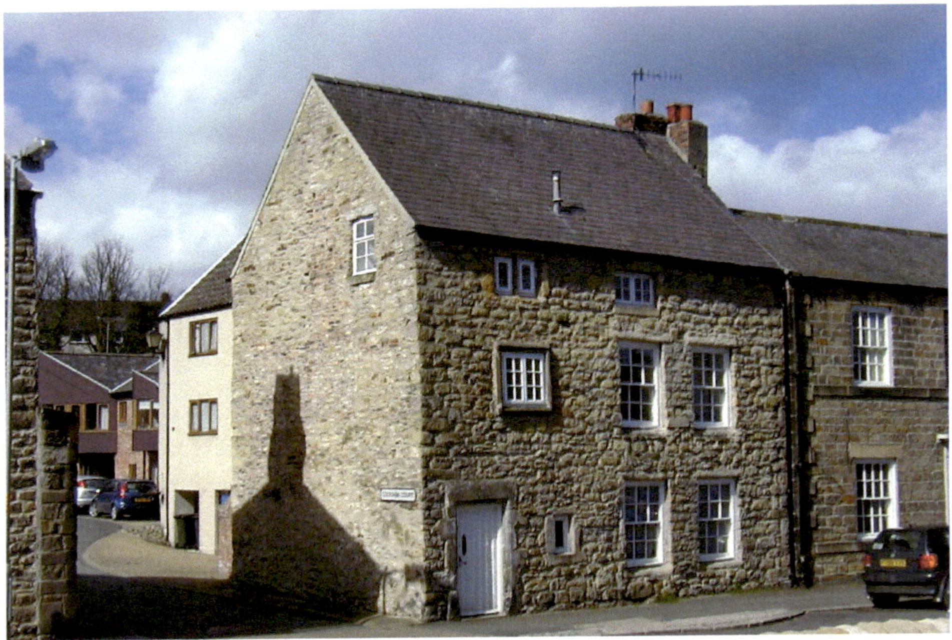

Priest's House

The seventeenth-century Priest's House was once used by Catholics as a Mass house. Behind it, later, was Robbs' warehouse. Below, the view down the burn today. At the end is the Old Tannery (The Skinners' Arms) and a chimney on the outside of one house is the result of a terrace being demolished, leaving a fireplace open to view. The new wall of the burn is part of a flood protection programme; it carries many words for 'water' in different languages and quotes a document reminding people not to wash 'puddings' (intestines) in the burn outside the permitted hours.

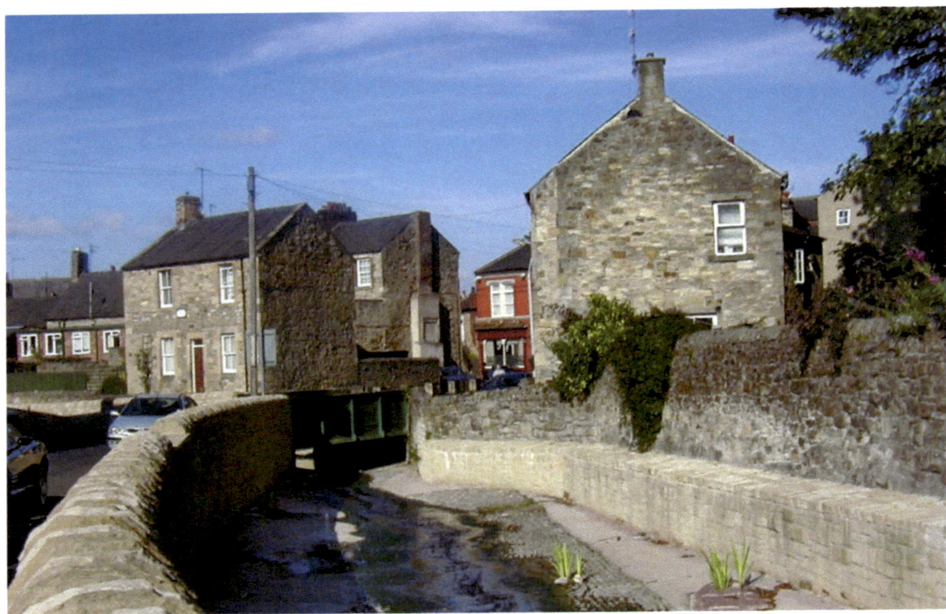

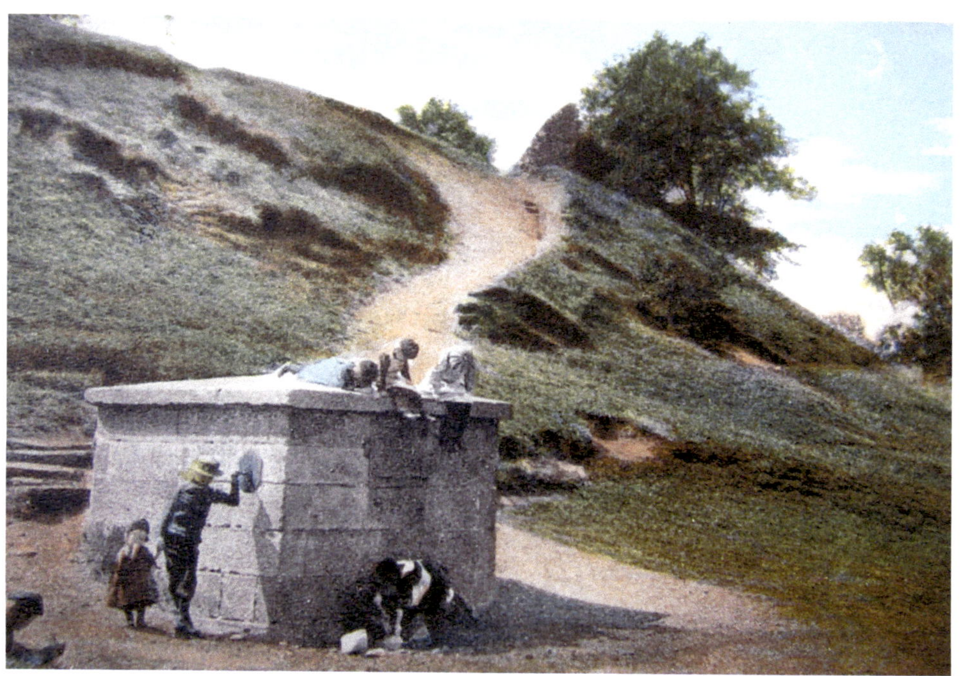

Water Sources

There are a few 'pants' (water sources) in Hexham of which two survive in Cockshaw. This one provided clean water when none other was available, and remains today. Others have already been seen in the Market Place, where the water quality was not good. Other sources of water were wells.

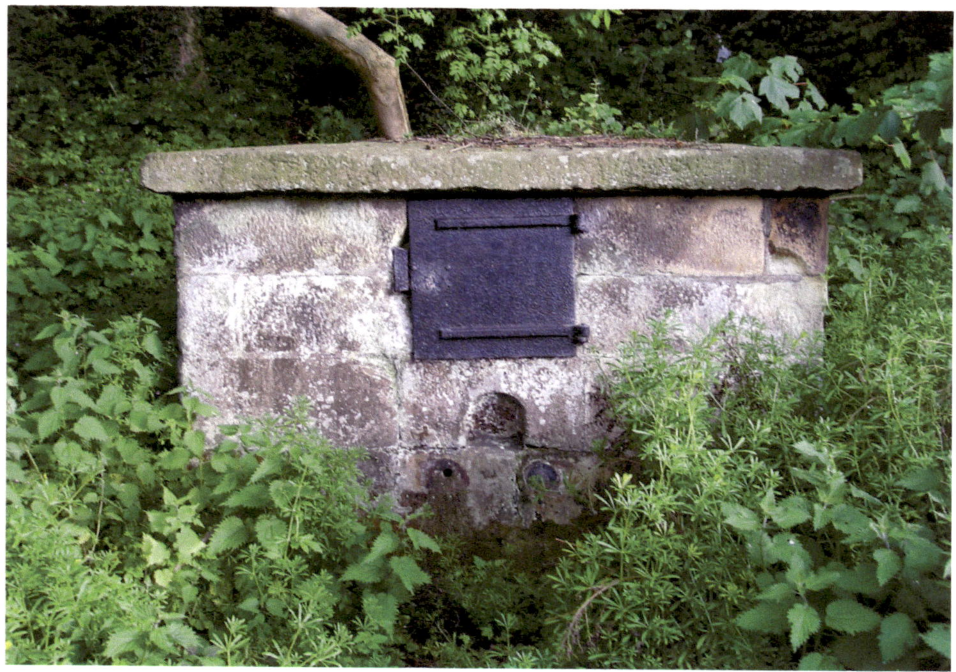

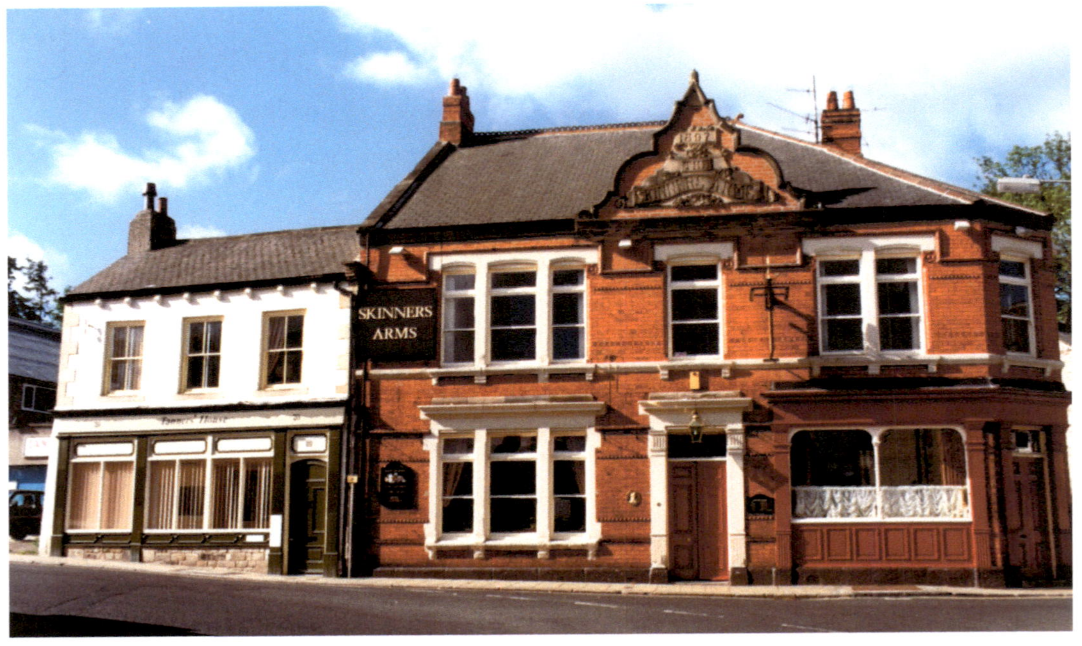

The Skinners' and Tanners' Arms

The Skinners' and Tanners' Arms lay side by side and remind us of the work carried out here. The former's name has been changed to the Old Tannery. Another surviving building further north along the burn is Smith Stobart's tannery. Opposite are the remains of the old House of Correction. The whole area has been recently extensively developed.

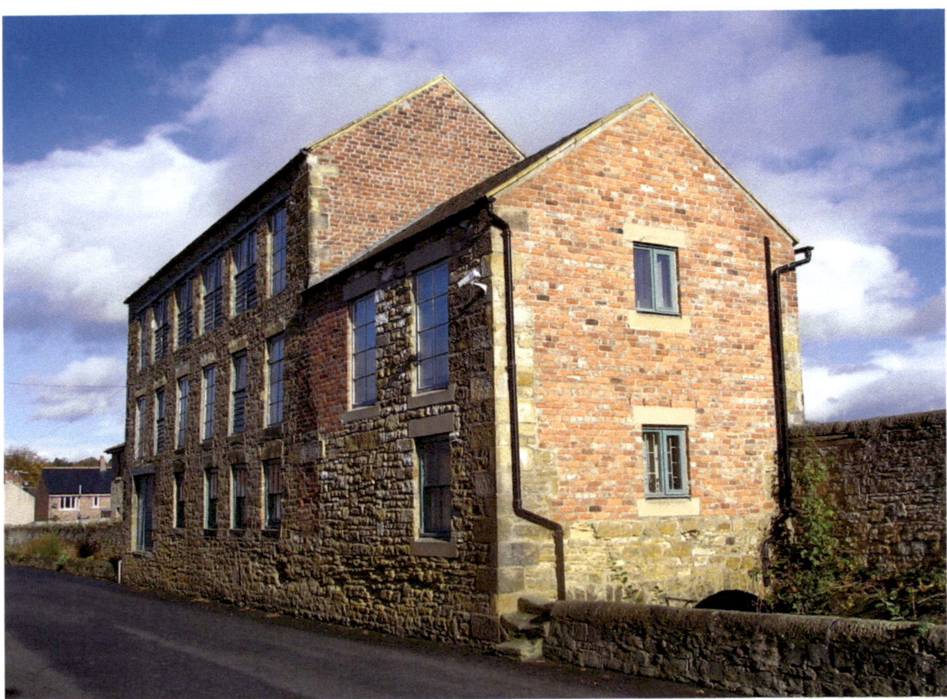

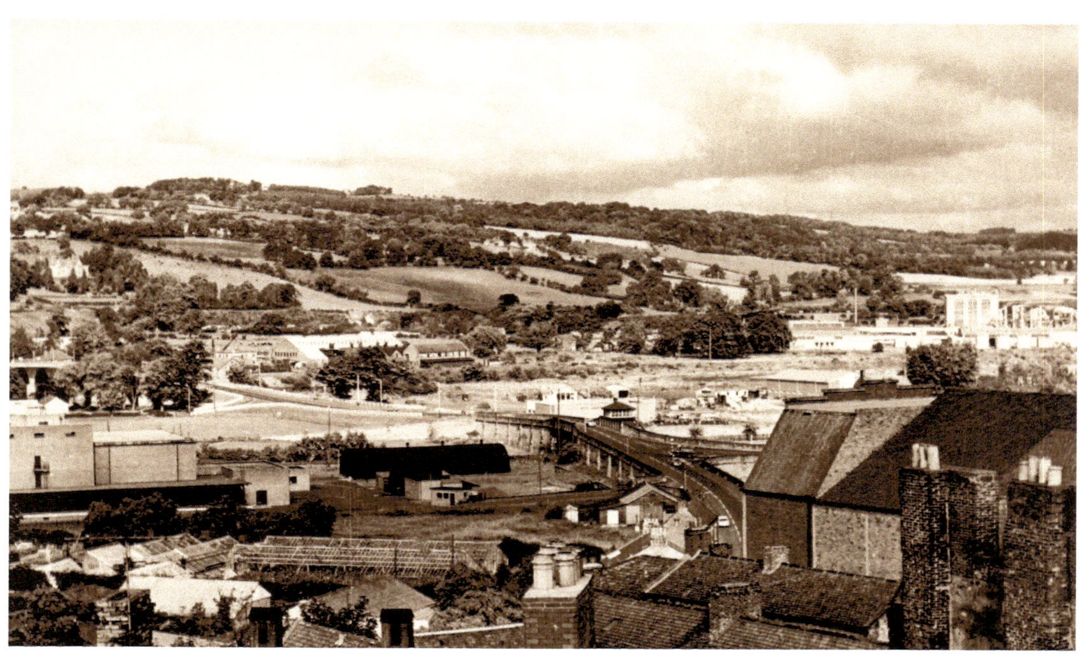

The Haugh

The flat alluvial plain known as the Haugh has been a growth area north of the old town. In this picture the now-demolished nuclear bunker rises to the left, and the road to the A69 cuts across. From Prospect House we see a large car park, Waitrose, and the Wentworth sports centre where a new swimming pool was recently added.

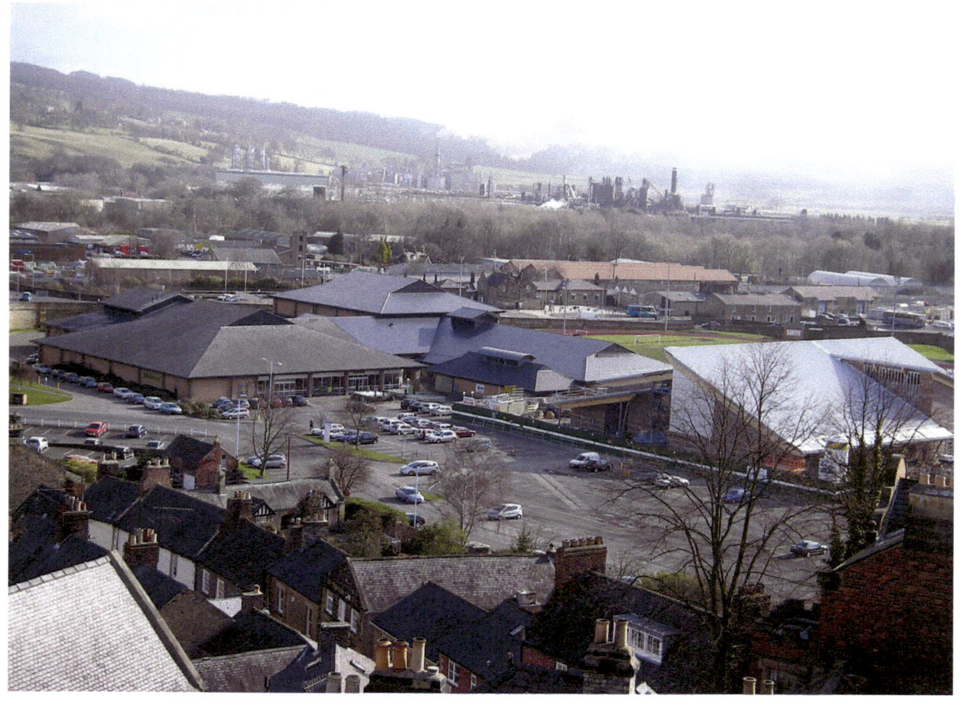

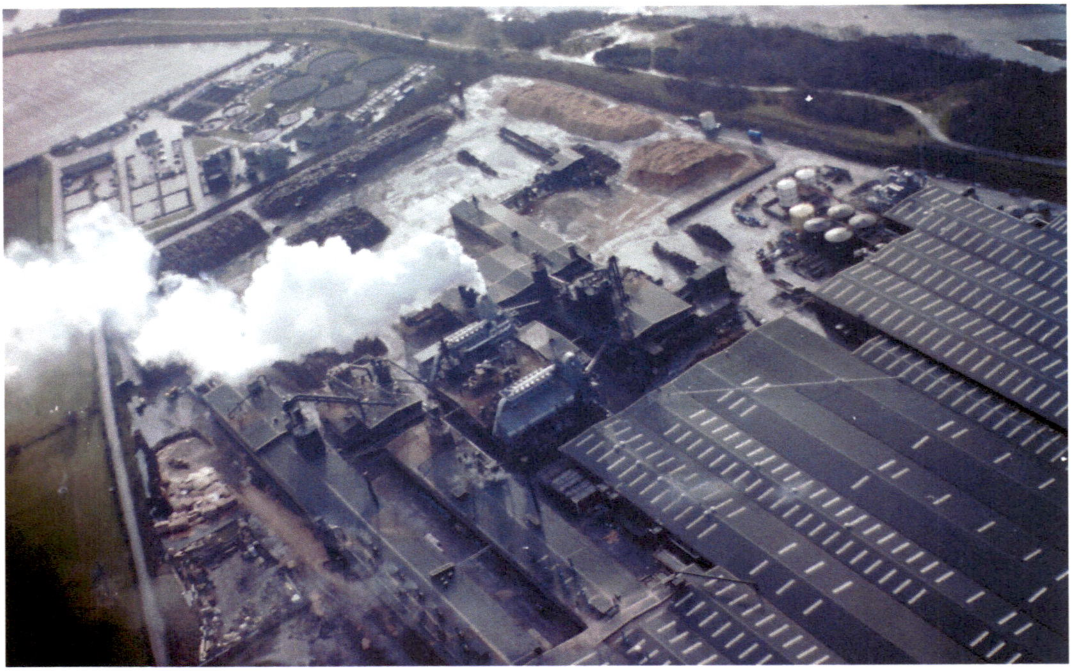

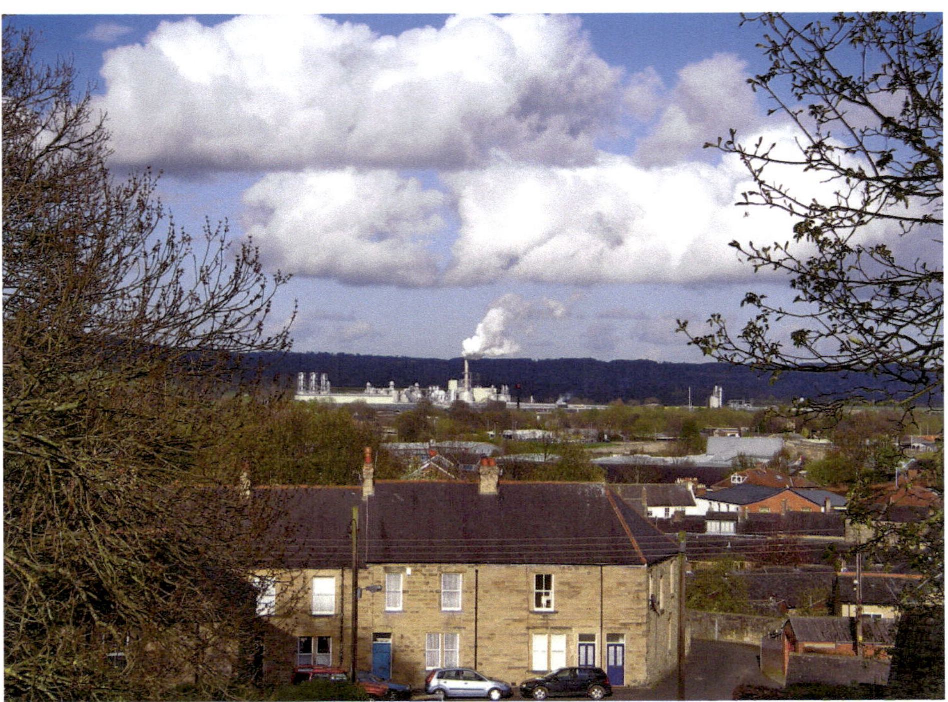

Ongoing Development I

A modern factory for chipboard manufacture, Egger, dominates the skyline to the east. From the air we see an earlier stage in its development, and the view below from Windmill Hill shows its continuing expansion.

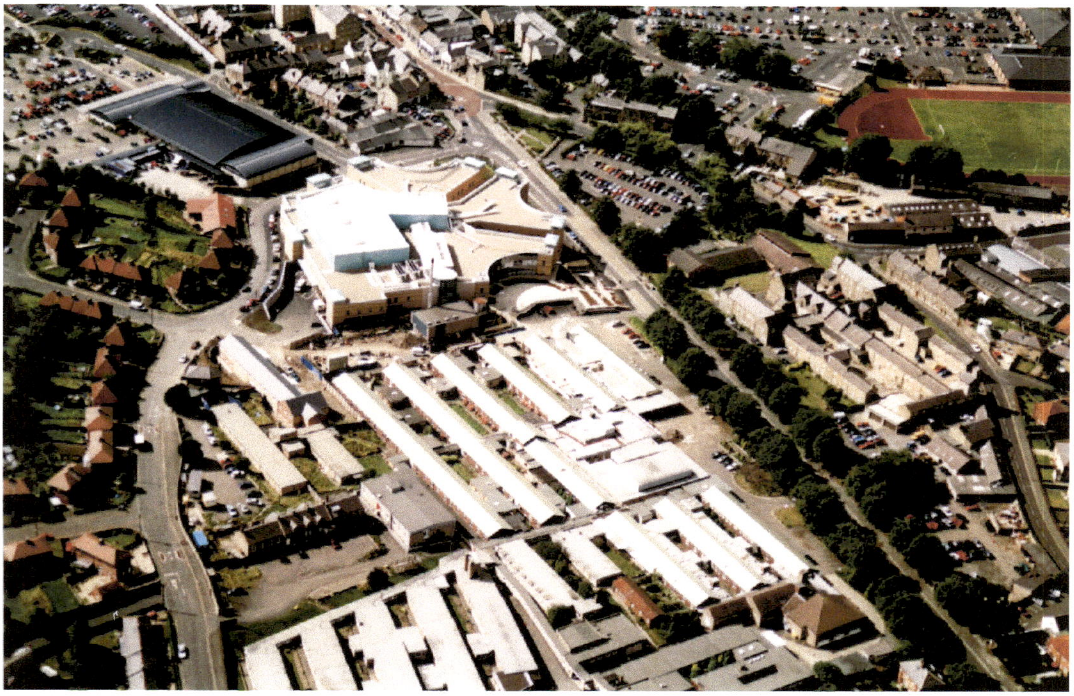

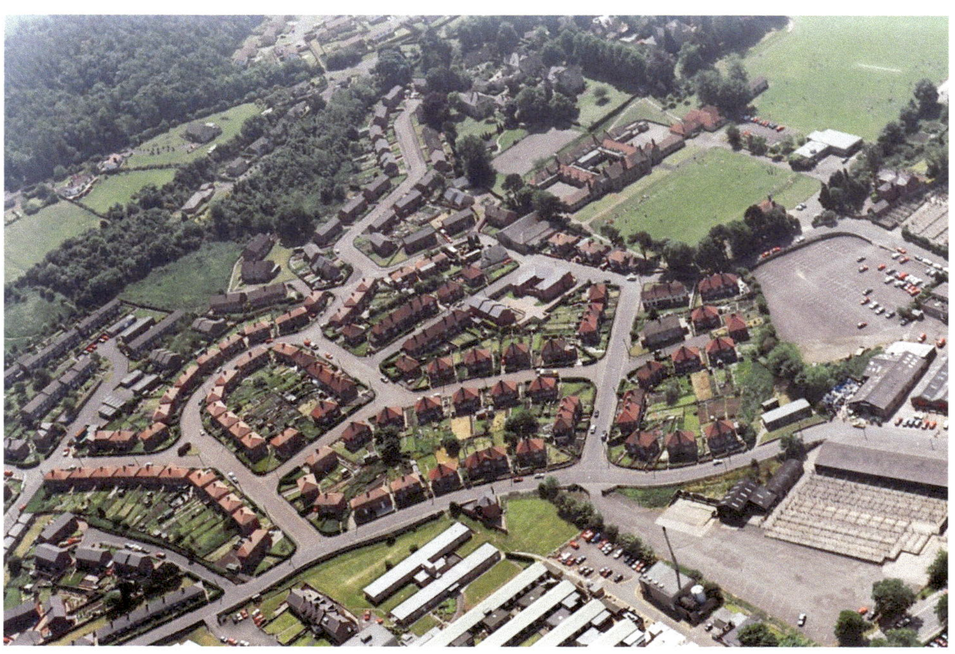

Ongoing Development II

An important development has been the building of a new hospital to replace the rectangular huts that we see here, when the west end was completed. To the north on its margin is an estate built to provide better housing for the people who were evicted from overcrowded areas like Cockshaw.

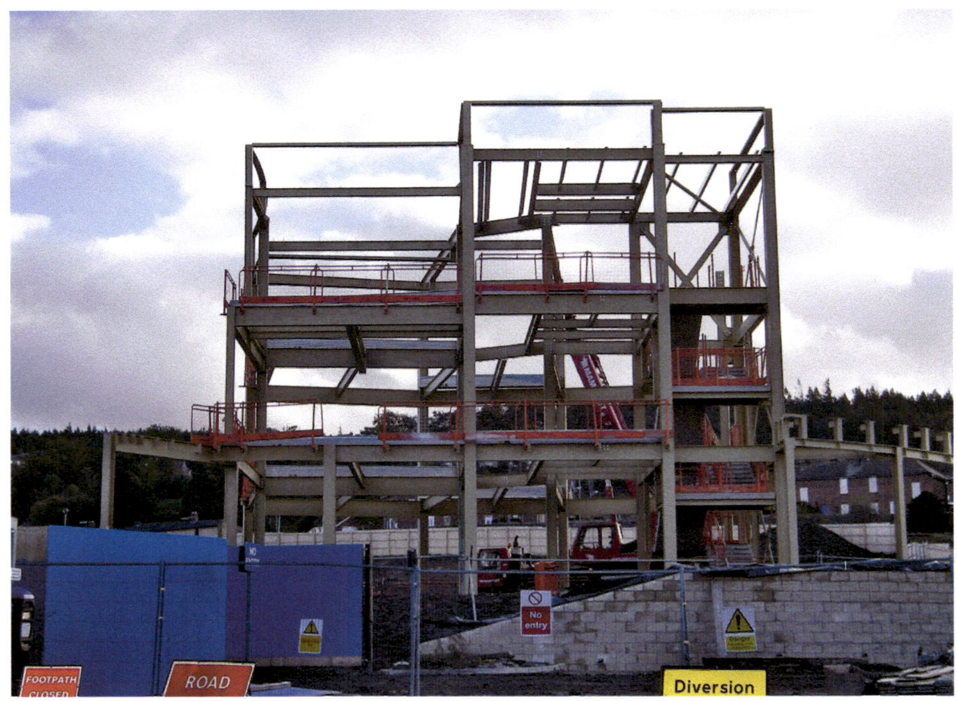

Hospital I

One part of the hospital is under construction above, and the completed building can be seen below from the Corbridge Road in 2012.

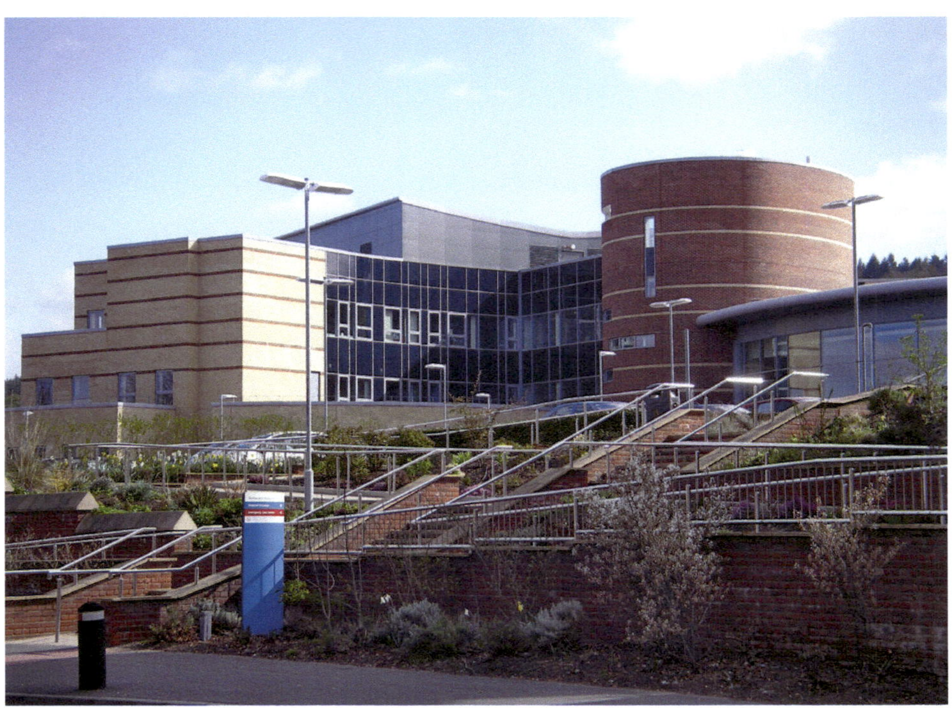

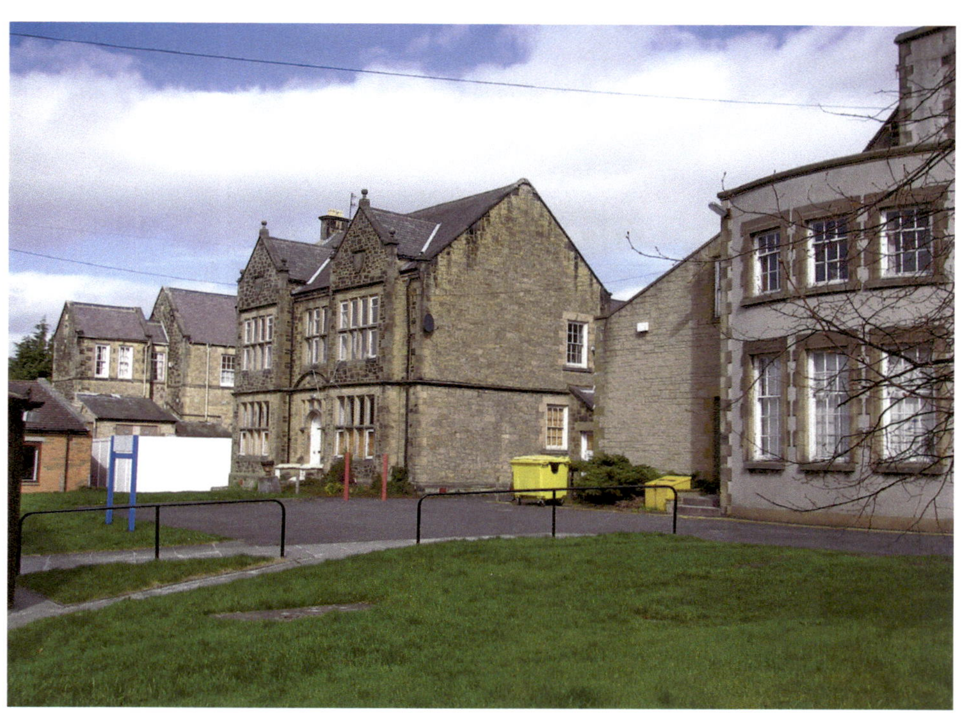

Hospital II

Opposite the hospital is a Workhouse, used now by the hospital. The large house belonged to the Master, and is dated 1883. It closed in 1939.

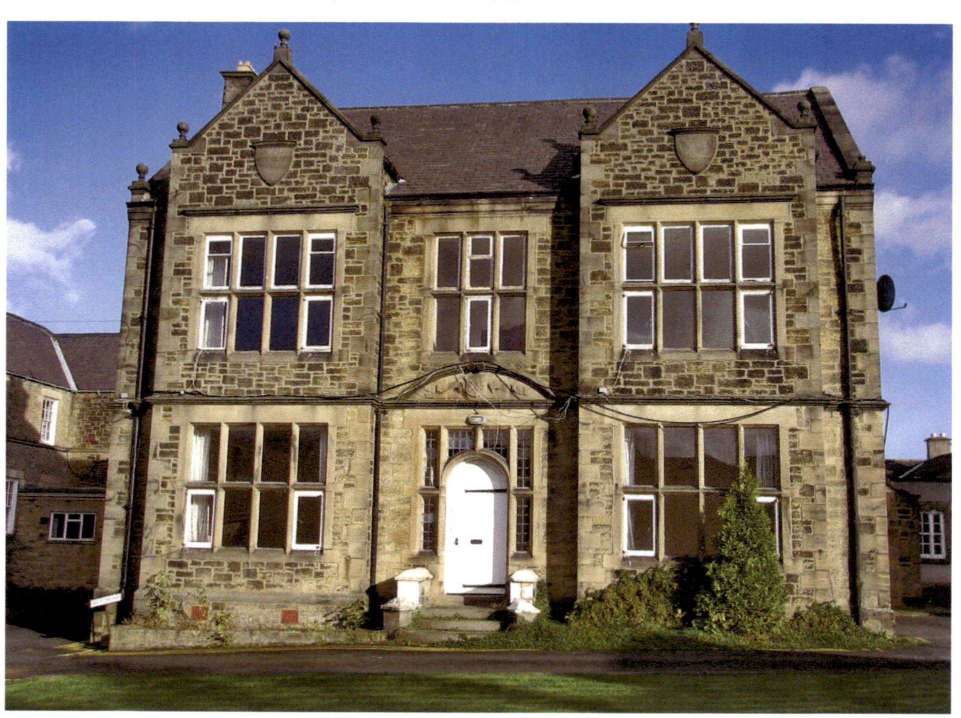

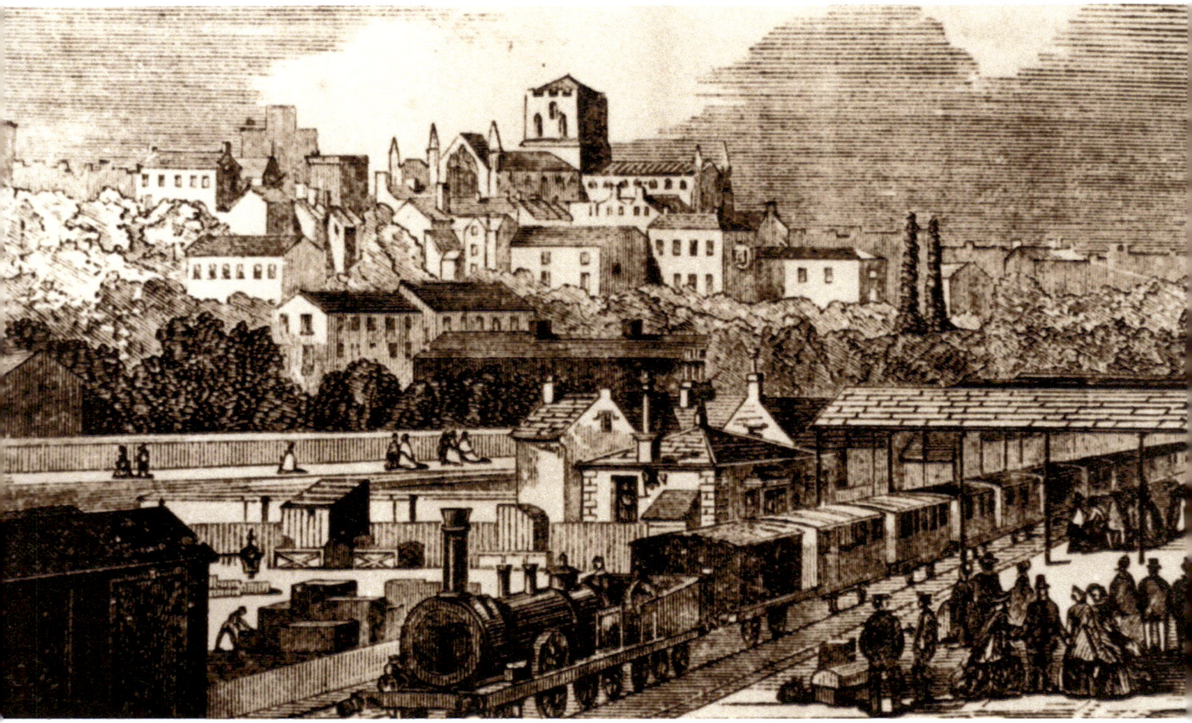

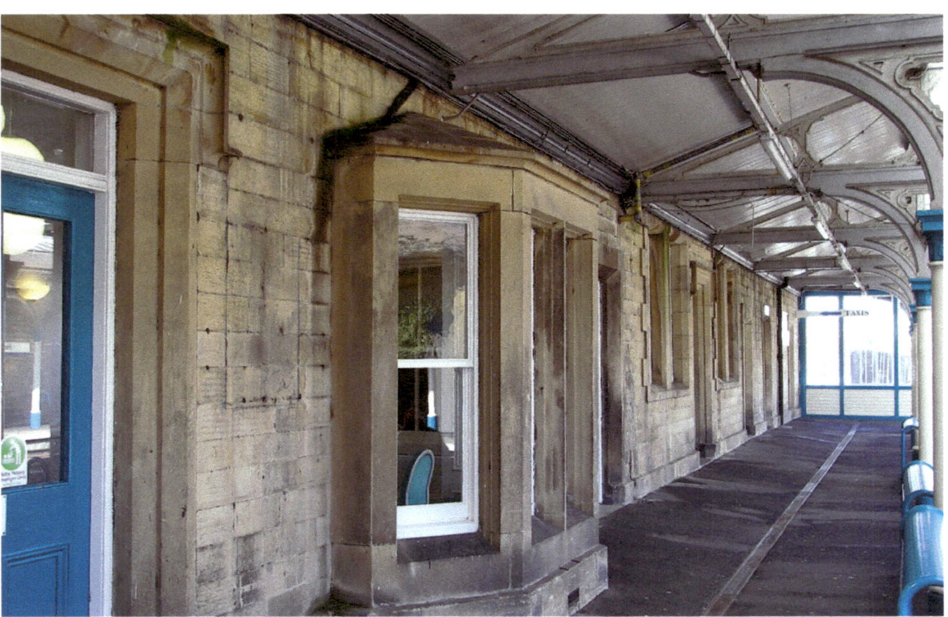

Newcastle & Carlisle Railway

A most important event was the opening of the Newcastle & Carlisle Railway in 1836. It had many platforms when it began to link up with other places, but is now down to a single east–west service. The station today retains some of the older features, like this bay window of the waiting room.

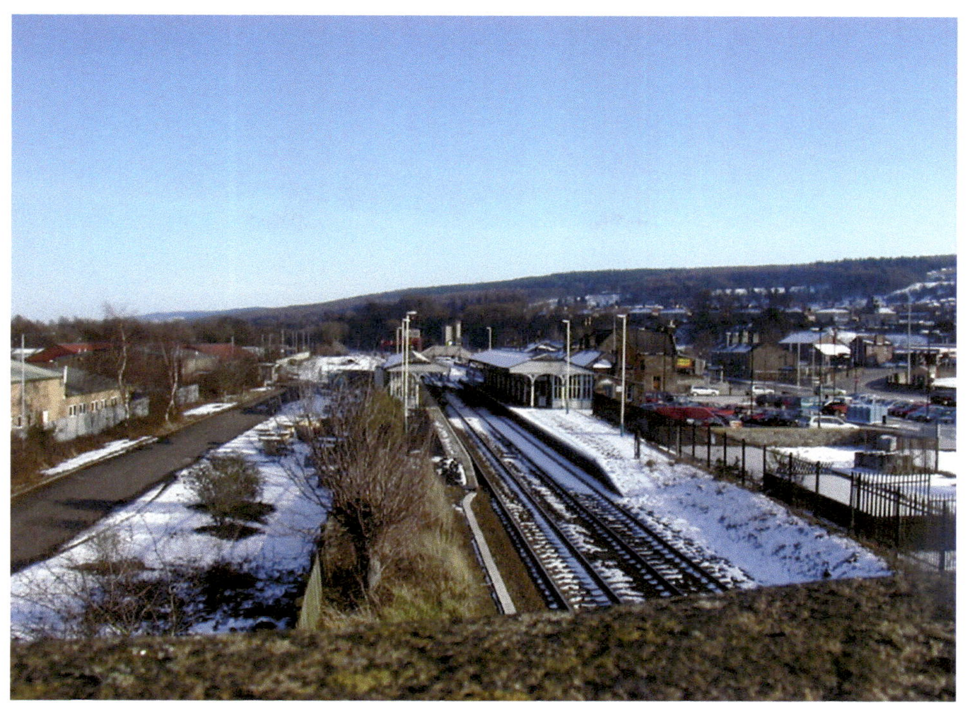

The Platforms and Lines Today
The quality of Victorian building is seen in the bridge over the lines.

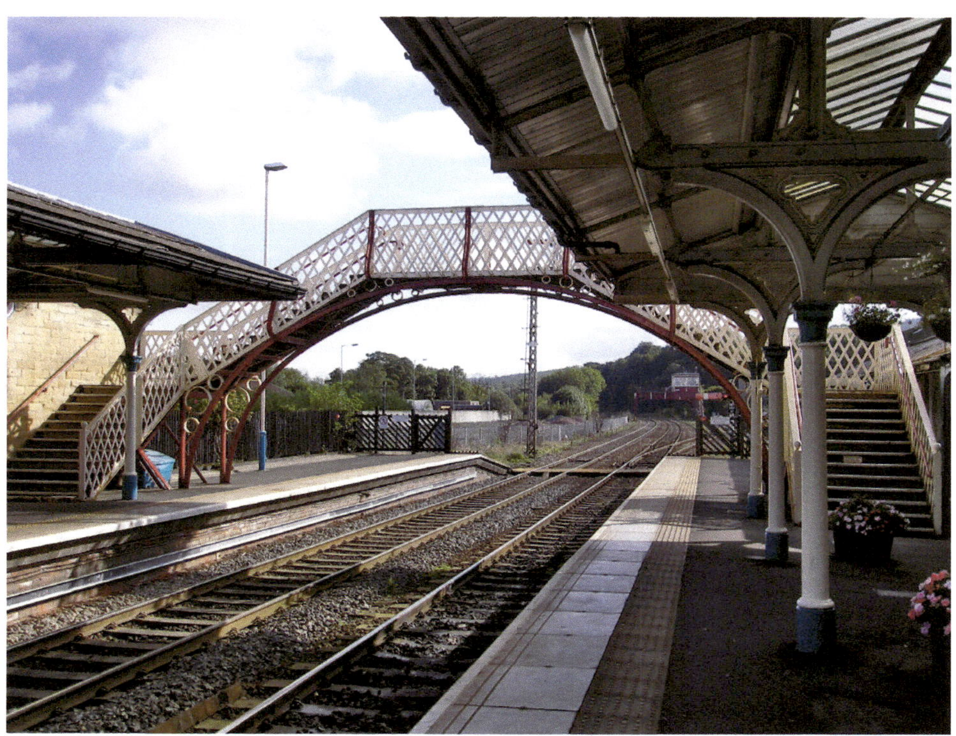

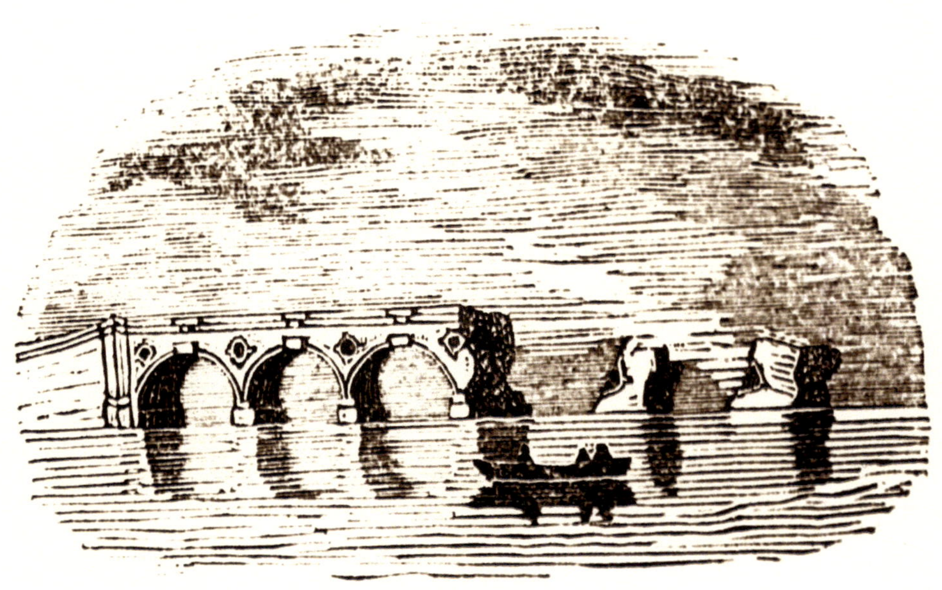

Bridges I

There was a fording place over the Tyne, replaced by bridges that collapsed like this one. The present bridge was built in 1793; here in 2012 the river is iced over. A scheme for hydro-electricity has now been approved and funded.

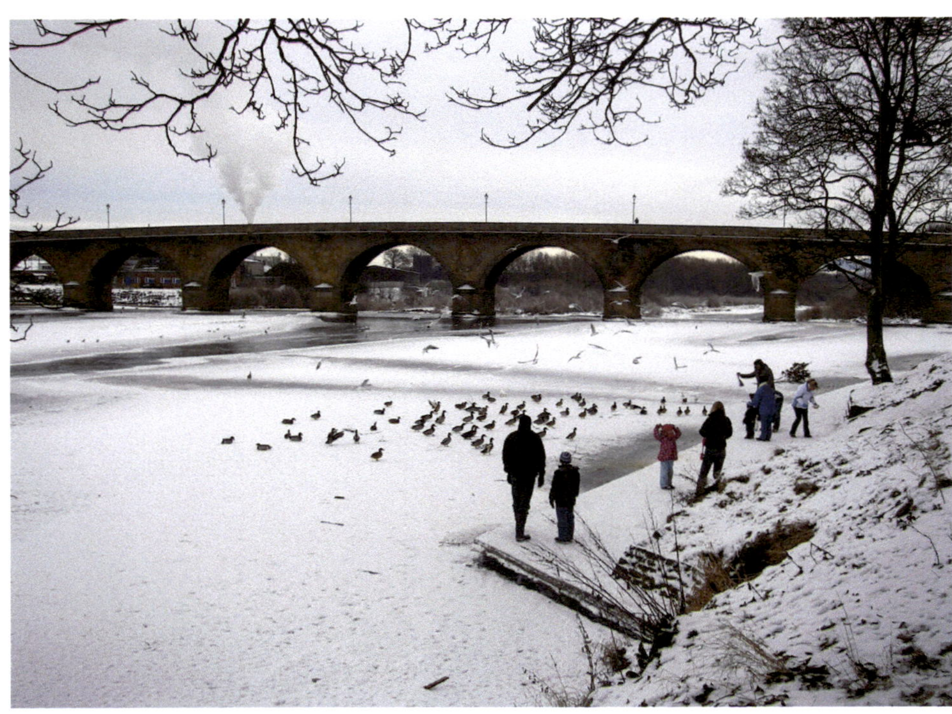

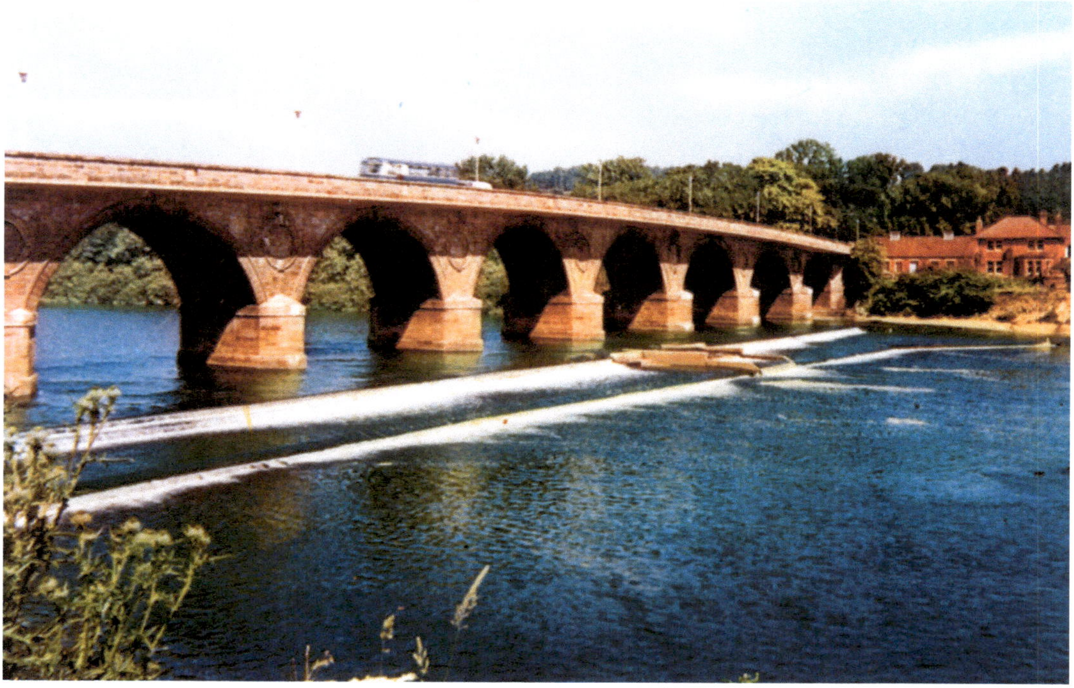

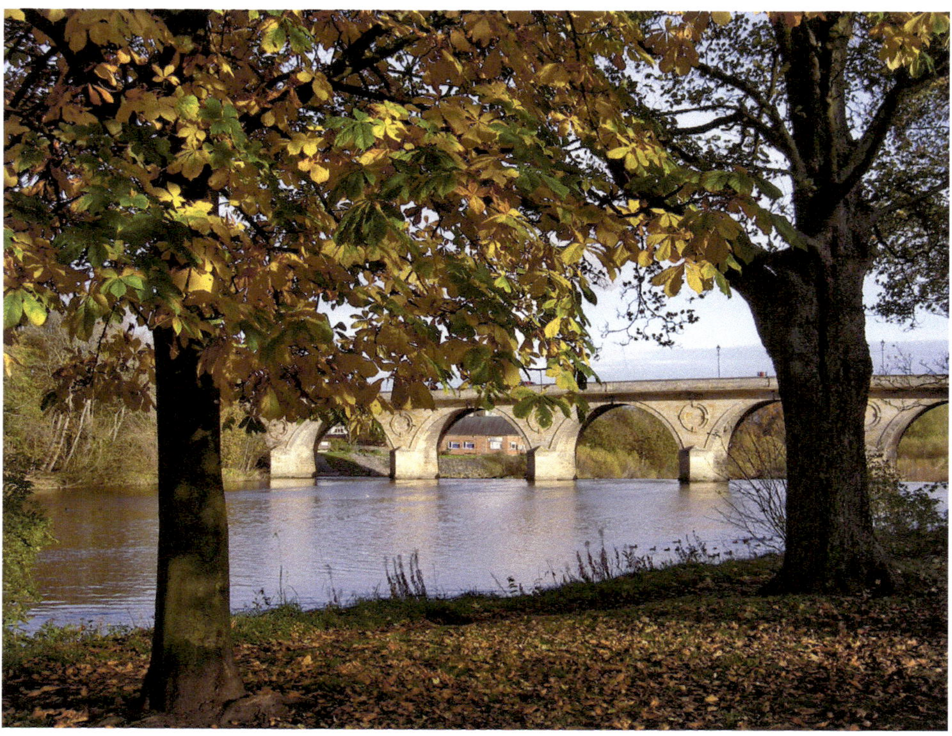

An old postcard shows the bridge from the east. The 2012 view is from the west.

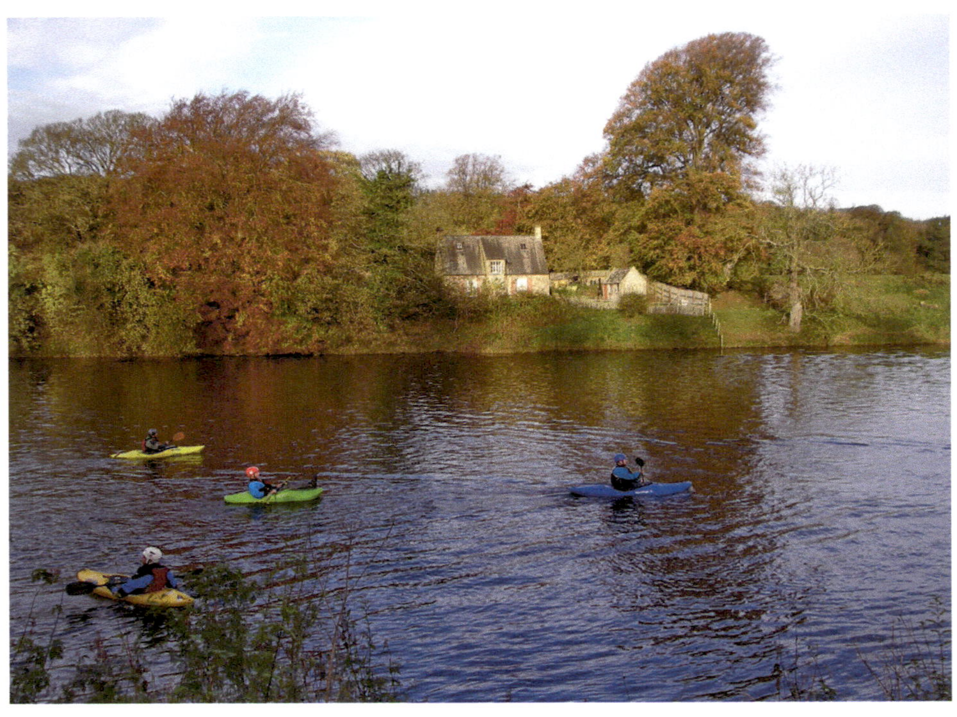

River Tyne

The river is well-used by boats and canoes. The tents under the trees in 2011 are part of a large camp for canoeists.

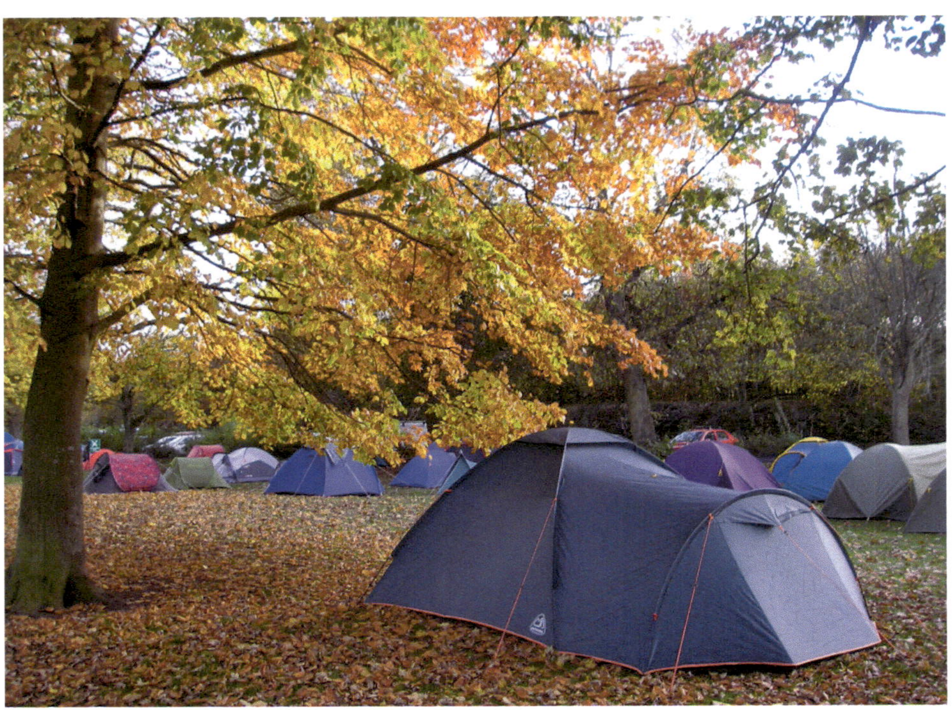

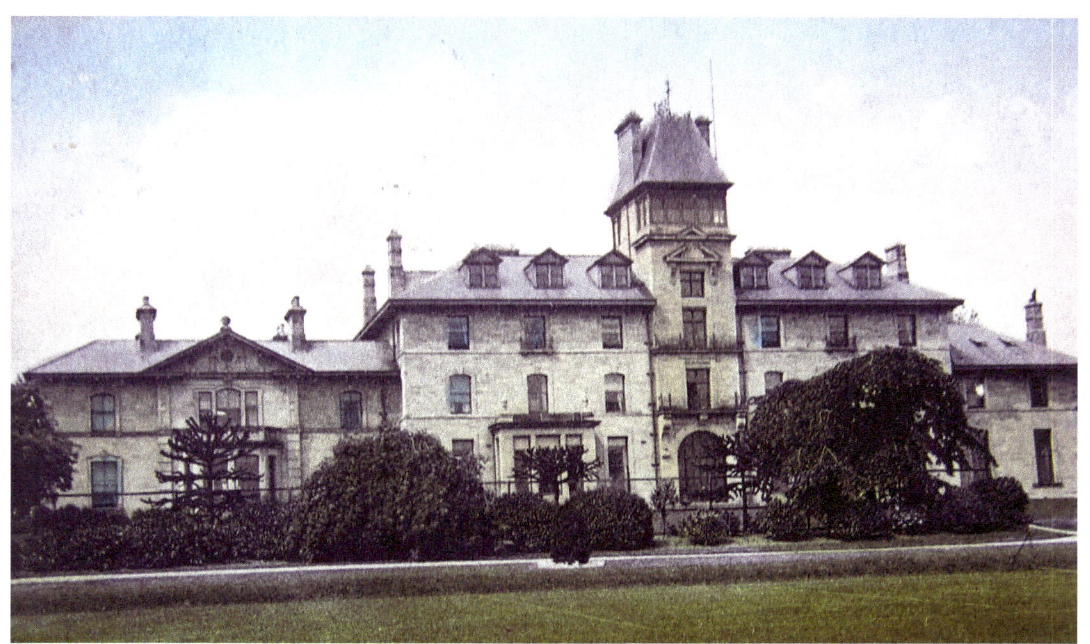

Hydro

An important building is the 'Hydro'. Built on the site of an older house as a health resort and spa, it has a fine view to the river across the town. It attracted not only people from outside the town, who came by rail, but also the local people for social occasions such as dances. Today it is part of the Queen Elizabeth High School.

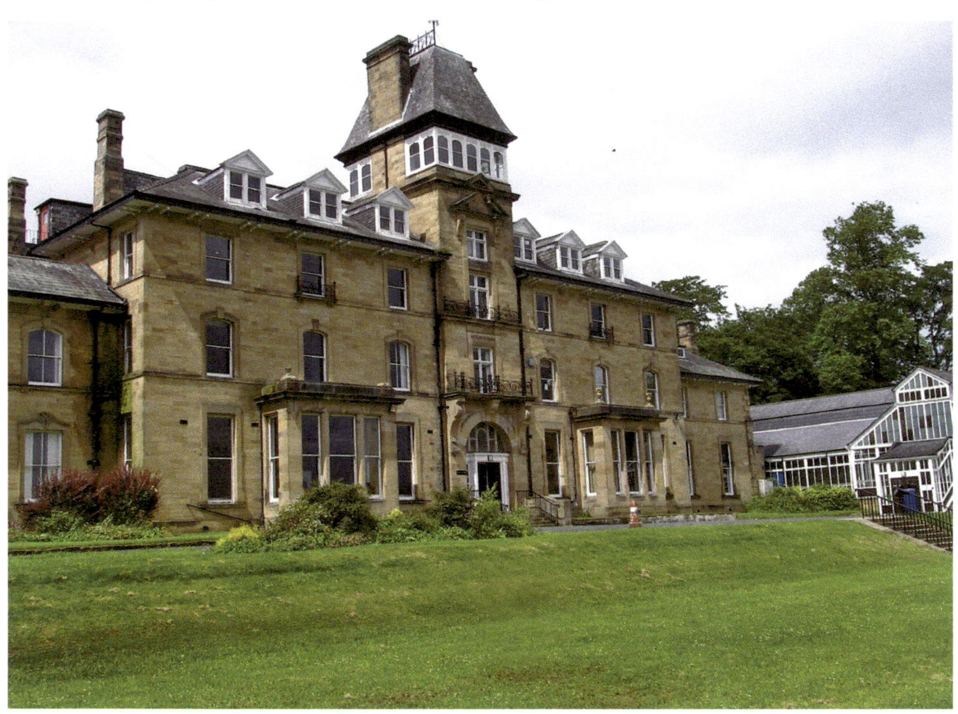

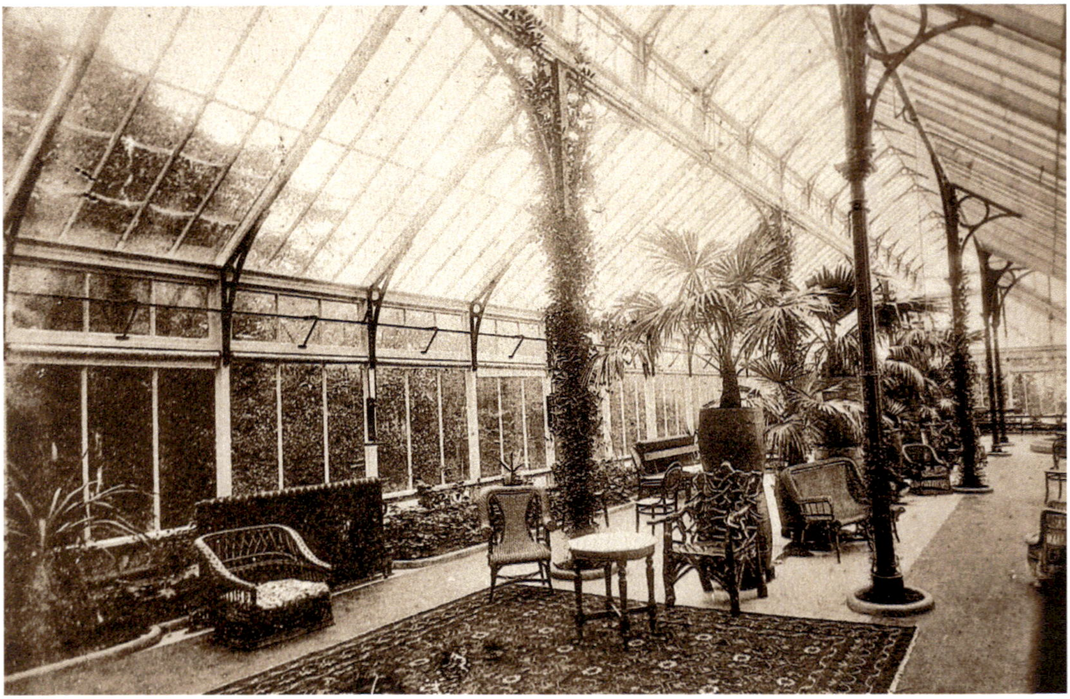

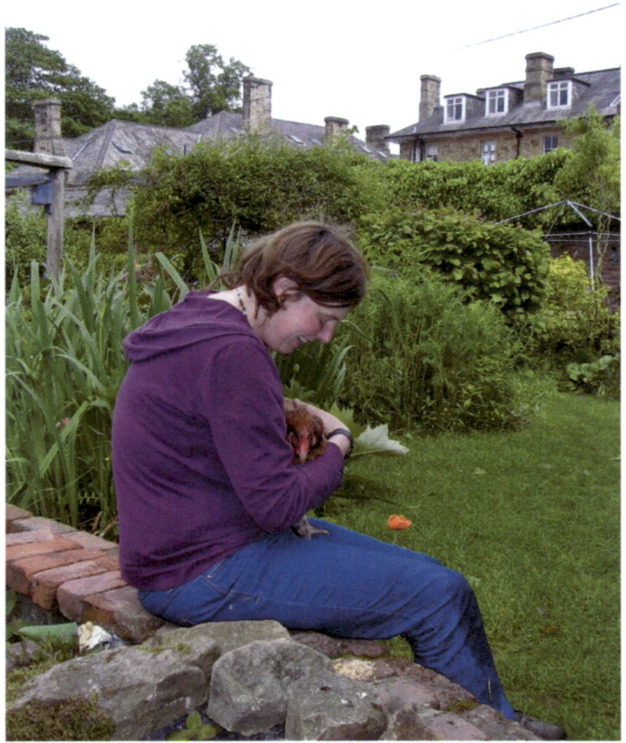

Winter Garden

Part of the Hydro is the Winter Garden, where dances and other social functions took place – and still do. Behind the Hydro are the kitchen gardens, re-discovered and transformed as part of the school's horticultural classes. Emma, the teacher, is seen here with one of the rescued battery hens in 2012.

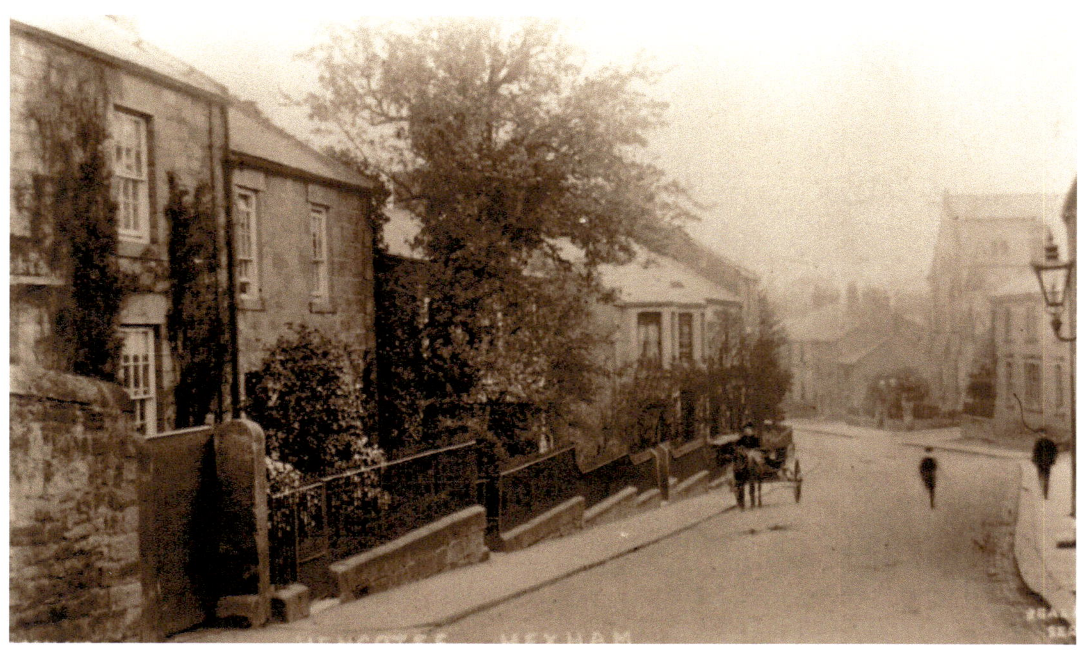

Hencotes I

Down the hill from the Hydro, the Allendale Road turns into Hencotes. The old photograph and the 2012 one show little change at the top of Hencotes at Temperley Place, in whose honour the Market Cross and Fountain were erected in 1902 as a gift from his family to the Urban District Council that he served.

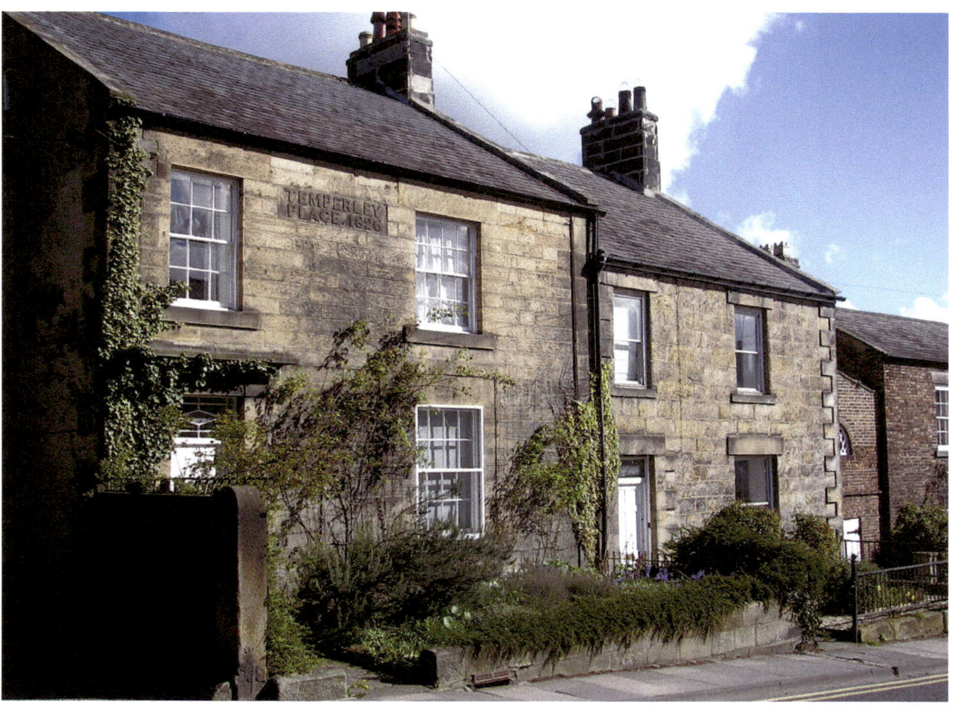

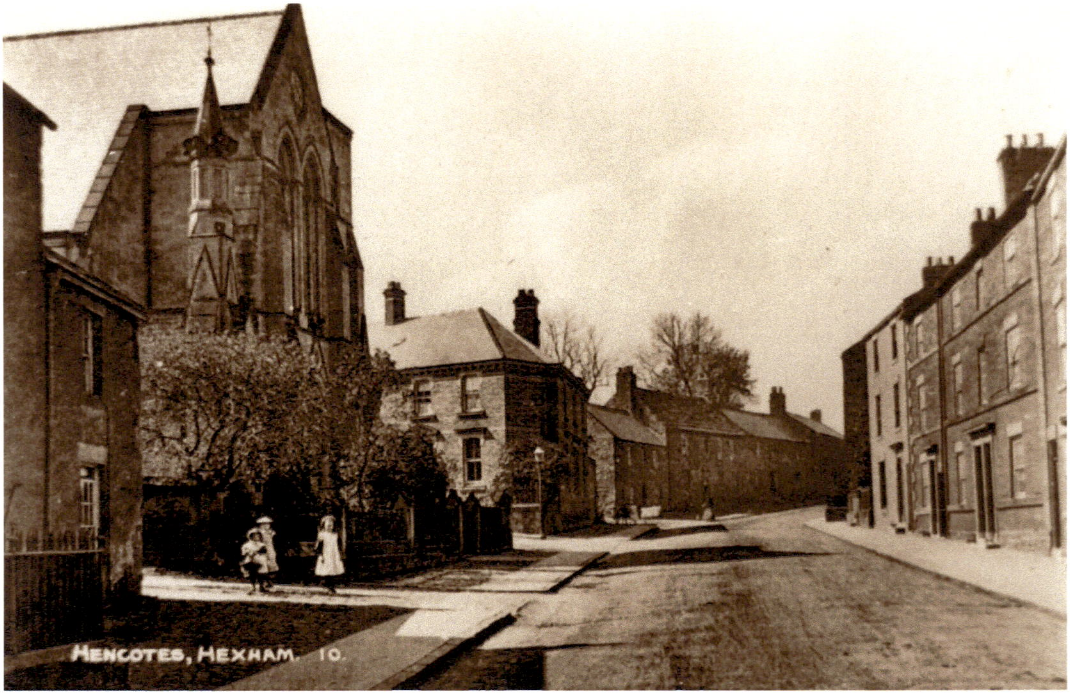

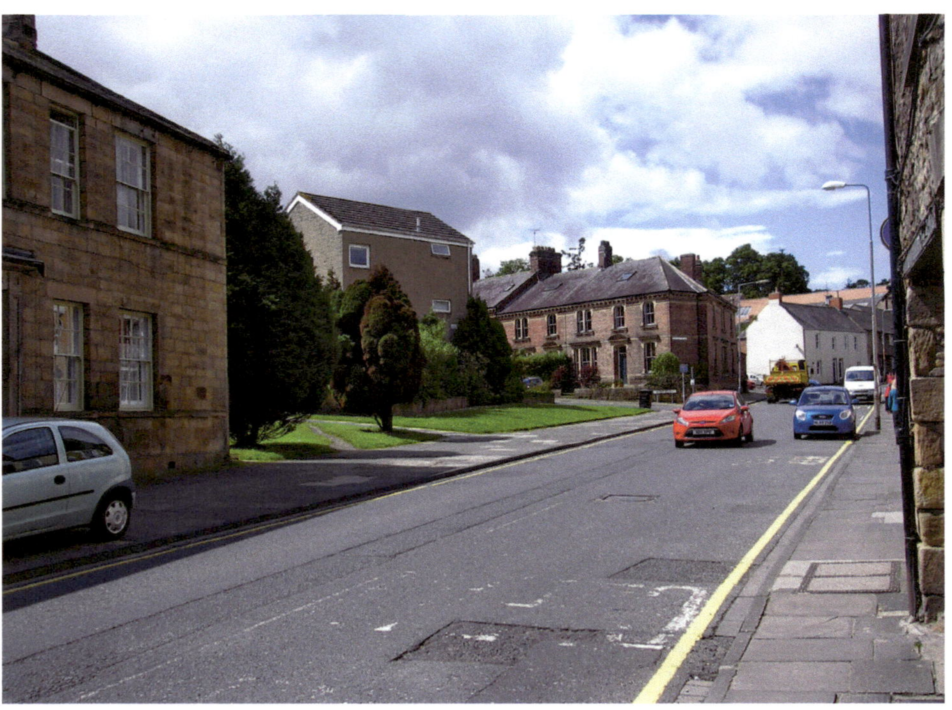

Hencotes II

In the central part of Hencotes this 1869 view shows a Congregational church. The church was demolished in 1967 and houses built there.

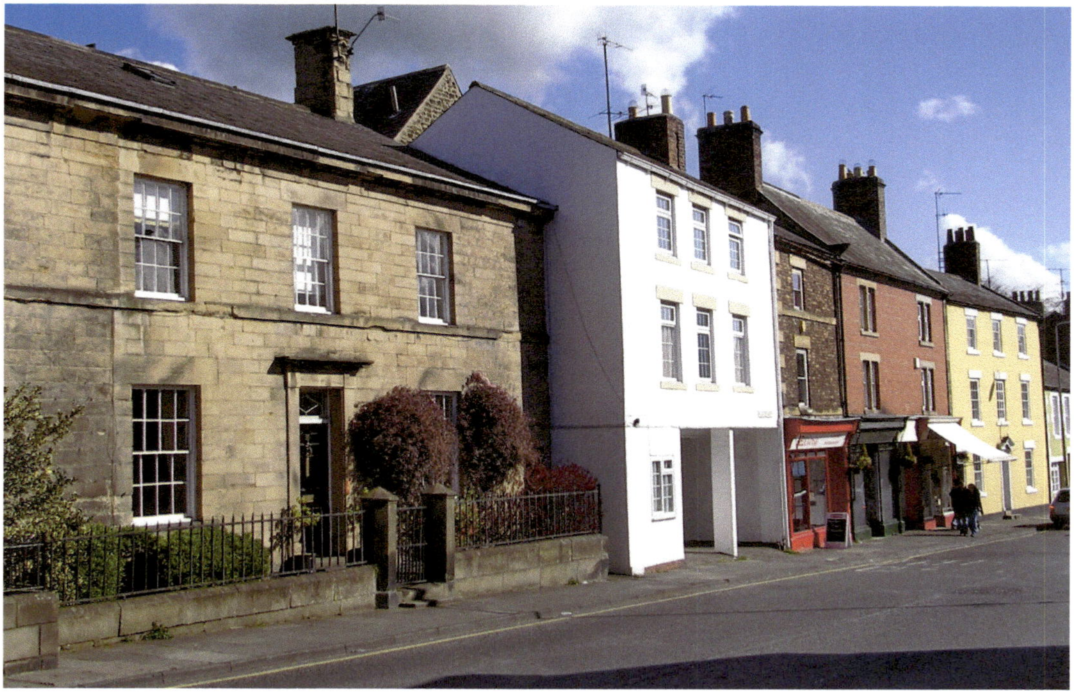

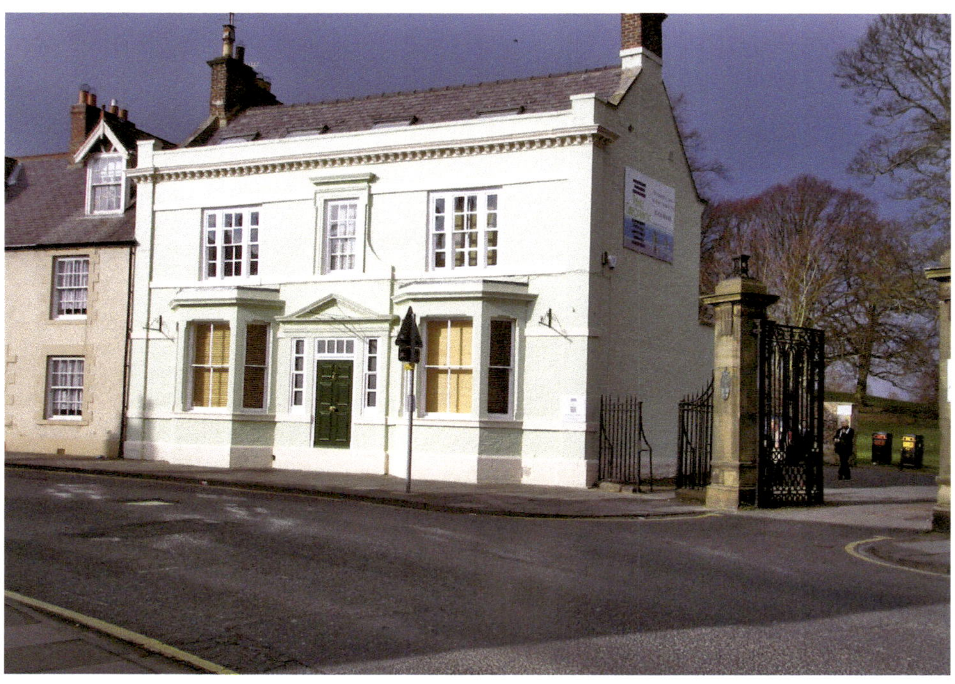

Hencotes III

The left-hand (north) side of Hencotes has some fine buildings, many with three storeys, some of which are shops. Towards the town centre Sele House was a surgery, now relocated to the hospital as a Primary Care centre.

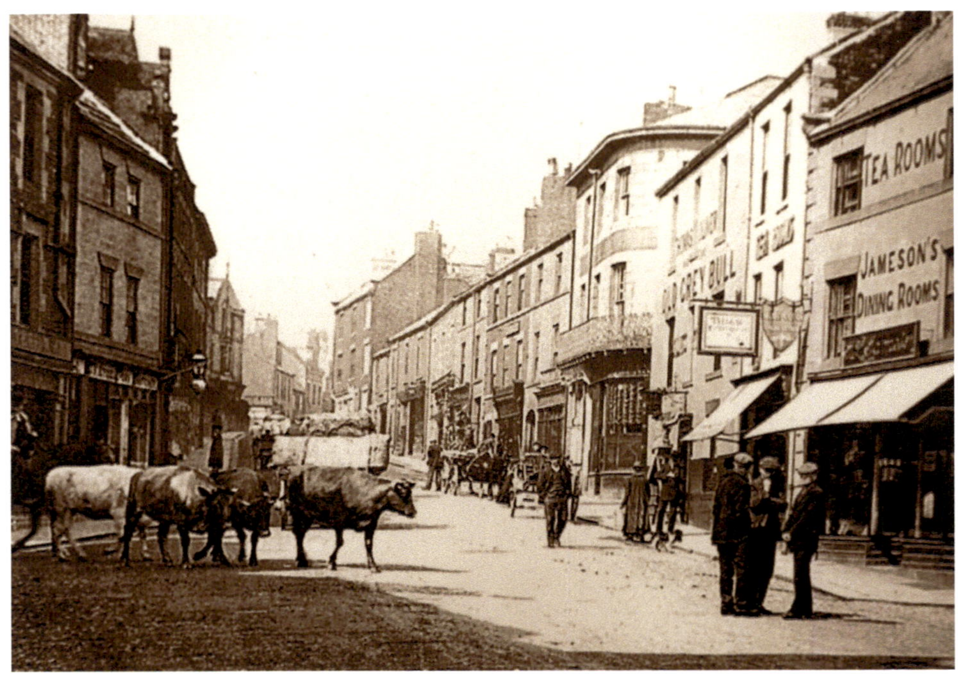

Sele House

It is difficult to believe that once the area to the north of Sele House was a place where cattle could be herded, but they were brought down Battle Hill to be sold at the Cattle Market. The Sele (probably named as a shieling where a herdsman had a temporary shelter) is a large open area, luckily preserved from development, and is used for recreation, including sledging.

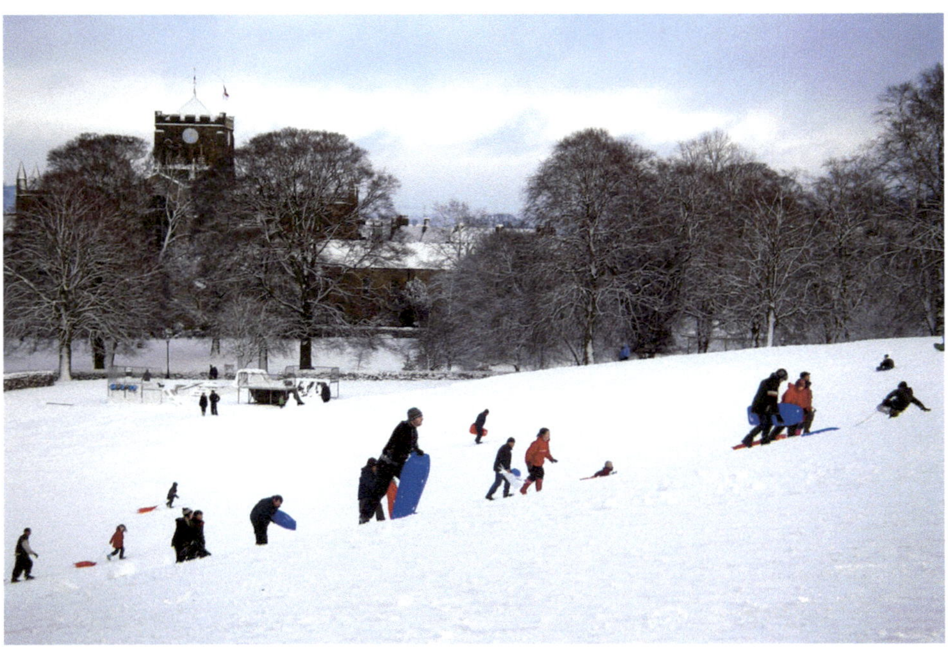

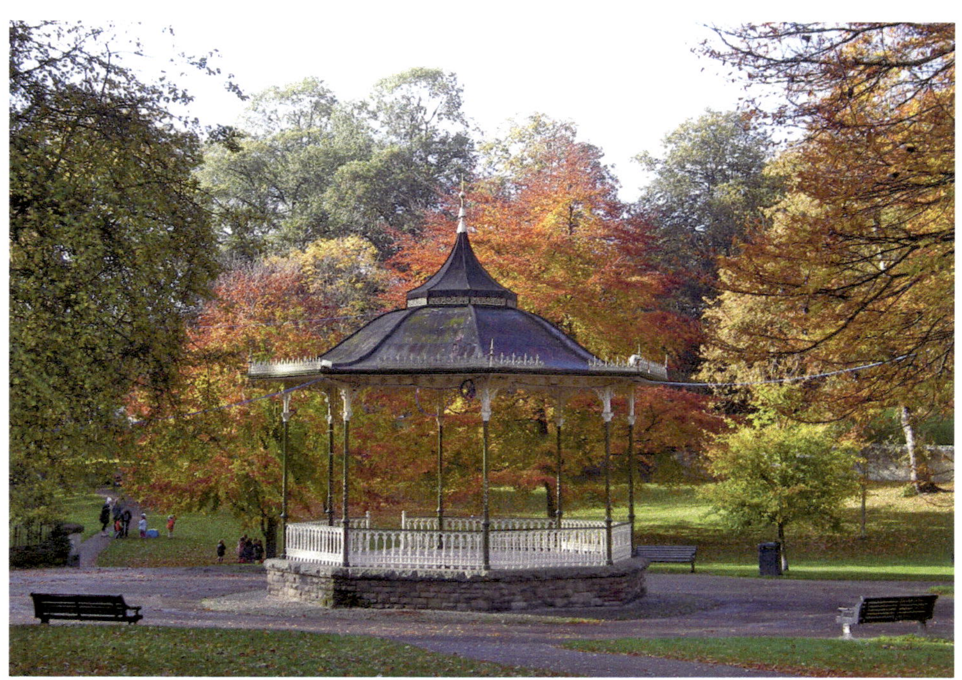

Bandstand

The Sele open space runs into the Abbey Grounds, where Henry Bell (wool merchant) built a bandstand over an area that was flattened and the stream culverted beneath it. The bandstand is attractive in all seasons, and is used for services, concerts and other town events.

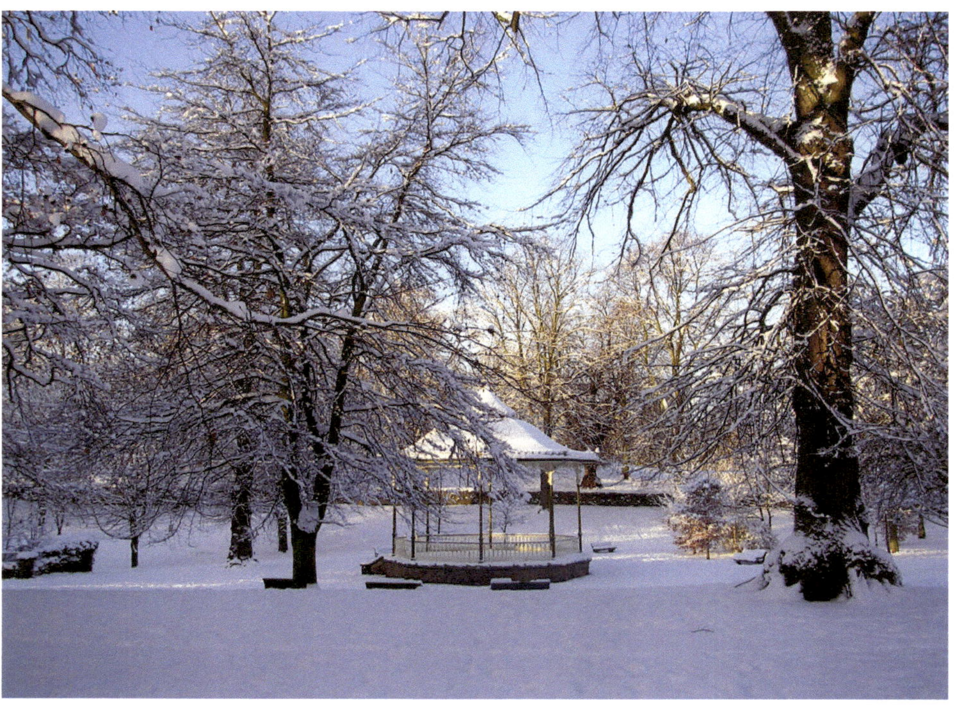

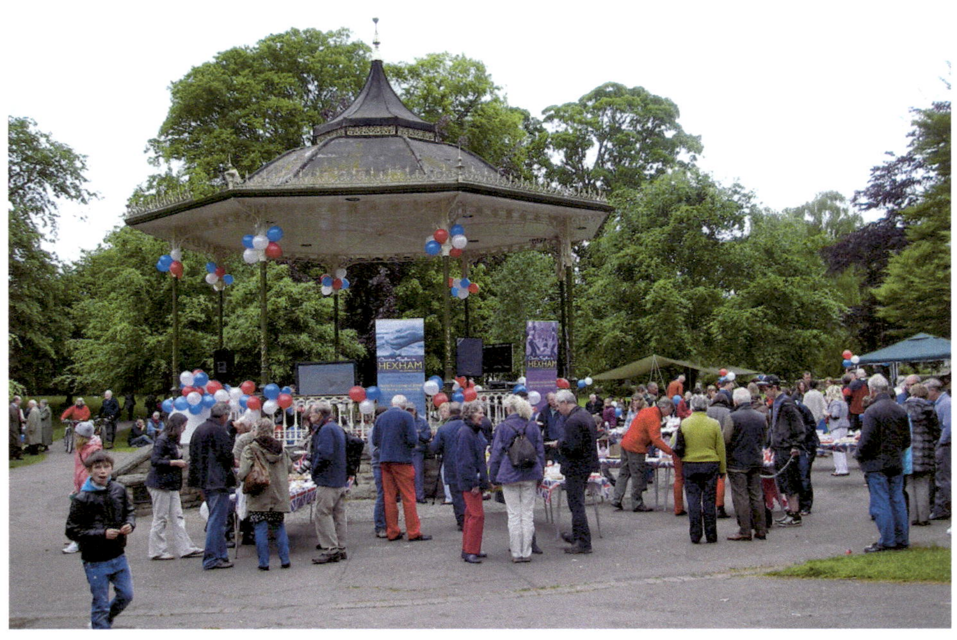

Celebrations

The year 2012 has seen many parties that celebrate royal occasions. The most recent is the Churches Together Lunch to celebrate the Queen's Diamond Jubilee, a lunch offered free to all from the town. Below, a folk concert is in session.

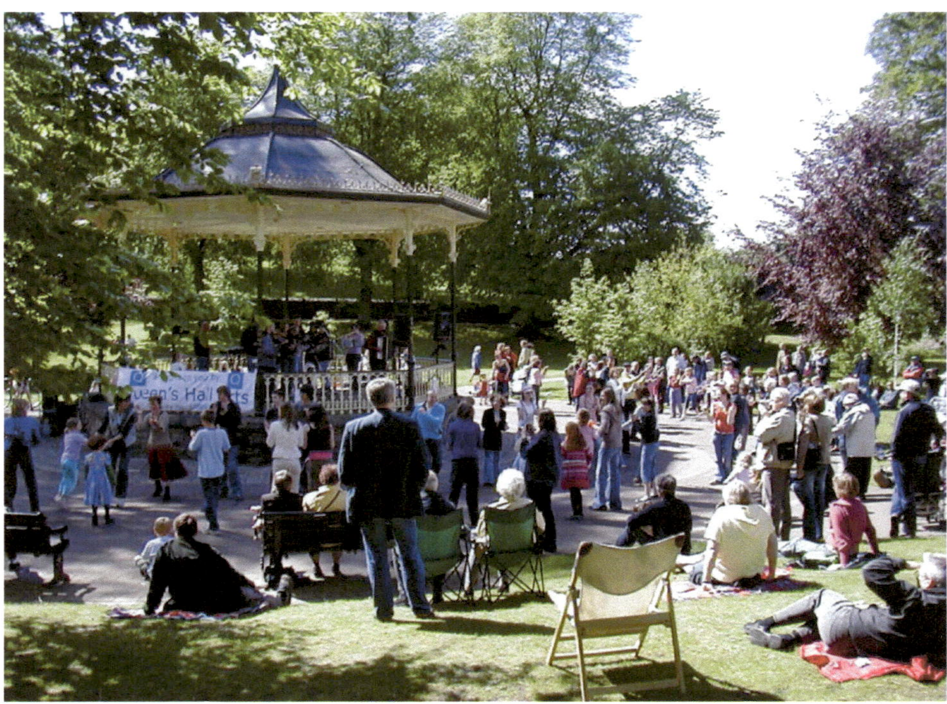

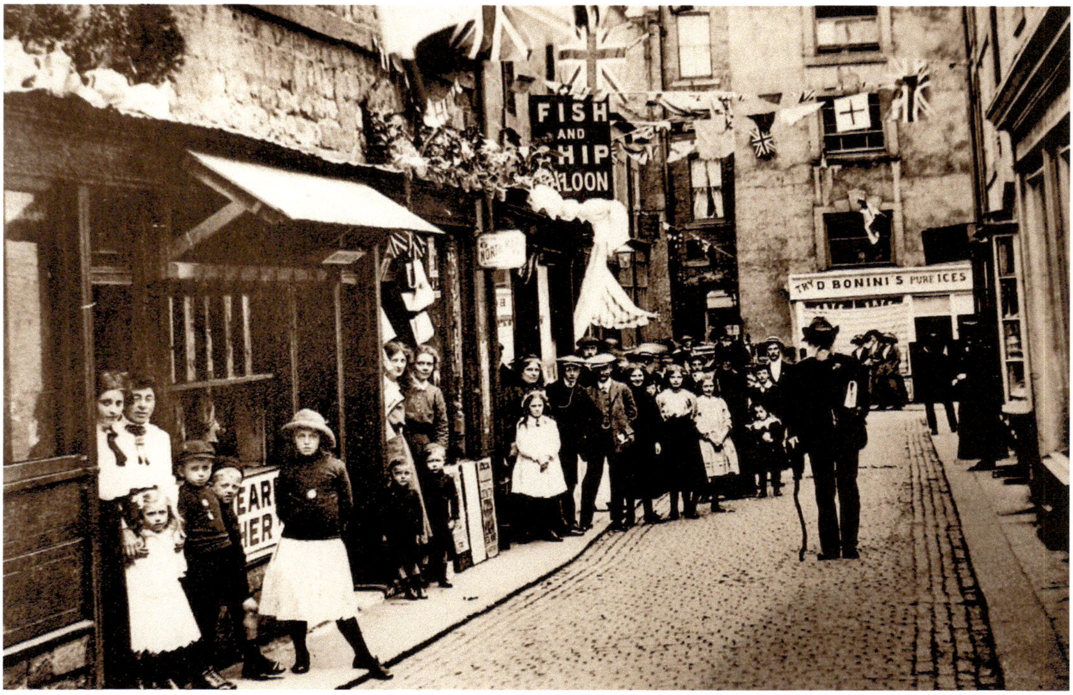

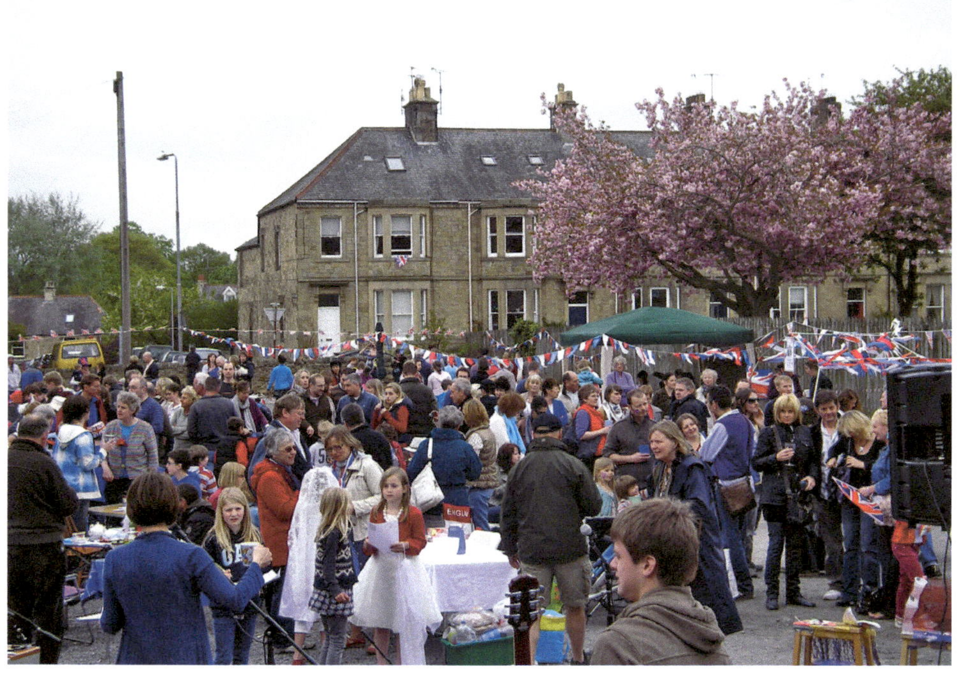

St Mary's Chare II

This subdued, posed, display of patriotism took place in St Mary's Chare (Back Street). In 2012 the people of the west end organised a more modern party to celebrate the Royal Wedding.

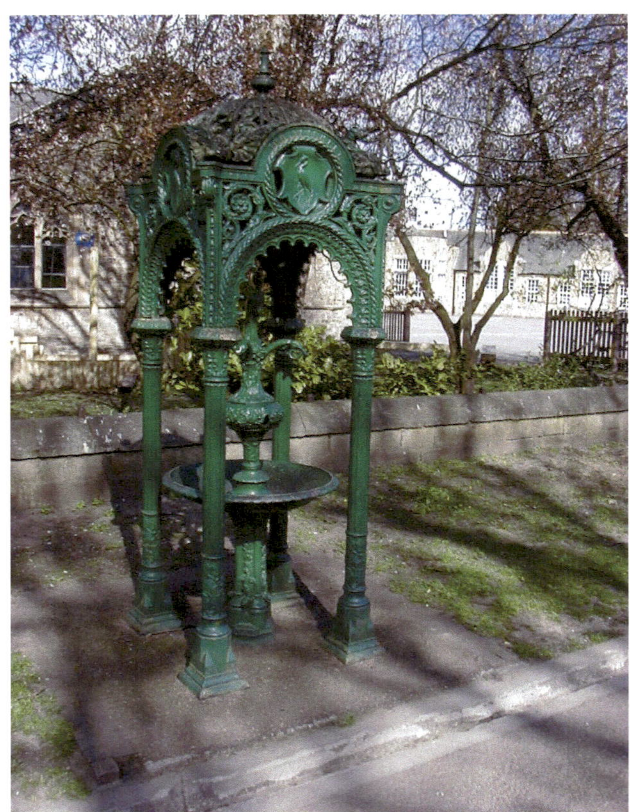

Fountain

At the north foot of the Sele, outside the school, is this fountain was erected in 1899 by the Abbey Temperance Society for Queen Victoria's Diamond Jubilee. The heron is a symbol of clear water.

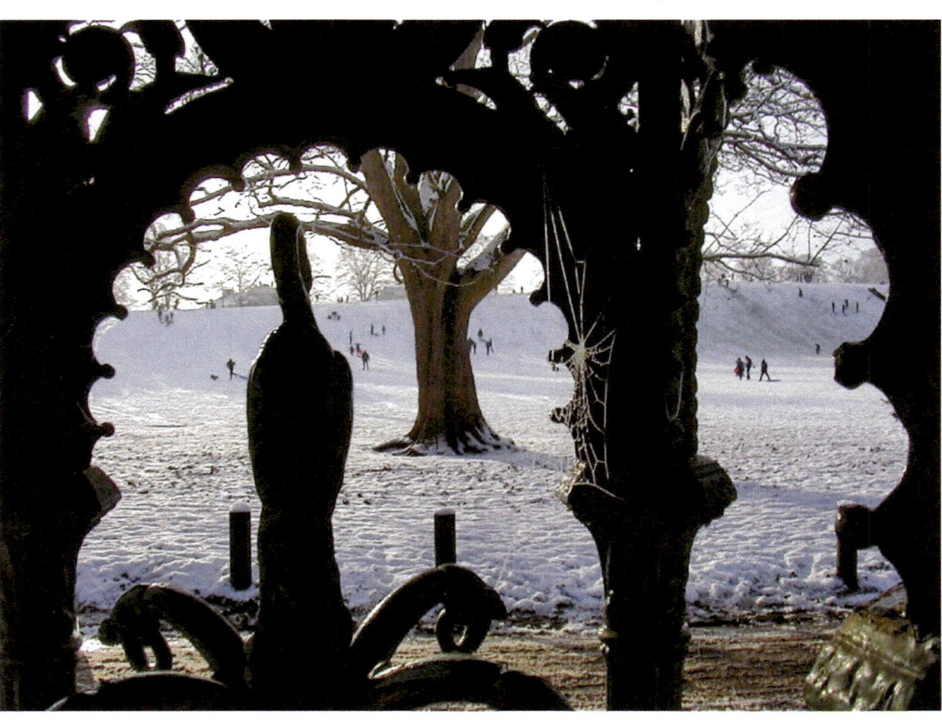

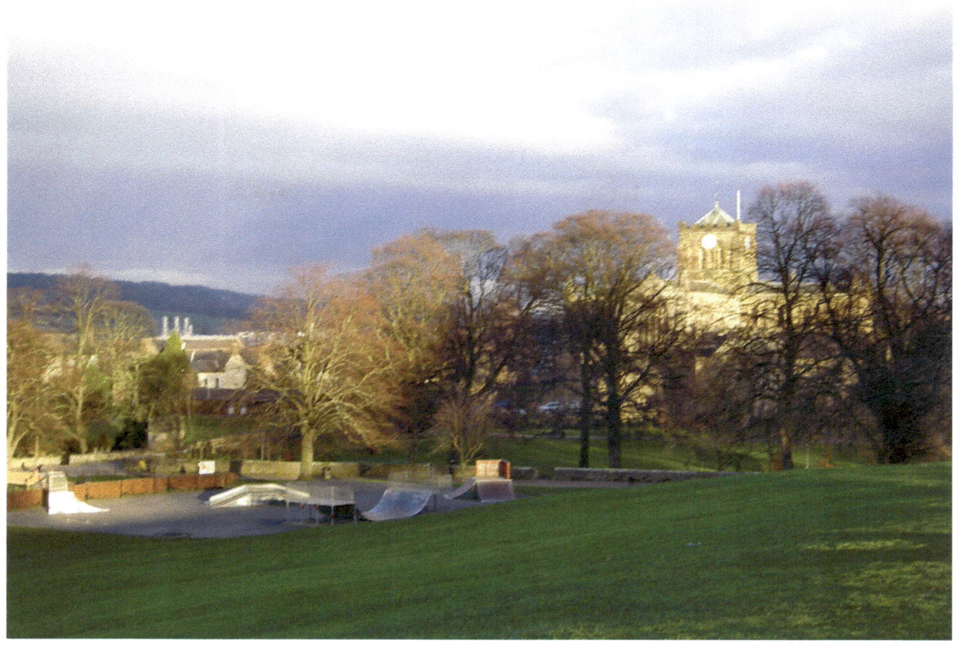

Sele

The view from the Sele to the river covers much of north Hexham. It is also a high place for the annual bonfire and fireworks display, organised by the Rotary Club, which attracts thousands each year and raises a great deal of money for charity.

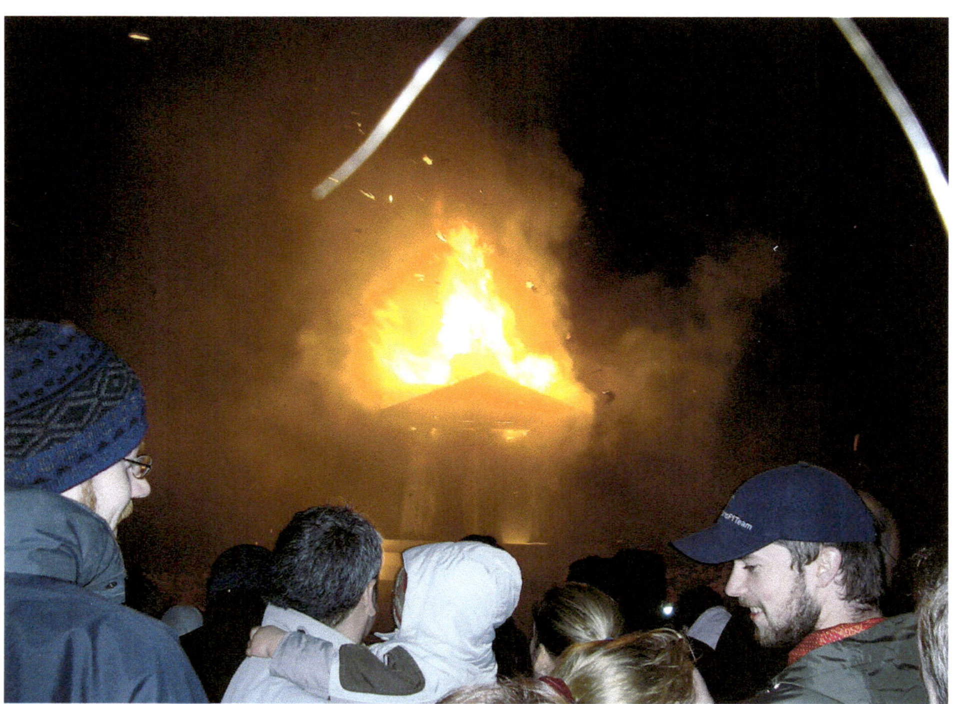

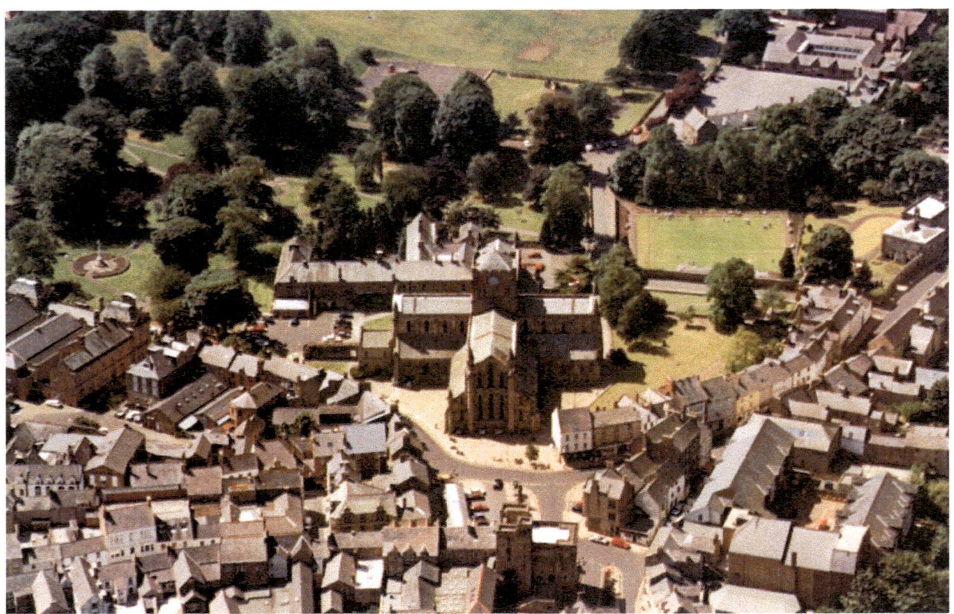

Abbey III

The Abbey is one of the most attractive buildings in the county. We see its position in relation to the rest of the town in my air photograph that was used as a postcard. The Abbey was without a nave until the beginning of the twentieth century, but whether the old nave was unfinished or destroyed in a Scot's raid is not clear. It became necessary to build a massive buttress to support the tower and this led to the discovery of the unique Anglo-Saxon crypt. The site of the nave was used as part of the town graveyard and called 'Campy Field'. The lower picture shows the south view without the choir school.

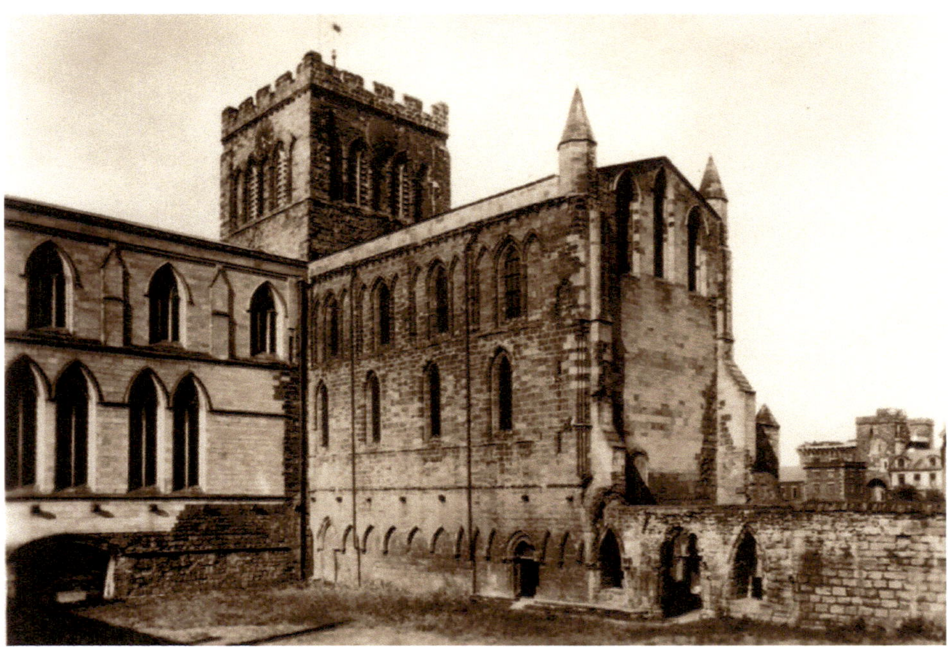

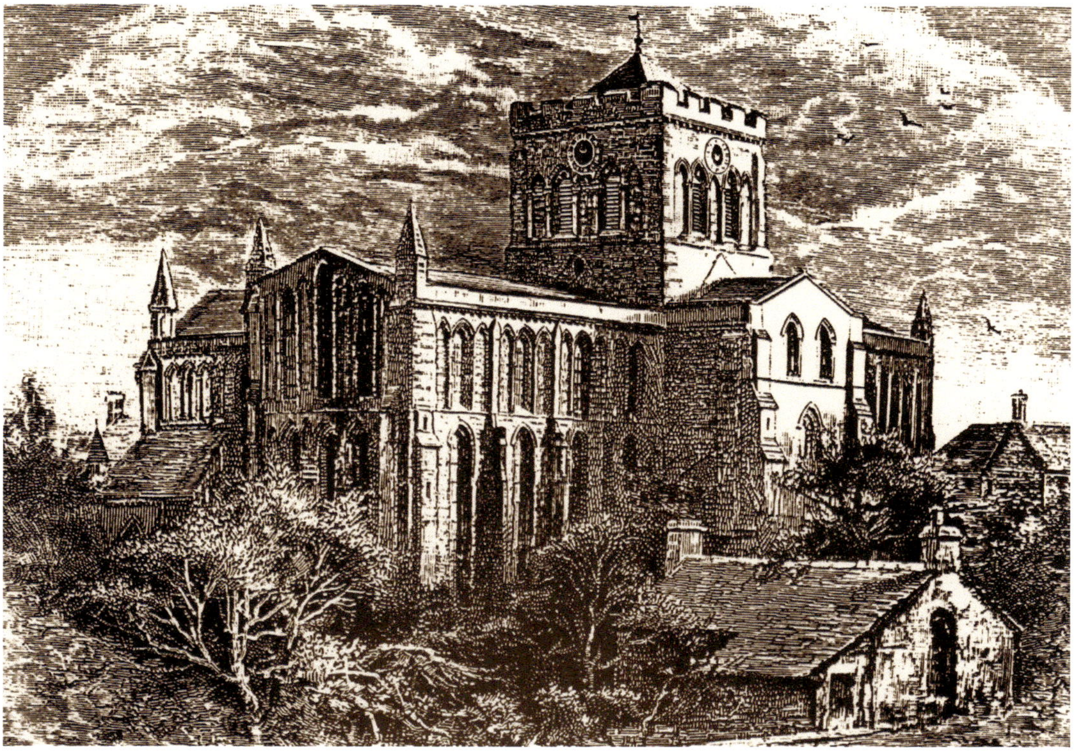

Abbey IV

Here is an etching and recent photograph of the Abbey from the north-west showing the addition of the nave, seen from the bowling green.

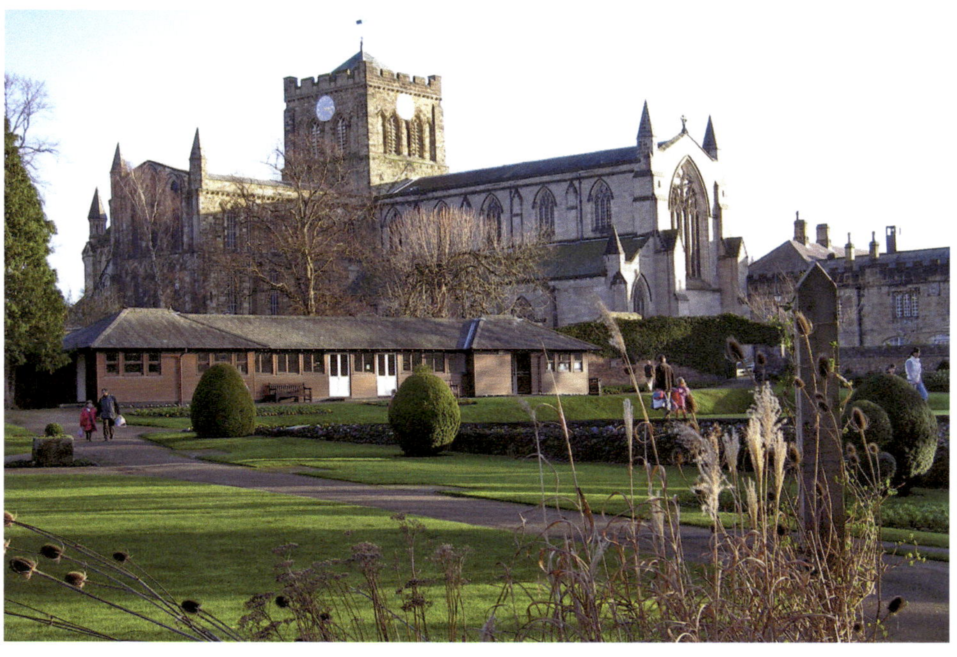

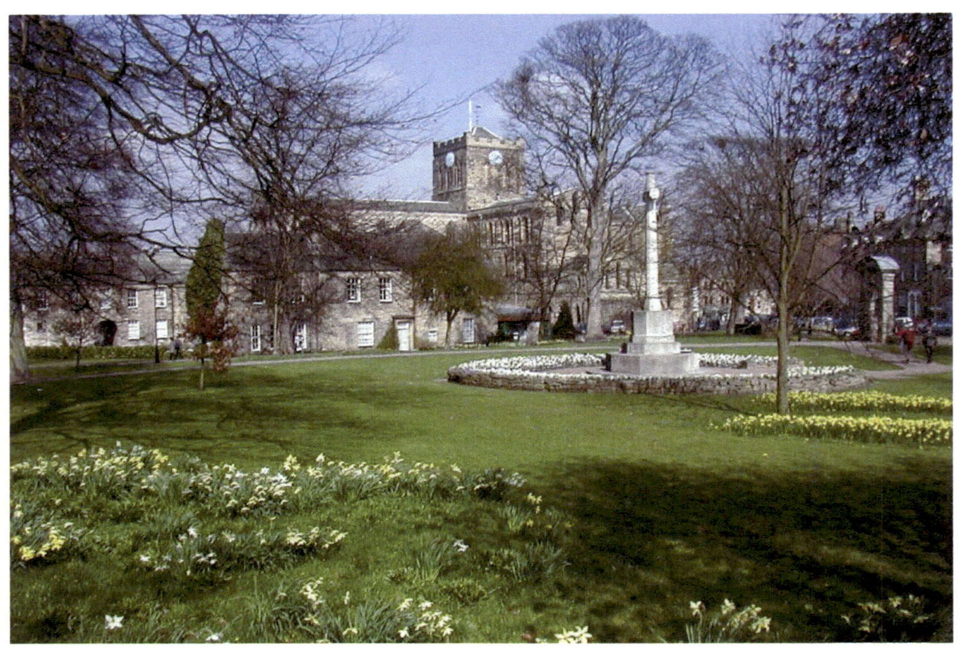

The Abbey in spring from the south-west. The Abbey grounds have been restored to their Victorian pattern. An addition to the Abbey is the Choir School, seen from the south. The ancient night stair leads from this inside to the church, and was the route from the canons' dormitory to the church.

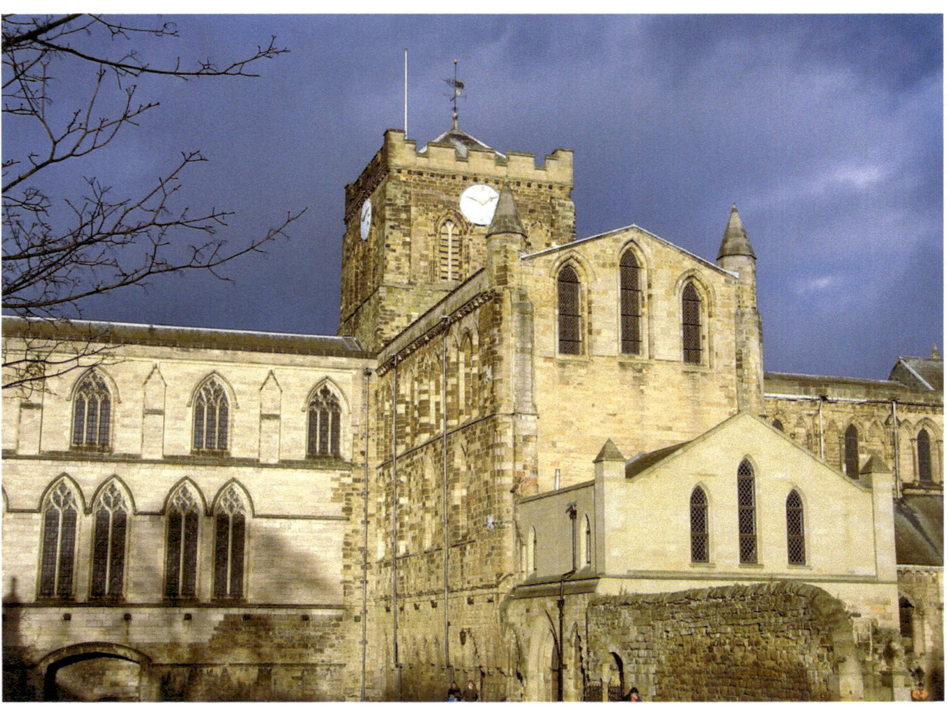

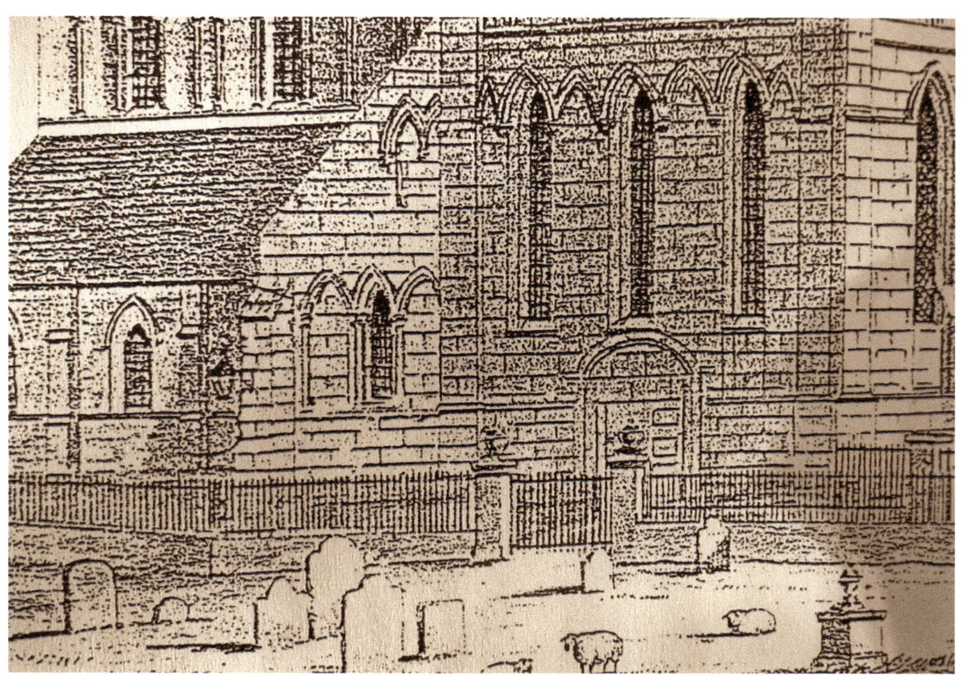

Abbey VI

The north transept once had a doorway built in 1670 by the Mercers' Company but it weakened the wall and had to be removed in 1869. The old northern graveyard became overcrowded and had to be discontinued.

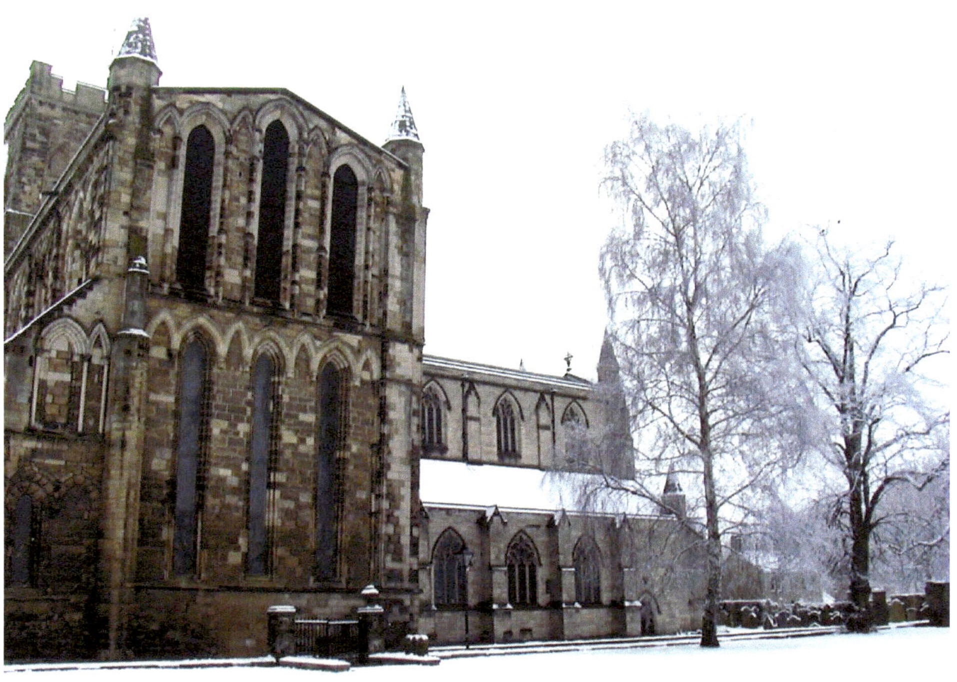

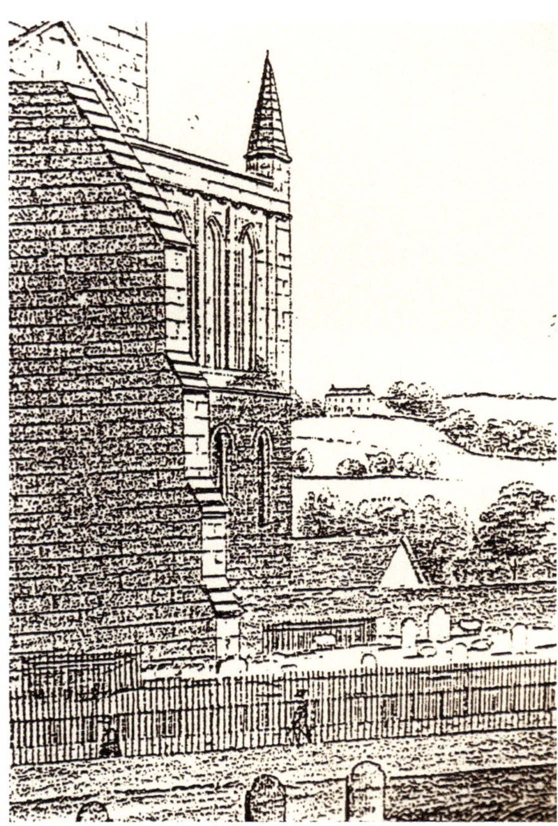

Campy Hill Cemetery
The Campy Hill cemetery is seen
in this mid-nineteenth-century
sketch before the new nave was
built. The same view today shows
the extent of the changes.

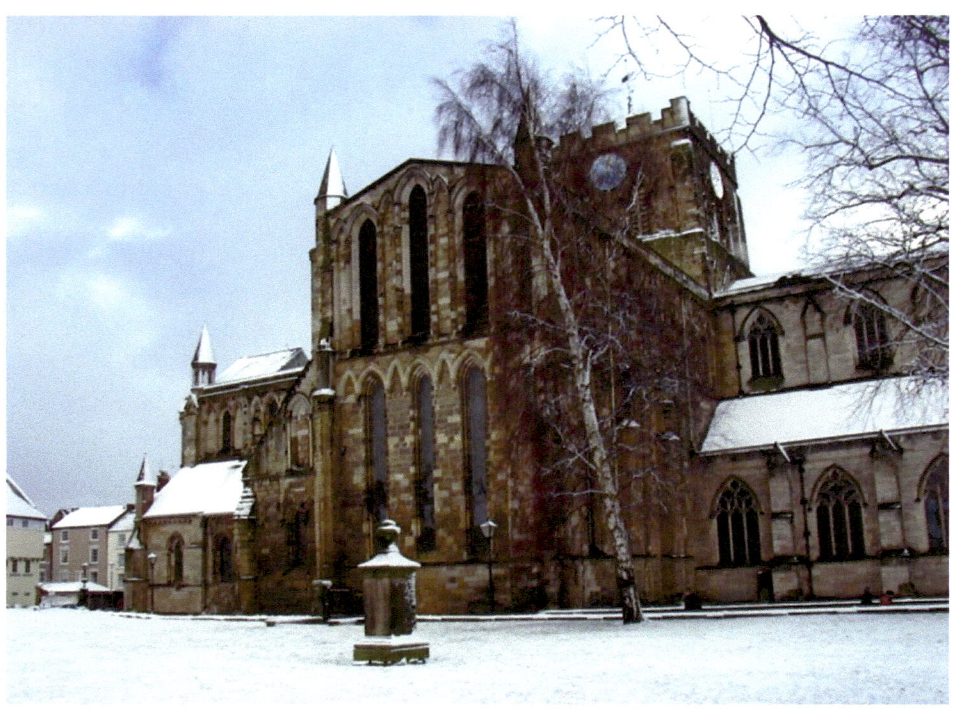

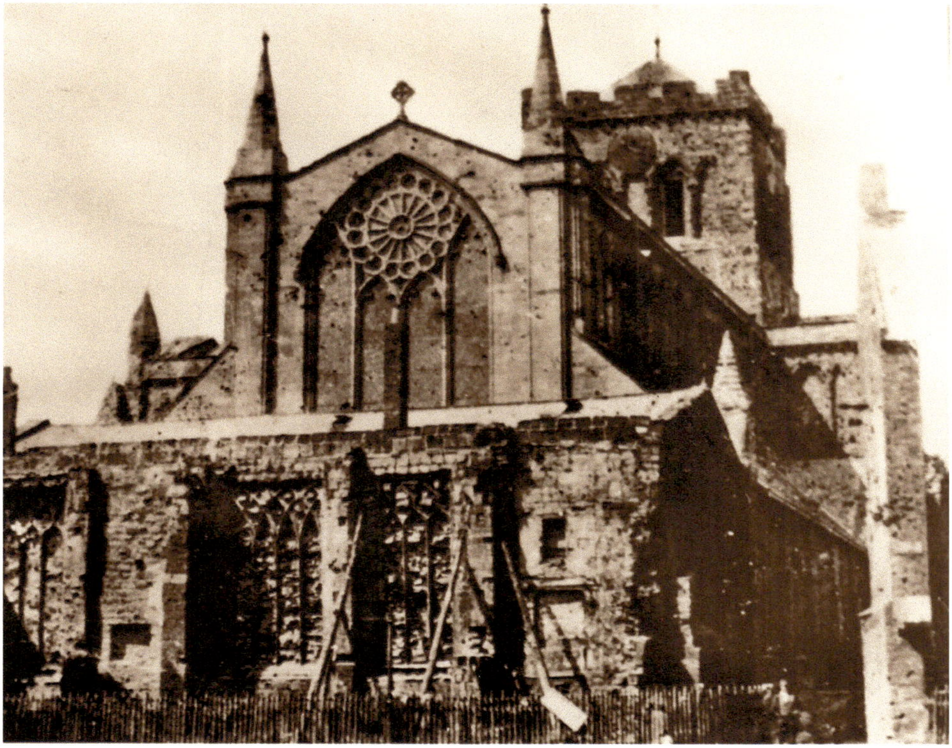

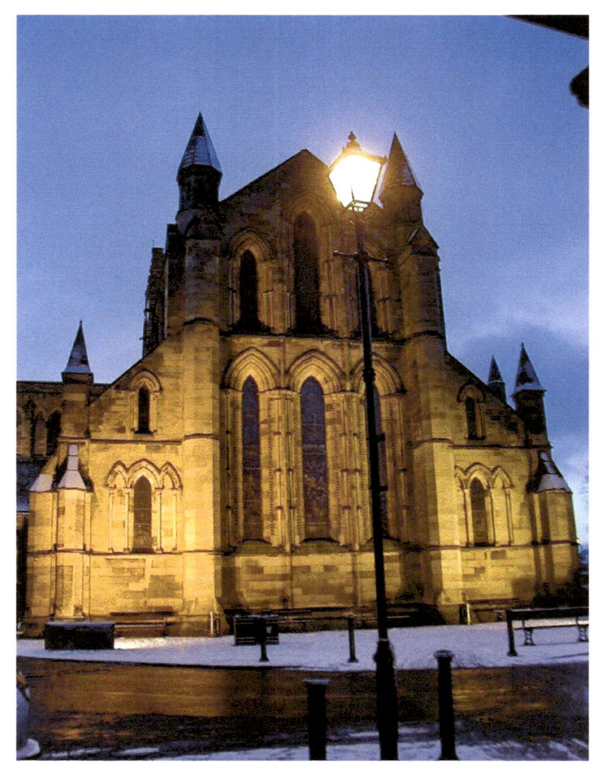

Medieval Chapels

The east end of the Abbey had medieval chapels behind it which became the back wall for shops and other buildings, which the town bought from the owners. Although townspeople wanted these chapels to be preserved, John Dobson destroyed them in his scheme for a new east end. He chose instead to model it on the east façade of Whitby Abbey.

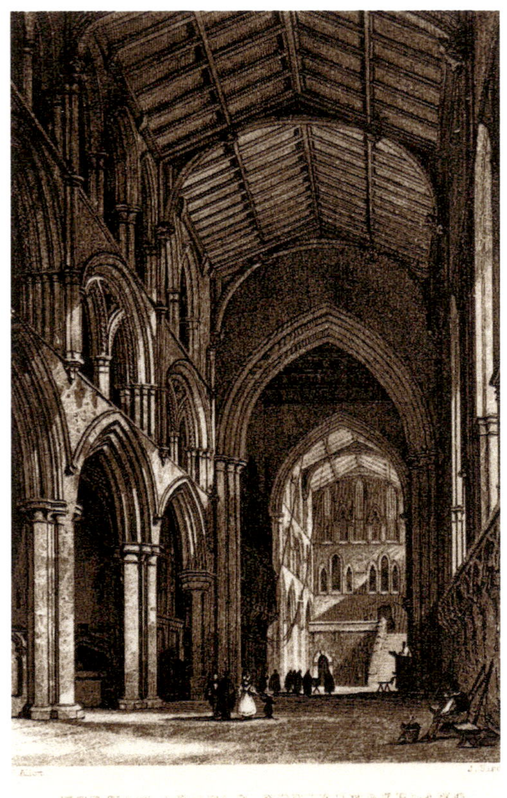

Abbey Interior I

An old etching of the Abbey interior towards the south transept before the new nave was built shows also the pulpit on the right, which is now close to the high altar with other painted wooden panels. Below, the picture shows the candles for an Abbey Festival of the Arts. The south transept is to have new stained glass windows to replace the plain glass ones. They are already being made, and will be outstanding in design, colour and symbolism.

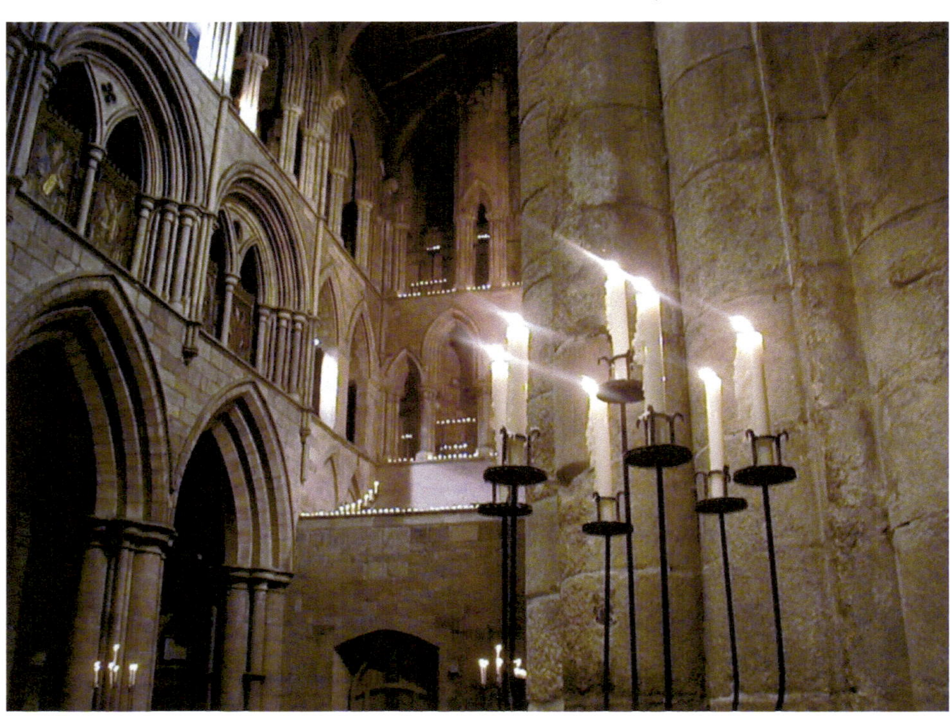

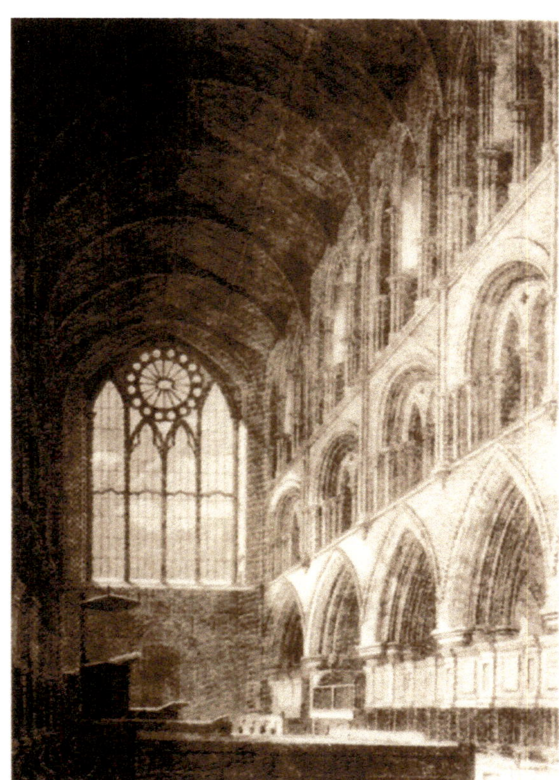

Abbey Interior II

From the inside we see the 'Catherine wheel' window that once fell out and was replaced. The new east end is seen from the organ loft during a Christmas service.

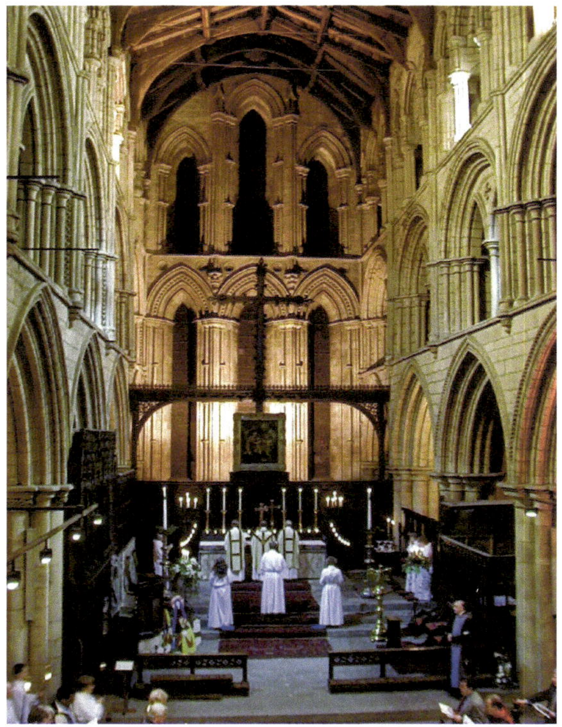

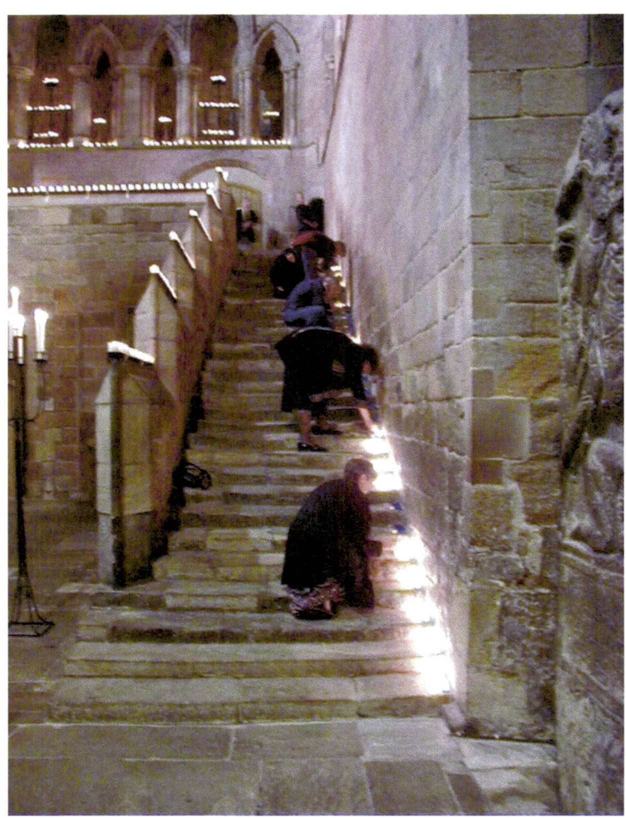

The Hexham Candlelight Concert is the culmination of the week's activities. The candles are being lighted on the Night Stair – a rare survival of a staircase from the canon's dormitory to the choir for the many services held.

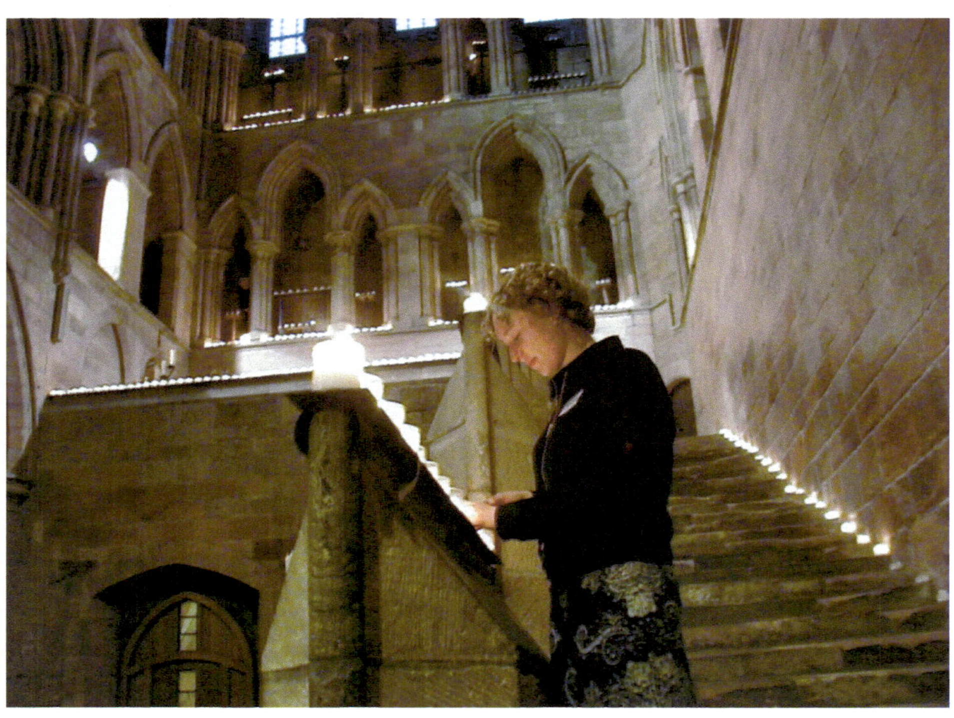

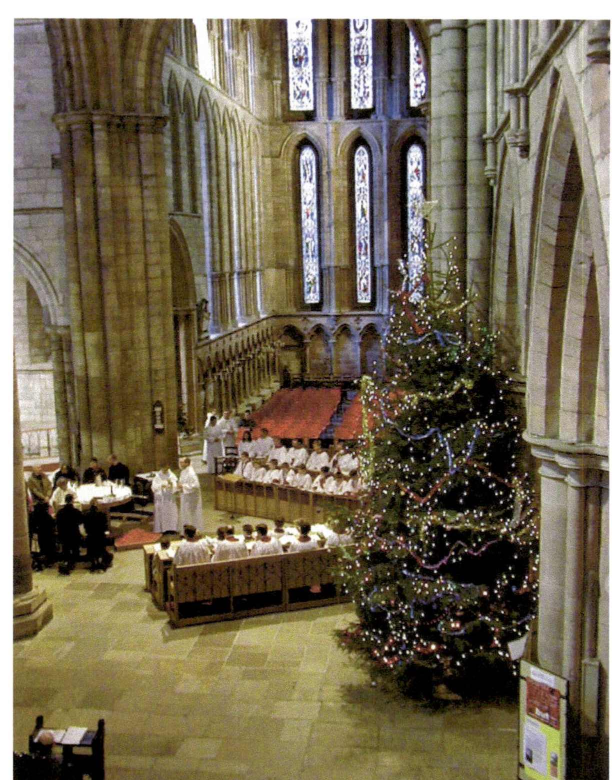

Abbey Interior III

The north transept is a very impressive building. It is now used for services, exhibitions, plays and music. The play being performed by the Abbey People is based on Chaucer's 'The Pardoner's Tale' from *Shepherds', Rogues and Angels*.

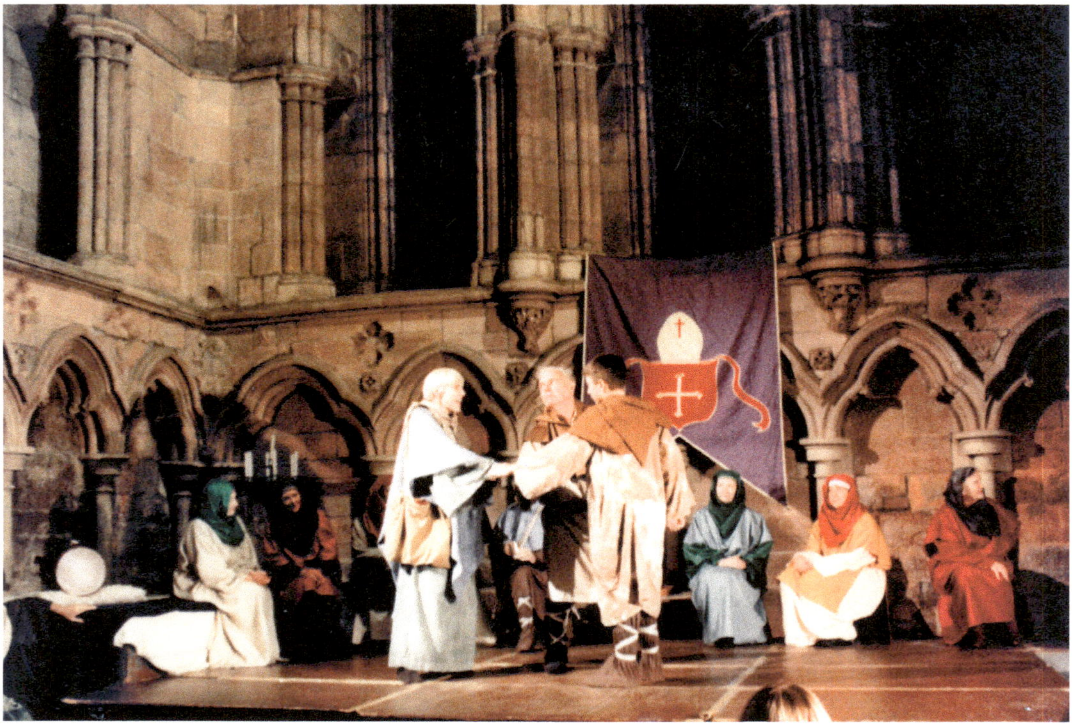

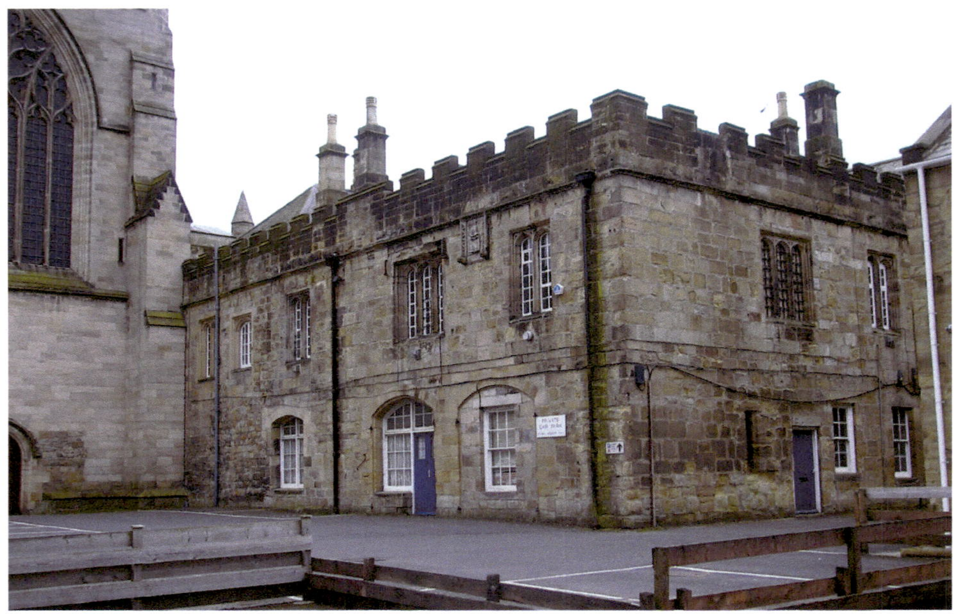

Carnaby Building

Sir Reynold Carnaby was granted land and buildings on the Dissolution of the Monasteries in 1537. His house is known as the Carnaby Building and has his crest in stone on the outer wall. It has been used for council services, but is now redundant. The Abbey has acquired this and other buildings, so the buildings are becoming unified. They will be used for exhibitions of the abbey and town's past, and for work with schools. Below is the wall of the west claustral buildings which are part of the project, and which will be extended for use by the town. To be able to report this progress is a good way to end a brief survey of the town's history seen through pictures. Hexham continues to change.

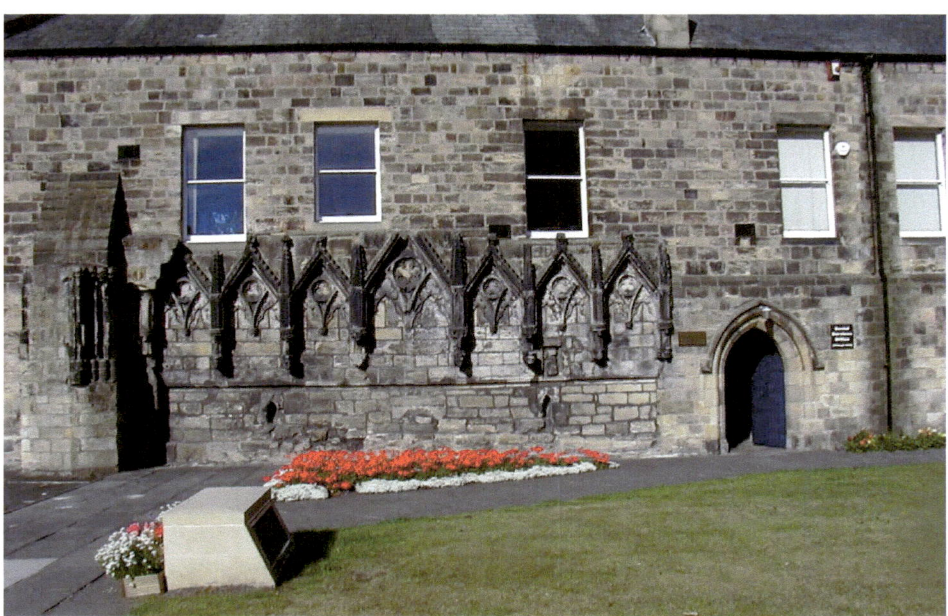